Where Bible and Life Connect

Reflections of a Spiritual Director

Lester Bach, Capuchin Franciscan

De La Salle House

A Liturgical Press Book

THE LITURGICAL PRESS
Collegeville, Minnesota

1   2   3   4   5   6   7   8   9

Library of Congress Cataloging-in-Publication Data

Bach, Lester.
  Where Bible and life connect : reflections of a spiritual director / Lester Bach.
        p.   cm.
    ISBN 0-8146-2247-X
    1. Spiritual life—Catholic Church.   2. Catholic Church-
  -Doctrines.   3. Bach, Lester.   I. Title.
  BX2350.2.B28   1995
  248.4'82—dc20   94-32432
                                                                  CIP

Contents

Foreword

It is with delight that I write this introduction to *Where Bible and Life Connect*. For a number of years the author has been for me a spiritual companion, friend, and co-worker in mission work. I have enjoyed his ability to use ordinary words and ordinary experience to give life to the *extraordinary good news* of the gospel. With this book, others will be offered new insights into Scripture.

Where Bible and Life Connect is likely to attract your immediate attention. If you are becoming thoughtful about the spiritual life, if you are asking questions, if you are seeking answers to the meaning of the gospel on a personal level — this book can help you.

The book is not intended for passive use. In fact, if it is read like a novel, you will miss the opportunity it offers to probe the deep places of your heart. This is a book to read and reflect upon, much as one lingers with a beautiful sunset or savors a favorite food. The questions at the end of each chapter offer an opportunity for plenty of reflection. They are meant to be an aid and to provoke questions of your own that may begin to surface.

Chapter One begins by calling us to be "truth seekers." One truth we can count on is that we are spiritual persons. Psychologists say that from the moment of birth we want to return to our mother's womb. As Christian believers we realize that our life journey is one of "created people." We search from the moment we are formed to return to our Creator. The

Word can be our guide on that return journey, but we must make that choice. Refusal to choose leaves us unsatisfied. The refusal to name the obstacles we encounter on the journey leaves us imprisoned in dissatisfaction.

Once we "own" what is ours, be it obstacle or anything else, we seem to have a better ability to move on. In naming and owning it, we continue to experience conversion in our life. The call of the gospel is also to name and own God's love for us.

Why is it that we yearn to hear that we are loved and lovable and yet refuse to accept that message fully? Page after page of Scripture reveals that God is with us. God loves us. God's power is within us. Chapter Five invites us to ask questions, to become informed, to seek a personal relationship with Jesus in order to receive the "graced power" of the Holy Spirit. We are not meant to be a people who just "exist." We are meant to be a people of abundance!

I often wonder what it is we fear in God's unconditional love. Is it perhaps that such love is unknown to us? Or is unconditional love inviting us to see ourselves as we really are — broken, limited human beings in need of God? This God is always with us. This God loves us without asking us to prove ourselves. This God challenges us to accept our own humanness with compassion. Is this what we fear? The chapter on love and intimacy may shed some light on how we have experienced love and our own limited ability to love. The shadow of our humanity is always present in some way in our experience of loving. If we look honestly at this shadow, we will find that we love with expectations. This is what makes God's unconditional love hard to understand.

Throughout my travels on our continent, I find that we as a people need to own our sexual selves in order to embody fully our spiritual nature. For various reasons we have split our body, mind, and spirit into different parts of self. *Where Bible and Life Connect* addresses this fragmented state of being. It helps us understand the importance of healing our sexual self so that body, mind, and spirit might come together. Lester states another truth. Healthy sexuality requires psychological and emotional maturity. I would simply add that it is our responsibility to seek any means possible to become the human persons God designed us to be. That means we are to own our wonderful bodies and realize that they are part of the *whole* creature God sees. Embodied spirituality believes the words of Genesis, that God gazed on the human creation and said: "It is good." God looks at us and is delighted. We, too, are asked to delight in our whole selves.

How wonderful it would be if we could each value ourselves as a spoken work of God — as sacramental. Perhaps we could then approach the sacraments the Church offers us with a deep sense of joy and aliveness. *Where Bible and Life Connect* helps us to look at the symbols, the "earthy" things we use in ritual as gifts to help us realize the presence of Jesus.

This book holds up for our concern both the "negative" and the "positive" that life offers us. It offers *hope* in the midst of chaos. The search for spiritual companioning, the interest in contemplative prayer, and the presence of people who seek to bring justice to the oppressed are signs that the Holy Spirit is at work among the people.

In reflecting on our own story, our own life journey, in our questioning of where God touches us in life, we have the opportunity to name and own our experience. The author tells us, in so many words, that we cannot remain containers that simply hold the experience. Rather, we are to be vessels that pour out what we have been given and thus give life to others. The gospel becomes living water that quenches the thirst of our brothers and sisters.

Where Bible and Life Connect offers good suggestions on how to "pass it on." Lester encourages us to widen our vision and realize that our spiritual journey, our God-moments, last a lifetime. To believe that we have already arrived is to fool ourselves, and we will soon suffer from spiritual anemia. Rather, we are to be a people of hope, willing to share what we have received, a people hospitable enough to receive another's shared story with reverence and attentive listening. Thus we become a living example of the gospel. Enjoy this book and go forth and spread the *extraordinary good news!*

Shirley Lembcke
Lay Spiritual Director
Sun Prairie, Wisconsin

Preface

Where Bible and Life Connect is a reflection on the connections between the signs of the time and the Bible. The Bible is not a dead word, hidden in a library of leather-bound books. It is a word of life waiting to be listened to and lived. It offers a way of life that holds the promise of joy and wisdom to a world sometimes lost in depression and ignorance. It is a word of hope to a world sometimes mired in despair. God's word bears the vision of God for the people who are God's people.

My reflections invite you to explore the gospel and life with fresh perspectives. Its vision may satisfy, confront, confuse, and even surprise. Persistence in listening to God's word is rewarded with life-giving discoveries. The Bible is less concerned with simplistic solutions and more concerned with faith-based reality. The Bible invites us to live in the reality of God's presence and love. No matter what life brings, God-with-us (Jesus) enables us to deal with it. With respectful and challenging words, God invites us to put skin on the word we hear. Each of us makes the personal decision to walk this path. God persistently offers the invitation.

At the cutting edge, we face the issues of newness, unity, and communion. We face our need for personal conversion. The revealing word of God does not permit indifference. Apathy and indifference bring only apathy and indifference. No light enters when we remain untouched by the word. Our world continues to be in shadow until we choose to walk in the light. Our commitment to Jesus brings light and life. *Where*

Bible and Life Connect explores ways of making the Bible our book for living. God alone gives the growth.

Some Native American people address God as "Grandfather." God is Grandfather, caring for the people. Grandfather listens especially to the prayers of the elders. Grandfather is concerned with the life of the young people. Grandfather looks with respect on woman, the life bearer, the one who is source of life for the tribe. Grandfather is concerned for all the people. The one who prays to Grandfather prays for all the people. When the traditions are forgotten and the ritual misused, the people are weak. Grandfather again calls them to respect and reverence. Respect and reverence surface again and again in the ritual and prayer of the Native American people. Always it is the *people* who are important to Grandfather.

But I am not a Native American. I am simply an American. My God, too, speaks of reverence and respect for the people. God's son, Jesus, speaks of respect and reverence for all. The community remembers the words of the God-who-came-among-us. They have been written down. The words God speaks to us are holy. The book containing these words is holy. They give life. They give light. They give meaning to what we do. They bring us as one people to God, who is one. The words of God must be heard with respect and reverence. From them comes the way of God, whose people we are. Listen to the word! Fill life with the word! Pass on to others the wonder of the word.

Trust your spirit-journey and your personal experiences. The Spirit will lead you beyond what I have written. Respond to the gospel with a firm commitment. Persistence brings joy, God's gift to those who are faithful.

"The word of God is alive and active. It cuts more keenly than any two-edged sword, piercing so deeply that it divides soul and spirit, joints and marrow; it discriminates among the purposes and thoughts of the heart" (Heb 4:12-13 — REB).

To Francis of Assisi I dedicate this book. It is he and his perception of the word of God that has been stimulus for my searching for life in the Scriptures. What a way to go! Many men and women who live the Franciscan spirit continue to influence me. To all of them: ''Thank you.''

Lester Bach
Capuchin-Franciscan

CHAPTER ONE

Here's Mud in Your Eye!

Truth is elusive. One of its original meanings was "loyalty; trustworthiness." We have come to consider it as the quality of being in accord with our experience, facts, and reality. It may also include a quality of sincerity and genuineness. Truth is not always believable. For example, friends tell us that we are good people. We brush it off. People affirm our compassion. We say: "Anyone would do the same." Young people find that being "young" is hard, and seek adulthood before their time. Middle-aged people face crisis and oftentimes seek multiple ways to look "young" again. Cosmetics perform a holding action on the inroads of aging. Middle-aged men find an artificial youth with women much younger than they. Getting past the midway mark of life is frightening. Death and mortality are no longer theoretical questions. It is not easy to live life in the truth of being our real self . . . age, mortality, beauty, wonderfully-made, warts, and whatever. I have never been as old as I am today. It is new to me. It is frightening. People frequently deny the reality of their own lives. It is not easy to accept truth — about ourselves or others or our world or our faith.

Technology enables us to communicate on a worldwide scale. But truth has not become easier to communicate. Denying the truth is a rather common practice. Technology has not made us more honest. Neither can it reveal the truth when we deny any growth in our understanding of the truth about ourselves, others, our world, our faith.

At its best, communication of the truth leads to communion. But our world doesn't have much communion, despite the fact that we get news almost as fast as it happens. It is not easy to discern the truth in all the news stories we see on TV or read in our newspapers. On the interpersonal level, we do not always share the truth with one another.

Newspaper truth is sometimes exciting, sometimes boring. Newspapers may be delightful or silly, informative or deceptive. Facts, opinions, rumors, and speculation vie with one another for headlines. Some newspapers feature sensationalism. Bold headlines proclaim their version of the "truth." Accuracy often suffers. Newspapers need to make a profit while informing the public. Stories sometimes tantalize the mind but offer few supporting facts. Partial information is often offered as the whole truth. Biased reporting is touted as "truth."

TV newscasts face similar problems with the truth. In thirty minutes TV newspeople try to cover the world. "They" make a tight selection of news items "they" consider important. Pilate's "What is truth?" is still a tough question to answer. It is difficult to know "the truth." Humans are limited. News corporations are subject to the human limitations of the people who work for them. Computers are fed facts and information. They compare and combine them faster than the mind can think. But "garbage in, garbage out" remains true. No computer can look into the eyes of a person to sense truth or falsehood. It doesn't have intuition. Neither is it able to explore intangible "hunches." There are dimensions of the truth not available to data-gathering machines no matter how refined they become. Claims to the contrary must be checked for their "truth."

Take an example. I say "I love you." You enter that data into a computer. But there is a dimension of the relationship that goes beyond computer data. Do computers compute your "feelings" that are part of a relationship? Do "cold facts" substitute for warm hugs? Human questions of this sort give us pause before our acceptance of computer read-outs as the "truth" about a relationship.

Opinion polls try to determine the truth about people and issues. Poll samplings are influenced in ways that may prejudice the data: how the question is asked, who is asked, how people feel when asked, people's perception of why the question is asked. Such variables influence the response. A "margin of error" tries to offer a margin for error. At best, polls offer a partial truth, sometimes touted as "the way people think."

A news organization is unable to give us the *whole* truth about the *whole* world. I heard one radio station boast: "Give us twenty-two minutes and we'll give you the world." This boast cannot be met. Yet the *idol* of the boast may convince us it is true. We need sound insights to avoid worshiping the claims of such a "golden calf."

We often believe as conclusive much of what we hear, see, or read. We have neither time nor resources to do our own research. We accept as factual what we see on TV, read in the newspapers, or hear on the radio. We cannot check the accuracy of every story! How difficult it was to get the truth when the USSR was breaking up. What a mixture of stories came into our living rooms. A roller coaster of frustration and hope touched us for a few days. Within a period of one week an earth-shattering change took place in the Soviet Union. Reporters did their best to interpret events for us. But the limitations were obvious. No one could be "all over" to cover the story and spell out implications not even imagined at the time.

We often use communications data as though they were the whole truth. In an office discussion, an argument over a beer, or a dialogue in the beauty parlor, there is little doubt about the truth of our "sources." Animosity or deceit is not involved. Neither are we trying to fool people. We believe what we see and hear. We may even trust what we read in the *National Enquirer*! That's "how conditions are" in America. A story may give us only partial truth. It may focus attention on one aspect of a story while neglecting others. Statements may be lifted out of context. The truth suffers when this happens, but it offers enough "truth" to get our attention.

I remember when I was transferred from a rather long stay in one place. I had worked in a parish for a number of years. When I left, the pastor and the people knew where I was going for my next assignment. Then we lost touch. About ten years later I began working for Isaiah 43 parish missions. At that time it was sponsored by Ferdy Mahfood and Food for the Poor in Florida. One part of the ministry was to visit the poor people in Jamaica or Haiti to get a feel for their awesome poverty. Somehow, word got back to the pastor that I had left the Capuchins. Another story had it that I had gone to the "missions" in a foreign country. Relying on some inventive reporting, the "truth" got waylaid. The truth? I *had* gone to a foreign country (Jamaica), and I *was* working with Food for the Poor. In addition I remain a Capuchin in good standing, and I am working in the USA in the preaching and retreat ministry of the Capuchins.

Sometimes disinformation is given by people in power positions. As a result, we develop a healthy skepticism. We recognize the need to get facts before accepting such "truth." Government people are prone to share only that portion of the "truth" that helps their cause. "They" decide what the public can hear. Cover-ups, as well as inadequate or biased information, are not unknown. Fairness requires us to use time and effort to seek the truth. Power people may put roadblocks in the way of such a search. Truth seekers are not always popular.

Searching for the truth requires us to put aside prejudices and biased opinions. We try to listen with minds open to the truth. This attitude is dedicated to discovering truth. We need this attitude when listening to or reading stories about the Church. People bring many ideas and attitudes to the listening process. Be aware of prejudice or bias that may influence your openness to the "Truth."

Thinking It Through

Consider what happens when we are confronted by an upsetting "truth." I am not very objective in dealing with such "truth."

When I dislike someone's ideas or theology, I take perverse delight if such people get into trouble. I have a sense of satisfaction when they get "foot-in-mouth" disease. No way will I invest time to discover if they are right or wrong or even partially right or wrong. On the other hand, I readily accept ideas that agree with my own. Anything that supports my ideas (prejudices?) is acceptable. I reject ideas (and people) that challenge my pet ideas or opinions!

Labels help me categorize people. It organizes my opinions. If I label people, I can listen to them with a certain mind-set. If they are liberal and I am liberal, they make sense to me. If someone is conservative, and I am conservative, he or she makes sense to me. If one is on the cutting edge of things and I want to be on the cutting edge, I admire that person. I find the ideas of such "wise" people to be personally acceptable.

On the other hand, if I am a liberal listening to conservatives, I reject their ideas. If I am a conservative listening to liberals, I call them "far out" and "a danger to the Church." My mind-set often determines my ability to "hear" the truth.

Labeling is an arrogant action. We decide who is right and who is wrong, who has the truth and who doesn't. We presume knowledge that permits us to decide what is best for Church and society. We accept infallibility for self that not even the Church claims. We claim open-mindedness even while closing our ears to challenging ideas. Clearly, some people have nothing worthwhile to say! It is prudent on our part to say so!

I remember how firm I was in my judgment of one of my Capuchin brothers. I knew that he was an arrogant person trying to shove his ideas on the rest of us. Everything I heard him say or other people's report about what he said tended to confirm my infallible judgment. Then I became part of a group of which he was a member. Little by little, I began to see him in a different light. My previous opinions had been highly prejudicial. Prolonged personal contact helped me see him in a new light. I hate to think what I would have missed if we had not been assigned to work together.

What a large amount of time I had wasted interpreting his words and actions to confirm my prejudice! Such "humble" arrogance is a poor substitute for the truth. It seemed so right and comfortable. Close the mind and heart to any ideas that confront preconceived notions. Reject anything that would be unsettling. What a great way to avoid confusion, challenge, and conversion!

In reality, I am conservative, liberal, progressive, on the cutting edge, a stick-in-the-mud, or most any label you want to use. It depends on what dimension of life you talk about. I get excited about new ideas. They are signs of life. They nurture an attitude of maturity. The more Scripture I read, the more I realize how much there is to learn. God's word cannot be confined to one particular meaning. The Spirit blowing through Scripture is astonishing, exciting, and frightening at the same time.

But — if you expect me to *do* what the Scripture requires of gospel people, I become very cautious. "Give me time to reflect and pray." "Let's talk it over." Begin a discussion club. Sponsor a seminar. Such "good" actions avoid personal conversion. I evade the personal commitment to *do* what Scripture says. I pick and choose positions depending on the price I may have to pay. If you'd like to "talk" about it, I'm ready! If you expect me to change my lifestyle — "Let's not rush into this!"

Reflect on your own positions. You may find similar feelings. Jesus calls us to accept the gospel truth. He expects us to accept all the consequences of the gospel truth. Things will change and life will be different. The power of Jesus' gospel truth will make a difference in our lives. Gospel truth is life-giving, enlightening, and tough to follow.

I have many ways to resist conversion. I am knowledge-able. I have good ideas about community life. I have read and written on the topic. People like my ideas and support them. However, when a demand of community (family) life inter-feres with what I'd like to do — the demands of a meeting or helping someone with their work or taking time for hospitality — watch my dust! Let a generous community person do it! I have so much to do that I cannot help! My written words and lived actions are often in conflict. If we talk in generali-ties, count me in. If you get specific and expect me to change, forget it!

Evading the demands of the gospel truth keeps us stuck in opinions that have little life. We need to sort the treasure from the trash. Comfortable opinions do not always satisfy or offer us new life. Ideas that are destructive or create animos-ity need careful scrutiny in the light of gospel truth. Honest reflection will keep us open to genuine gospel reality.

> "But I say to you that if you are angry with a brother or sister, you will be liable to judgment; and if you insult a brother or sister, you will be liable to the council; and if you say, 'You fool,' you will be liable to the hell of fire. . . . You have heard that it was said, 'You shall love your neighbor and hate your enemy.' But I say to you, Love your enemies and pray for those who persecute you" (Matt 5:22, 43-44).

These words offer uncomplicated truth. They make de-mands. Putting them into practice requires personal forgive-ness of enemies. It means abandoning the power that anger or resentment give me. It requires dealing with feelings that give "legitimacy" to my actions. I am invited to surrender inner hurts. I do *not* use them as a club against another. I will *not* use them to impose my will on others or to wallow in guilt feelings. I will *deal* with them and not allow them to control my life.

The gospel truth is a call to conversion. It doesn't matter if I am conservative or liberal, progressive or traditional. The gospel requires conversion no matter what label I use for my opinions. I can't excuse myself to Jesus by having good discussions on the Bible if I refuse conversion! Jesus wants us to give flesh to gospel truth in our lives. It seems obvious that our response to the gospel will change as we mature. Differing circumstances will influence our understanding of the truth. The worst thing we can do is refuse to change. Being static in life is to join the walking dead.

> But be doers of the word, and not merely hearers who deceive themselves. For if any are hearers of the word and not doers, they are like those who look at themselves in a mirror; for they look at themselves and, on going away, immediately forget what they were like. But those who look into the perfect law, the law of liberty . . . being not hearers who forget but doers who act — they will be blessed in their doing (Jas 1:22-25).

The Lord will ask us questions dealing with relationships rather than labels. If I substitute talking for action, I stand condemned. If I demand change in others without any change in myself, the Lord will ask tough questions. Labels or prejudices, laziness or fear will be useless excuses to offer to Jesus. Jesus looks at the quality of my response to the gospel truth, not how I managed to evade it.

> "The men of Nineveh will appear in court when this generation is on trial, and ensure their condemnation, for they repented at the preaching of Jonah; and what is here is greater than Jonah!
> "No one lights a lamp and puts it in a cellar, but on the lampstand so that those who come in may see the light. The lamp of your body is the eye. When your eyes are sound, you have light for your whole body; but when they are bad, your body is in darkness. See to it then that the light you have is not darkness. If you have light for your whole body with no trace of darkness, it will all be full of light, as when the light of a lamp shines on you" (Luke 11:32-36 — REB).

Choose to take time for reflection. Do not substitute labels for reality or discussion for action. It can be fearful to have my ideas challenged. It is risky to leave the shelter of what I know for the unknown. The unfamiliar territory of fresh ideas and/or a call to conversion seems frightening. A dedicated Christian walks the way of conversion and growth. Security does not come through brilliant deductions, but through Jesus' presence. His presence is evident in the brothers and sisters who walk at my side.

> But now that faith has come, we are no longer subject to a disciplinarian, for in Christ Jesus you are all children of God through faith. . . . There is no longer Jew or Greek, there is no longer slave or free, there is no longer male or female; for all of you are one in Christ Jesus (Gal 3:25-28).

Seeing and Believing

"Some things have to be believed to be seen" (Ralph Hodgson). John's Gospel has a story about seeking truth. John often uses the symbol of "seeing" to describe faith. Its opposite is "blindness" or refusal to see (believe). "Blind" is John's description of people who refuse to believe Jesus. John speaks of light and darkness. Faith brings light. Refusal to believe brings darkness. These issues are addressed in the story of the man born blind in chapter 9 of John's Gospel. As you read the story, keep in mind what "seeing" and "blindness" mean for John.

The blind man asks for nothing. He is simply present, a kind of "everyman." The first thing Jesus does is to deal with the "blindness" of his disciples. They *presumed* that the common belief about blind people was true — either the blind man or his parents had sinned. Blindness is a punishment (so "they" say). Somebody had sinned! Everybody knows that! It is an obvious religious "truth."

Jesus deals with this "blind" prejudice without hesitation: "As he walked along, he saw a man blind from birth. His disciples asked him, 'Rabbi, who sinned, this man or his parents, that he was born blind?' " (John 9:1-2).

The disciples had no hesitation. They *knew* it had to be one or the other. All Jesus had to do was take one side or the other. No problem! "Jesus answered, 'Neither this man nor his parents sinned; he was born blind so that God's works might be revealed in him'" (John 9:3).

The blindness of the disciples was the worst kind — they *thought they were right!* They believed there was no alternative to their version of the "truth." They were in darkness and didn't know it — a very dark darkness. Jesus challenged their prejudice. Imagine their surprise at Jesus' answer. Prejudice thinks it has looked at every angle of the issue. That is part of its problem. It is closed off from the truth by its narrowness. The awful truth is: *It doesn't see and thinks it does!*

Such confrontation is threatening. The gospel truth asks me to examine *my* opinions. It threatens labels I use to put people in their "place." It requires me to change my attitudes about some people. How do I feel about homosexuals? Or Catholics who get a divorce? What about criminals? Child abusers? Can I ignore them and/or condemn them out of hand? What about gang members who shoot innocent children? What about people of other cultures? Do I really "know" all about them? Listen to your opinions and attitudes. Notice how readily light and darkness surface in life. It takes persistent effort to reshape stubborn, longstanding opinions and attitudes and allow the gospel truth to critique them.

Jesus has the audacity to say: "As long as I am in the world, I am the light of the world" (John 9:5). Christians are committed to walk in the light of Christ. Reading Scripture tends to pour light on the dark places of life. If we choose to follow the gospel, be ready for truth that calls for change. If we blot out the gospel and ignore its call, we walk in darkness.

The blind man still hasn't said or done anything. He has not seen Jesus, since he is blind. But Jesus sees him and enters his life. "He spat on the ground and made mud with the saliva and spread the mud on the man's eyes, saying to him, 'Go, wash in the pool of Siloam' (which means Sent). Then he went and washed and came back able to see" (John 9:6-7).

Discipleship requires many things. Among them is trust. What I like about the blind man is his trustful response to Jesus. He had nothing to say about what was happening. Jesus' touch calls for a response. Jesus smears his face with mud and tells him to wash. My initial reaction is that if Jesus hadn't put mud on his face he wouldn't have had to wash!

I find myself in similar situations. If Jesus didn't "touch" my ideas and opinions with his light, I wouldn't have to reevaluate them. I wouldn't have to accept new "truth." I could live contentedly without any commitment to change. After I've tried to reconcile with someone for five, six, or seven times, I figure I've done my part. Then I hear Jesus tell Peter that he should forgive another person seventy times seven times (Matt 18:22). Jesus messes things up for me. I can't leave things as they are. I hate getting mud on my face!

I must deal with what I know. Like the blind man, I have to wash off foolish ideas and opinions and habits. As I wash at the pool, I am surprised to see things differently. My former "truths" seem harsh, even foolishly arrogant. Jesus brings me to my senses. The foolishness (getting mud on my face) becomes a gateway to hope. When the blind man finished washing he could see!

Seeing brings consequences. The rest of chapter 9 looks at some of the consequences for the blind man. No one can escape the consequences of "seeing." I may have to apologize to people I have misjudged. I may have to discard labels I used to keep people in their "place." I may have to question long-standing personal prejudices. I may have to realize the depth of my ignorance. I need more steady effort to *follow* the gospel truth instead of merely hearing it. The gospel truth makes a difference. To refuse the consequences of "seeing" is to remain blind. "If you were blind, you would not have sin. But now that you say, 'We see,' your sin remains" (John 9:41).

What an awe-full statement! Physical blindness is no problem for Jesus. That can happen to anyone. But if people say they "see" when they are "blind," that is bad news! The good news that Jesus gives is simple. Go! Wash! See! Listen! Follow! Act! We are not in a hopeless position. Jesus offers a way to walk in the light as surely as he condemns blindness that masquerades as sight.

Another Story

Conversion is part of another story in John's Gospel. Jesus prays at the tomb of Lazarus: " 'Father, I thank you for having heard me. I knew that you always hear me, but I have said this for the sake of the crowd standing here, so that they may believe that you sent me.' When he had said this, he cried with a loud voice, 'Lazarus, come out!' The dead man came out, his hands and feet bound with strips of cloth and his face wrapped in a cloth. Jesus said to them, 'Unbind him, and let him go' " (John 11:42-44).

These last words tell me to go and "loose" people. Wherever I have bound people by my attitudes or verbal attacks, Jesus asks me to unloose them and set them free. I am the only one who can offer this freedom to others. My willingness to "let loose" of ideas, opinions, and judgments that "bind" people is a clear demand of the gospel. The truth of the gospel demands a change in my inner self! What I do for others I also do for myself. If I have put my "self" in a category that is untrue, Jesus calls me to change the ideas that "bind" me.

———————

Reflection

Which of my attitudes keep people "bound"? What do I intend to do about it? How blind am I? Can I risk asking others what blindness they see in me? How will I deal with the consequences of their answer? Have I been arrogant in my attitudes? Do my normal reactions to people (family) offer affirmation or rejection? How strong is my desire to change? Am I happy with my prejudices? Do I use physical or emotional force to prove that I'm right? Does a nation's use of force *prove* that it is right (Might makes right!)? What kind of blindness do I have? What will it take to admit light into my darkness? Must I walk alone on the path of change? What does Jesus say about the need for help on the journey? In what area(s) of life is my "seeing" good? What does "washing in the pool'' mean for me? What times in my life did I feel the Lord put "mud" on my face? Do I "bind" people (family / self / others) by a domineering attitude? Do I bind them by never sharing my needs? Do I bind them by refusing to share my "true" self with them? Do I condemn them for indifference when I haven't made my needs known? What is the source of "truth" in my life? How do I determine what is true? What (who) are the most reliable sources of truth for me? How do I deal with others who are "blind" to the truth? How do I "see" the gospel truth working in my daily life? What techniques do I use to avoid discovering the truth about myself? How do my magazine subscriptions reflect my search for the "truth"? How can I improve my openness to the "whole truth" — wherever I find it?

So Ananias went and entered the house. He laid his hands on Saul and said: "Brother Saul, the Lord Jesus, who appeared to you on your way here, has sent me so that you may regain your sight and be filled with the Holy Spirit." And immediately something like scales fell from his eyes, and his sight was restored (Acts 9:17-18).

Like Saul, we need an Ananias to help us "see" the truth. May friends help us as Ananias helped Saul. May truthfulness and compassion remove the scales of "false self" perceptions that block the light of Jesus. "Everyone who belongs to the truth listens to my voice" (John 18:37).

CHAPTER TWO

Give Me a Break

"Rat race" often describes the work-world of today. In this rat race people hurry and scurry about. People jet hither and yon to make a profit and achieve success. People are obsessed with "projects." They demand perks and expect others to say "How high?" when they say "Jump!" Some "rat racers" seem unable to withdraw from the fray. They are chained as firmly as hostages, trapped in an inhumane value system. These values say: "Work is more important than personal growth." "Profits are more important than relationships." "The gross national product is more vital than peace." For some people, it is easier to work with data banks than people, with sale of products than with intimacy with loved ones. For some, work provides an escape from intimacy. For others, it fills the gaps that come with lack of intimacy. For some, it may be a way of serving people.

Many folks are in the rat race because survival requires it. Lack of jobs paying an adequate wage makes it necessary to hold several jobs. It is tiring. It is disheartening to see the suffering of loved ones because of lack of money. The hopelessness depresses the spirit. When even extreme efforts yield meager results, frustration and despair grow rampant. Reasons for addiction in rat-race people are numerous and diverse. It seems unreal to think that the rat race is for the human race! Many good people get chewed up in the rat-race grinder.

Our focus on success and achievement-at-any-cost has consequences. The rat race is not a place where everyone is cared for. It is not always a place of human happiness. To fall victim to the rat race often absorbs so much energy that little is left for the people in our lives. For people whose survival puts them on the rat-race treadmill, life tends to lose its vibrant edge. Many of the consequences are devastating to a full life and solid relationships. Let's explore some of these consequences.

It is difficult to argue with success. Society offers an abundance of consumer goods. We are free in ways unknown to many people. We have elaborate systems for managing research and development. Rewards come to people for designing better systems. We are a rich society. Except for the Revolutionary War and our tragic Civil War, we have managed to keep war from our land. The horror of bombed-out cities and wartime destruction by other nations has not touched our lives.

But we do have a crisis of spirit. We face issues of human despair in the face of apparent plenty. There is a loss of the spirit of commitment to one another. Failure to take time to know each other can lead to commitments that quickly fall apart. The substitute of success-at-all-costs for successful relationships hampers a relaxed personal growth. Concrete and asphalt keep us from touching the earth that supports us. Amoral use of power and violence keeps our inner spirit at a dwarf level. Over-use of the intellect and under-use of the heart gives us an unbalanced view of life and success. The gentling power of nature is unavailable to millions of people. It is simply another resource to be used without respect. Lacking an inner core to guide life, we are subject to external influences without discrimination. Cults, literalism, and business practices tell us what to do and how to live. They replace our taking personal responsibility for our lives. The ''system,'' whether secular or religious, often supports such unreflective ways of living.

We pay a high price for this. Justice is sometimes a victim on the road to riches and progress. Gospel people need to examine our social systems and find ways to improve them. Gospel people are challenged to change the imperfect elements in our justice system. We are faced with the cost of decaying urban areas as well as economic inequality. Many people get lost "in the cracks" of our system. Gospel people need to address the issues of the "lost people" in our system. We cannot tolerate the spectacle of thousands of homeless teenagers living on the streets of our big cities. The reign of God does not grow when millions of people are homeless and hungry throughout the world. We Americans have more goods and products than we can use. We face a problem of waste disposal while millions are starving. Landfills overflow with castoffs while many people have no shelter and little food. " 'Tis a puzzlement!''

> O house of Jacob,
>   come, let us walk
>   in the light of the LORD! . . .
> Their land is filled with silver and gold,
>   and there is no end to their treasures. . . .
> Their land is filled with idols;
>   they bow down to the work of their hands,
>   to what their own fingers have made (Isa 2:5, 7-8).
>
> The LORD rises to argue his case;
>   he stands to judge the peoples. . . .
> It is you who have devoured the vineyard;
>   the spoil of the poor is in your houses.
> What do you mean by crushing my people,
>   by grinding the face of the poor? says the Lord God of
>   hosts (Isa 3:13-14).

Sprays and insecticides that give us freedom from insects also cause disease. Specialization in many professions brings growth. It also lessens our awareness of how one thing impacts another. The "big picture" is lost in a race to develop new products that turn a profit. Morality and people-needs may be overlooked in favor of the need for profitability. Reasonable profits are not evil. But choices that favor profits over people cannot bear the gospel light.

We sometimes ignore the impact products have on our earth, our lakes and streams, our forests and environment. When tragedy strikes we get concerned. But we quickly forget as other crises grab our attention. We provide jobs through defense contracts without asking whether we need more weapons. Would it be possible to have a better life, building the tools of peace rather than war? New office buildings arise, wonders of architectural design and engineering. But housing for the poor and homeless lags. We state that more production will solve our problems. Yet such a solution often leaves meager moments for family and friends. Poor people become anonymous "thems" we never meet. But we dutifully design programs to help "them." "'Tis a puzzlement!"

Can gospel people design programs without knowing the people they wish to help? Can gospel people design programs for the handicapped without listening to them? Can gospel people remain distant from people in need? How do we decide where to spend tax money? Are we spending wisely? St. Francis of Assisi learned about lepers when he embraced a leper. Gospel people discover what Francis discovered. As Francis put it: "What before seemed bitter, was changed into sweetness of soul and body." "'Tis a puzzlement!"

We expect the private sector to care for the needy. We expect it to deal with social issues on local and regional levels. But at the same time, some businesses fail to give workers a living wage. At times, workers demand wages beyond what a company can absorb. Then bankruptcy leaves everyone a loser. It adds to the problem of poverty. Corporations get caught in an economic bind and move to where labor is cheaper. The cycle begins again — unemployment, frustration, crime, depression, anger — consequences that diminish human life. Gospel people know that ignoring these issues is suicidal for the human spirit.

Church and State *talk* about justice for all. But we do not always practice what we preach when it touches our pocketbook. It is entertaining to have shows on the "rich and famous." Yet the reality for many people is: "Poor, unknown

— and uncared for!'' We claim the right to get whatever we want or desire. But if poor people lack *necessities*, can gospel people fulfill personal *desires* in the presence of these ''poor ones''? '' 'Tis a puzzlement!''

There are inconsistencies in our society and in each of us. Solutions are not easily found. Sound-thinking men and women are needed to tackle these problems. That includes you and me. There is a need for growth in interpersonal relationships as well as in profit-taking. We must find ways to meet people-needs as well as business-needs. These *do not have to be* enemies. However, if greed and power become more important than people, we are left with a shabby society with rich tastes.

I contribute to this problem. I am an ''addictive consumer'' when it comes to electronic devices. A few years ago, I received a fine, portable cassette recorder/radio combination. It gave me fine sound. I really liked it. Then I read an ad for a portable cassette with automatic reverse. ''What a great idea,'' I said to myself. ''If I had one of those, I wouldn't have to keep changing cassettes.'' The desire for such a product grew. Being creative, I found a way to get one. Now I have just what I wanted. My desires were met. Isn't life wonderful! The problem for me arises from my feelings of guilt. Where is my personal concern for the poor? How can I so readily fulfill my own desires and still talk about caring for the poor and needy? Conversion is needed. But, practically, I'd like to find a way to keep the cassette recorder and stop feeling like a hypocrite at the same time. '' 'Tis a puzzlement.'' I know the direction the answer will take. Trying to be a genuine gospel person will require *my* personal conversion.

It seems grossly unjust for one person to have a salary of $200,000 while poor people scrounge in dumpsters for food. It is not a matter of depriving the rich. But luxury becomes abominable when human beings are dying for lack of food and shelter. No one *needs* $500 a day ($3500 a week) to live! Anyone can become accustomed to such a lifestyle. But there is no inherent right that such lifestyles must be maintained. (Nor do I really need another cassette recorder in the face of survival needs of my brothers and sisters.)

Each of us has the right to live a human life, with a future full of hope and a reasonable livelihood. Everyone need not have an absolutely equal share of the world's goods. Each person does have a right to whatever is required to live in dignity. *That right comes from God.* It is not given by economic power. God demands it! It is not a vague wish on God's part. An extravagant lifestyle is not right for a gospel person when people are living in destitution. No one should have to live in destitution! A life of dignity is a *right* for all people. Sharing resources is one way to move in that direction. Wise men and women will find ways to accomplish this.

Technology is not the villain. The instruments of technology are run by people. If I am greedy and indifferent to others, I need to change my heart. Blaming progress or technology or electronics would miss the mark. Things are directed by people. The human heart is the place where real changes must happen. When enough people *choose* generosity instead of greed, we will have made a start. When enough people *choose* people instead of profit, we will have made a start. When enough people *choose* gospel-values instead of rat-race values, we will have made a start. When *I choose* gospel-values instead of merely meeting desire-values, *I* will have made a start. The *good news* is that many gospel people are already doing such choosing! They need to multiply and fill the earth. Business is not the villain. Many business people show real care for their workers. Executives are not the villains. Many of them seek to develop policies that reflect concern for people over product. Workers are not the villains. Many of them give quality work for their wages. The list could continue.

But there are weaknesses. There are business people who are callous and hard. There are executives whose only concern is corporate profits and personal perks. There are workers whose indifference and poor work habits debilitate a sound business.

Technology *can* be used to put others out of business. It's a "dog-eat-dog" atmosphere in the market place. "If you can't stand the heat, get out of the kitchen!'' Some people think this is the way it *has* to be! Little consideration is given to a gospel alternative.

Couples often need two jobs (or more!) to make ends meet. Such a necessity puts a heavy burden on relationships. The consequences of doing *nothing* are enormous. If we value relationships over the gross national product, people over profits, compassion over competition, gospel people will prove it by action!

> Strengthen the weak hands,
>   and make firm the feeble knees.
> Say to those who are of a fearful heart,
>   ''Be strong, do not fear!
> Here is your God. . . .
> He will come and save you.''
>
> Then the eyes of the blind shall be opened,
>   and the ears of the deaf unstopped;
> then the lame shall leap like a deer,
>   and the tongue of the speechless sing for joy.
> For water will break forth in the wilderness,
>   and streams in the desert; . . .
>
> A highway shall be there,
>   and it shall be called the Holy Way;
> the unclean shall not travel on it,
>   but it shall be for God's people;
>   no traveler, not even fools shall go astray. . . .
>   But the redeemed shall walk there. . . .
> everlasting joy shall be upon their heads;
>   they shall obtain joy and gladness,
>   and sorrow and sighing shall flee away (Isa 35:3-6, 8, 9-10).

Law

We need to take a gospel look at the laws of our land. Law is a tool meant to serve the human race. It has the possibility of offering guidelines in dealing with problems between people. It serves people and society. Law has a place in any society that recognizes and respects the value of human life. No society can long exist that does away with just laws.

But law can become oppressive. When it is applied unequally because of wealth or lack of it, it becomes oppressive. When it allows clever schemers to circumvent its provisions, it is a mockery. When it tolerates unjust practices and allows them to flourish, law becomes a sham. Law is a mix of *both* good and oppressive applications. It is in need of constant critique and relevant reform. Without such critique, law can be a dictator rather than a servant. When laws are applied with prejudice; when law favors one group over another; when law is so complicated it cannot function because of overloaded courts — then changes are needed. When law is unbalanced in its application or unjustly favors those who can afford good lawyers, it needs change. When law unevenly condemns people because of race or nationality or sexual preferences, it is in need of reform. Both civil and church law is subject to the criteria of true justice as revealed in the Bible.

> "The scribes and the Pharisees sit on Moses' seat; therefore, do whatever they teach you and follow it; but do not do as they do, for they do not practice what they teach. They tie up heavy burdens, hard to bear, and lay them on the shoulders of others; but they themselves are unwilling to lift a finger to move them. They do all their deeds to be seen by others. . . .
>
> "Woe to you, scribes and Pharisees, hypocrites! For you tithe mint, dill, and cummin, and have neglected the weightier matters of the law; justice and mercy and faith. It is these you ought to have practiced without neglecting the others. You blind guides! You strain out a gnat but swallow a camel!" (Matt 23:2-5, 23).

Law is a human instrument. It is not infallible. It *needs* change and is constantly being changed. Gospel people support the legal profession and legislatures as they work for change. There is plenty of work for reformers. We need wise men and women to deal with this issue.

Our goal is not simply new laws or the cessation of old, bad laws. Law is meant to reflect human and societal needs and promote the pursuit of liberty and human happiness. If we were angels, always obedient and understanding one another, we wouldn't need law. But we are human beings who are weak, sometimes greedy, often more concerned with our own advancement than with others' welfare. We need law to govern our relationships and deal with our arguments. Law's goal is a society where human beings are treated with human dignity. It is a challenge to achieve such a goal.

Law is not solely the servant of government, allowing rulers to do whatever they want. It is not the slave of influential people, doing as they please at whatever cost to ordinary folks. Neither is it merely a tool to punish those who don't fit into society and must be "put away"!

Law is meant to direct society/church in a way that is both human and humane. Society's need to punish criminals is its right. But the punishment must be human and humane even for the harshest criminal. The goal of law is not revenge, but a peaceful society. It is not meant to diminish human life, but to enable people to live humanly in society. The enormous problems of our criminal justice system cannot be dealt with in an atmosphere of fear and vengeance. Whether in civil society or church society, laws springing from fear generally prove to be ultimately ineffective.

Our "feelings" toward rapists, mass murderers, and drunk drivers who kill is not surprising. Such feelings are human reactions to pain and fear and loss. If they become the basis of law, however, they become self-serving rather than society-building. Getting revenge may be self-satisfying, but it is not the basis for good law. We are not always wise in dealing with these issues. We tend to choose the same, familiar solutions over and over. Creativity is lost in a swamp of legitimate feelings of anger and hatred. Lacking creativity, we do nothing new. We repeat "old" solutions that fail us again. Peace is not our final product! We need wise and dedicated men and women to deal with these issues. Gospel people, competent in the law and dedicated to the gospel, must address this issue.

I remember a personal frustration with the law when I was

trying to help a friend. This friend (Let's call her Abby) had many personal and mental problems. There was a need to get her into a psychiatric clinic before her family suffered any more trauma. The law bent over backwards to protect Abby's right not to be arbitrarily institutionalized. I was helpless to do anything because I had no blood relationship with Abby. The family refused to do anything. I experienced frustration with a law that refused me the right to help someone. I was glad there was protection for Abby. I was frustrated and angry that there was nothing the law allowed me to do. It prevented the kind of help Abby needed. Because there was no way around it, the family misery continued until it burst into violence. Then action was taken. I appreciate how much wisdom is needed to write laws that allow for healthy help without taking away personal freedom. Gospel people need competence in helping to write such laws.

Quite a Journey

From rat race to law is a challenging journey. Law and business, compassion and justice, mercy and a peaceful society are linked to each other. To neglect any of them will keep us from building a world suitable for living a human life. It will keep us from having a church that supports growth and development. It might help us to be efficient while we lose the heart of the gospel — love.

When Jesus addressed these issues, he was not a visionary with his head in the clouds. He knew the human heart and its foibles. He chose not to let the dark side of human nature dictate choices.

"For if you forgive others their trespasses, your heavenly Father will also forgive you; but if you do not forgive others, neither will your Father forgive your trespasses" (Matt 6:14-15).

"But love your enemies, do good and lend, expecting nothing in return. Your reward will be great, and you will be children of the Most High; for he is kind to the ungrateful and wicked. Be merciful, just as your Father is merciful'' (Luke 6:35-36).

''That slave who knew what his master wanted, but did not prepare himself or do what was wanted, will receive a severe beating. But the one who did not know and did what deserved a beating will receive a light beating. From everyone to whom much has been given, much will be required; and from the one to whom much has been entrusted, even more will be demanded'' (Luke 12:47-48).

Jesus ''lays it on the line.'' Gospel people are committed to this message. It requires more than intellectual assent. It requires a personal *commitment* to follow the gospel. The rat race can distract us from the gospel. It absorbs time and energy, perspective and focus. The need for results is so demanding that there is little time for gospel reflection. A rat-race attitude convinces us that gospel reflection is a waste of time. What counts is what happens in the board room! The rat race becomes obsessive, absorbing every waking moment of life.

We take it home. We take it to work. We talk about it at lunch. It infiltrates our recreation. It tends to muffle, even stifle, any gospel word that seeks entry. It is difficult to be compulsive about work and committed to Jesus. Promoting the reign of God requires the integration of gospel and life. It will not happen if our contact with God and gospel is only a Sunday affair.

Then he told them a parable: ''The land of a rich man produced abundantly. And he thought to himself, 'What should I do, for I have no place to store my crops?' Then he said, 'I will do this: I will pull down my barns and build larger ones, and there I will store all my grain and my goods. And I will say to my soul, ''Soul, you have ample goods laid up for many years; relax, eat, drink, be merry.'' ' But God said to him, 'You fool! This very night your life will be demanded of you. And the things you have prepared, whose will they be?' So it is with those who store up treasures for themselves but are not rich toward God'' (Luke 12:16-21).

Compulsive pursuit of law and order can hinder the gospel life. Both law and order can be good. Obsessive pursuit of them can minimize compassion. The everyday experience of violence, both physical and psychological, can make us defensive. The chaos of terrorism frightens us. The threat of economic bankruptcy leads to despair. Like a trapped animal, we fight back, often with the same weapons used on us. Violence and anger multiply. The last state is worse than the first.

The cry for punishment and vengeance seems legitimate in the face of violence. Obviously, these reactions do not support gospel attitudes. Human reactions are understandable. We would be strange creatures if we had no fear or anger in such situations. But the gospel calls us to deal with these feelings in ways that are not violent. We are expected to deal with the reality of our feelings and not deny them. We point them in a direction that is life-giving and not destructive. The gospel asks us to forgive when we prefer to seek revenge. It asks us to pray for persecutors when we would prefer to see them punished. It is our task to confront the evil that people do. We demand that they are made to deal with their ''crimes.'' But the gospel invites us to renounce actions that make them enemies. So long as hatred and anger linger in our hearts, we are not free. Forgiveness is the way to life and freedom.

The gospel does not oppose order. Neither does it deny the value of just laws. The gospel offers plans for building a society where punishment leads to *conversion*. The gospel seeks to bring people together rather than divide them. The gospel supports laws that serve people rather than oppress them. With a gospel vision, we have a perspective from which to design laws, policies, and practices that are life-giving.

Gospel people know we may never complete the task. But we are not free to desist from it. Whatever we can do, we will do. Compassion is not a luxury for us. It is part of our identity as Christians. We accept responsibility to promote the reign of God in our world. We will make our lives as genuinely gospel-oriented as possible.

> ''Would any of you think of building a tower without first sitting down and calculating the cost to see whether he could afford to finish it? Otherwise, if he has laid its foundation and

then is unable to complete it, everyone who sees it will laugh at him. 'There goes the man,' they will say, 'who started to build and could not finish' '' (Luke 14:28-30 — REB).

Realistically, we cannot live the gospel in isolation. We need the support of a faith-community. Such support strengthens us to challenge people's unreflective worship of law and order. We need other Christians to dialogue with us. We need them to pray for us. We need them to hold us when we fail. We need them to love us when we act foolishly. We need them to heal our wounds, offering the balm of love when we have been rejected. We need to hear their ideas and varying viewpoints. Building a gospel-world is a community affair.

Alone, isolated in a hostile world, faith easily collapses. Trusting "practicality" may mock gospel values. Ideas learned in business school may make the gospel vision seem like a trip to never-never land. Without support and love, we succumb to the false values of society. Within a faith-filled community we are enabled to offer hope and life to both civil and church society.

"The sower sows the word. These are the ones on the path where the word is sown; when they hear, Satan immediately comes and takes away the word that is sown in them. And these are the ones sown on rocky ground: when they hear the word, they immediately receive it with joy. But they have no root, and endure only for a while; then, when trouble or persecution arises on account of the word, immediately they fall away. And others are those sown among the thorns: these are the ones who hear the word, but the cares of the world, and the lure of wealth, and the desire for other things come in and choke the word, and it yields nothing. And these are the ones sown on the good soil: they hear the word and accept it and bear fruit, thirty and sixty and a hundredfold" (Mark 4:14-20).

God wants us to plunge into society just as Jesus plunged into our world and presented an alternative way of life. The world keeps changing and so must we. Our proclamation of the gospel will be made in ways our world can understand.

Our best proclamation is the way we live. In the course of a lifetime, we will change often. We grow from babyhood to adolescence to adulthood to maturity to old age. The changes are obvious. In our faith-life we also change. We do not remain babies forever, expecting "Big Daddy-God" to do everything for us.

We reach an adolescence that seeks independence from God, questioning everything. It is a healthy time that brings us to a more mature faith. This newfound faith will be formed and reformed through experience, listening to the word, through prayer and reading, in crises and pain. Our faith will face public issues and require study and dialogue. We will experience suffering and struggle, trying to understand how our God is present in such situations. We will experience great joy and discover a God of delights. Change is part of the gospel life. God is too big to be confined to a catechism or a book on theology. The search will continue until we die.

Our manner of living the gospel will change as we know Jesus better. We will apply the gospel to new situations as they come along. Gospel people discover fresh insights as God's revelation continues to unfold. We face new experiences that require plunging anew into the gospel. The *Rule for Secular Franciscans* puts it well:

> Motivated by the dynamic power of the gospel, let them conform their thoughts and deeds to those of Christ by means of that *radical* [italics mine] interior change which the gospel itself calls "conversion." Human frailty makes it necessary that this conversion be carried out daily! (Secular Franciscan Order Rule #7).

Reflection

Am I caught in the rat race? How do I like it? What attracts me to the rat race? Am I caught in the gospel race? How do I like it? What attracts or repels me about the gospel race? How do I handle conflict between the two? Which one is most in-

fluential? How strong are the relationships in my life? . . .
with my spouse? . . . with my family? . . . with friends?
. . . with employees/employer? . . . with fellow workers?
. . . with people in my parish administration? . . . with
God? How can I prove that I care about them? Do I presume
that they know of my care? Is law always fair? How do I feel
about Church law, e.g., about marriage, divorce, demands for
baptism? Is the law implemented without prejudice? How do
I administer the "law" of my office? . . . home? . . . group?
. . . family? . . . parish? How do I show compassion? Do I
use law as a club to make people do what I want? How good
am I as a listener? Can I prove it? Am I a grudge-holder or
conflict-avoider? What are the consequences? Do I stew rather
than deal with touchy issues? How do I deal with stress? Is
there creative, positive stress in my life that pushes me to new
horizons? Do I refuse help from others? Am I an individualist
or a team person? How often does the gospel influence my
decision-making? Do I listen to people of other cultures in order
to understand them better? How good is my ability to "hear"
different ways of doing things? Where do I get my gospel
nourishment?

Be committed as a follower of the gospel. Don't rationalize
to evade change. Don't dawdle along the gospel journey. We
need time to relax and reflect. But don't linger so long that you
die on the vine. Ask others for help when you need it. Offer
help when it is asked. Develop competence in understanding
the gospel. It takes time and effort. It takes energy and dedication. It takes faith and persistence. It takes openness to the
work of the Holy Spirit in everyday life. But it happens to be
the way Christians choose to go. Jesus brings life and light.
Christians, in turn, bring life and light to others.

As for those who in the present age are rich, command them
not to be haughty, or to set their hopes on the uncertainty of
riches, but rather on God who richly provides us with every-

thing for our enjoyment. They are to do good, to be rich in good works, generous, and ready to share, thus storing up for themselves the treasure of a good foundation for the future, so that they may take hold of the life that really is life! (1 Tim 6:17-19).

CHAPTER THREE

Button Up Your Overcoat

Trust and security are important for people. In a world caught in a web of terrorism, violence, rising drug use, and irrational crime, we want to feel safe. Criminal statistics escalate regularly. From the pulpit to the congress people abuse trust. Dishonest business deals and questionable activities by government officials chip away at our trust. The failure of friends to support us at crucial moments leaves us feeling isolated and alone. The awesome race to make money puts things of the heart in cold storage. Efficiency often drowns affection. Intellectual growth often outdistances the growth of the spirit within us. Because relationships are often neglected, we find it hard to trust one another. The words of the king in the musical *The King and I* say it well: ". . . unless someday somebody trusts somebody, there'll be nothing left on earth excepting fishes."

Advertising often betrays trust. Advertisers cannot always fulfill the promises they make. Claims that a product can rejuvenate old bodies to youthful vigor are hard to fulfill. Advertisements attempt to seduce buyers with pictures of gorgeous people enjoying themselves. Products that are addictive are touted as an inspiration for joy.

Even a brief examination of advertisements shows that fear is often used as motivation for buying. Fear of growing old. Fear of being out of sync with society. Fear of wearing the wrong clothes or not looking like the "beautiful people." Fear of being fat or fear of having pimples. Obtaining the right product will put you in the top ten of popular people. Driving the right car will be your ticket to life in the fast lane. How tragic should you fail to buy! You could become a social outcast! Instant gratification is the only way to go. What a tragedy if you should have to wait for gratification. Get it and get it *now!*

Buy now, pay later! Pictures of a lonely repair man touch our hearts and invite us to buy. Rebates and long-term payments keep us from the need to wait for what we want. Spending now will bring instant satisfaction. The whole of life will be transformed! Small wonder that advertising seems untrustworthy even at its effective best. It offers little for the human spirit.

Technology seemed to be an answer to our human needs. But the idol of technology has clay feet. The atomic "accident" at Chernobyl and the Challenger explosion left us uneasy about trusting "fail-safe" devices developed by technology. Things that can serve us can also make us less human. "Smart bombs" keep us from seeing these bombs kill living people. Push a button and people die. On the other hand, technology also offers cures for devastating diseases. It provides life-giving possibilities. But it must remain a servant of people, not an idol people must serve. Genetic engineering may intrude on the relationship of man and woman. An unchecked need to control may push us into practices and processes that require a great deal of serious examination and reflection. Respect for the dignity of human persons must not be lost in the race for progress. We remain God's special creation. It is too easy to ignore the spirit of the human person while making money through intellectual discoveries. Neither mind nor heart can be ignored if we wish to nourish the whole person.

Is there no way to achieve a secure life? Are we trapped by a technology that can as easily blow us apart as serve us? Do people's attitudes change through computer programming? Does concern for their images make leaders more effective in seeking peace? Can strict law enforcement solve our drug problem? If nobody cares about me, can I be helped by a streamlined advertising campaign? Can preachy sermons about heaven bring comfort when my child has died? Can dogmas make life more livable when meaning disappears?

It is not easy to answer these questions. They may be threatening to our sense of security. But they also help us get to the root of some of our societal and religious issues. Healthy reflection and consistent searching for creative answers enable us to take responsibility for our lives. We need to address these kinds of issues if we want to live gospel values in the marketplace of everyday life.

Some people believe nothing can be changed. It is too much hard work to develop alternatives. Yet we invest considerable time and energy in producing and acquiring material goods. We work feverishly to be Number One. Research and development programs keep designing new and different products. The business of changing products and developing new technologies is a common competitive project. Changing our obsession to be Number One is no fly-by-night project.

We probably sell more cars than any other country. We rank near the top in weapons sales. We may sell more gadgets than any other country. We may have more sports events and TV channels than other countries. We have taller buildings and a well-developed infrastructure. We have more jails than many countries. We produce more food than most countries. We educate millions of people. We have absorbed millions of immigrants. We have more psychiatrists than most nations and more people who need them. We have people who earn millions of dollars each year. We have street people who earn nothing and depend on hand-outs and street-smarts to stay alive. We have an image-building industry second to none and people who use it to create artificial reputations.

The energy we expend in trying to be Number One in all things is enormous. We sometimes succeed and sometimes fail. But the image of being Number One is the carrot that drives many people. Being Number One is not evil, but the energy we use can destroy something in our spirit. It can also destroy healthy values and principles that nurture relationships. At best it is an ambiguous "treasure." It can insidiously eat away at gospel values in the lives of Christians. The gospel way of life calls for sharing of resources. The hard-headed economics and single-mindedness required to be Number One may not tolerate sharing resources. People who follow the gospel counter this headlong drive for success. They spend less time worrying about being Number One. They spend more time trying to create a world where everyone is treated as though they were Number One. There are few spots at the top. Many people will never come close to being Number One. We may reach for the heights and seek to make our dreams a reality. But success does not come to all of us. What we need is a healthy ability to live within personal human limitations. We seek to push out our horizons while acknowledging our limitations. At the same time, we attempt to open society to all people. The society we seek acknowledges economic realities but submits them to gospel evaluation. Unless we develop an openness to each other, there is little reason to trust one another. Trust becomes another victim of that thing we call "reality." It seems obvious that a change of perception is in order.

We are ordinary people living in a society that is often unsure of itself. It needs to prove itself again and again. Jean Vanier says that this drive to be Number One leaves many people at the bottom of the ladder of success. It leaves many people exhausted, stressed-out, and surrounded by fractured relationships. Few reach the top. Many more waste away, scratching for a "place in the sun." The ladder of success has a scarcity of room at the top. Trying to get there can use up great amounts of time and energy. Life itself may pass us by as we are trapped on the treadmill of success-at-all-costs. The cost of health care for these stressed-out people is enormous. The cost of the "escape addictions" is out of sight. The price paid by families and friends is exorbitant in terms of physical, psychological, and emotional pain. How can people trapped in such prisons find any reason (or have any energy) to build trusting relationships?

I remember my own drive for success in my first years in ministry. I found myself relying on *doing* things to gain acceptance. At one and the same time, I was involved in formation work in our friary, I was chaplain at a county convalescent home, director of religious education and assisting with the pastoral ministry in a parish, I was active in the Cursillo movement, working with young people through the Search Program, developing an adult education center at the friary, working with the Secular Franciscans, writing, doing spiritual direction and counseling, and trying to be a good community person. I loved it. With no time to spare, I easily avoided serious reflection about whom I was serving. In all these ministries (jobs?) I was at least adequate. I was appreciated and affirmed. It was traumatic when I was moved from my ''escapism.'' Little did I realize how empty all this activity left me. The idol of personal success and busyness had claimed another victim. After all, ''My work was my prayer''!

There are few people at the top of the ladder of success. Many people live lives of quiet desperation at the bottom. Some successful people may be concerned about others. They are not necessarily evil-spirited. Some share the fruits of success with others. But other successful people idolize the acquisition of wealth and/or power. They show meager concern for the needs of others. What they earn is ''Theirs''! No one benefits but they! Now and then some scraps are given from the table of plenty to hold guilt at bay. Trusting people comes hard when concern for the bottom line dominates one's thinking.

As wealth and power grow, so does the need to protect it. Ways are found to protect acquired goods and power. Growth in the security industry, local and worldwide, is a natural consequence. Raw force, whether economic, physical or psychological, may be used to protect investments and maintain wealth and power. This doesn't sound like the road to the city where trust dwells!

These issues are complex. It is not a case of bad people versus good people, greedy folks versus generous folks. It is human folks caught in systems that seem good and look as though they are working. It may well be that both the poor and the rich need to be liberated from the desire for riches. No matter how great the fortune, the human heart and spirit require something wealth cannot buy — love. Christians who are serious about the gospel face many challenges. The values of society and the values of the gospel come into conflict. Gospel-people cannot disregard this conflict and remain genuinely Christian. Without some degree of love for one another, it will be difficult to develop trust.

Inconsistency, indifference, misuse of power, destructive policies, and lack of compassion cannot be ignored. Christians who take the gospel seriously face tough choices. Gospel values can be lost in the race for success and security. The sense of what is ''real'' can be lost in a sea of possessiveness.

Jesus is realistic about human limitations. His perceptions are down to earth. For example, he was aware of Peter's limitations. Put under pressure, he knew Peter would crack and deny their relationship (Luke 22:55-62). He knew that the man cured of paralysis could get involved in situations worse than paralysis (John 5:14). Jesus knew that interpretation of the law was not a guarantee of holiness (Matt 23:1-7). Jesus asked hard questions. Is law meant to serve people or dictate to people? Are people made for the law or the law for people? Jesus was able to be realistic and still find room to trust people. He shows that his continued trust is often the tool that helps people change.

Jesus was practical. He was not naive about his apostles. They were not sophisticated, influential people who were politically astute. They were ordinary people — fishermen, tax collectors, rebels, married and single. He knew them well. He was frustrated with their slow pace of understanding. But he stuck with them. Their success as disciples brought him joy. The disciples, in turn, knew where their power came from.

Jesus sometimes avoided the spotlight because people would make him the wrong kind of king. Jesus knew what he wanted and set about achieving it. With consistent persistence, Jesus proclaimed the reign of God and his role in it. Glory belongs to his Father. He would not be detoured from the path laid out by his "Abba." *Faithfulness* is a hallmark of Jesus. He would trust his belief in people's ability to change. His anger with the Pharisees did not close the door on the Pharisee Nicodemus, the seeker (John 3:1-8).

Jesus knew that a gospel society cannot be built on the presumption that nothing can change. People possess a resource called "heart and spirit." This power can overcome enormous obstacles. Jesus knew that dedication makes a difference. Supportive relationships enable people to stretch their limits. Jesus proclaimed a way of living that offered new life to faithful people. Trust would be a part of that life.

Jesus was not content to leave things as they were. His Father sent him to reveal a richer way, the way of the reign of God. This gospel-way offers a vision of hope. Without hope, life is a burden to be endured rather than a dream to fulfill. Jesus would not deny the dream of his Father. Jesus' faithfulness to the dream got him killed. But death could not destroy the life-giving vision. "And this is eternal life, that they may know you, the only true God, and Jesus Christ, whom you have sent. . . . Righteous Father, the world does not know you, but I know you; and these know that you have sent me. I made your name known to them, and I will make it known, so that the love with which you have loved me may be in them, and I in them" (John 17:3, 25-26).

Jesus' intimacy with his Father was his source of life. His vision was the Father's vision. Jesus shared with us everything the Father had given him. He held nothing back. Jesus did not rely on accumulation as the way to life. He taught that intimacy is more important than acquisition; relationships are more important than bank accounts; life and living are more important than the security provided by wealth, insurance, and weaponry. Jesus offers an alternative to values society holds dear. Christians who live the gospel learn to trust God and God's people rather than things and structures.

Do not store up for yourselves treasures on earth, where moth and rust consume and where thieves break in and steal; but store up for yourselves treasures in heaven, where neither moth nor rust consumes and where thieves do not break in and steal. For where your treasure is, there your heart will be also (Matt 6:19-21).

Therefore do not worry, saying, "What will we eat?" or "What will we drink?" or "What will we wear?" For it is the Gentiles who strive for all these things; and indeed your heavenly Father knows that you need all these things. But strive first for the kingdom of God and his righteousness, and all these things will be given to you as well. So do not worry about tomorrow, for tomorrow will bring worries of its own. Today's trouble is enough for today (Matt 6:31-34).

Jesus is concerned that we might rely on the accumulation of things as reliable security. Realistically, houses, cars, bank accounts, even health, are very uncertain securities. One fire can destroy a house, one accident demolish a car. One failed bank or savings and loan can wipe out savings. Much of what we rely on is very unreliable. The biblical word speaks to the heart. When the word of God calls for change, change! Happiness comes when we *act* on what we know. As Jesus puts it: "If you know these things, you are blessed if you do them!" (John 13:17).

Security

The desire for security is not evil. People need to feel safe and secure. No one wants to lose personal possessions through theft or fire. The need for security springs from deep within our humanity. It is not bad to have possessions that are necessary for life. Everyone needs food, companionship, shelter, and love to live a human life. The Lord does not want people to live in destitution. Nor does Jesus expect us to live in fear, scratching for survival. Such things bring bitterness and lives without hope. They even cause people to revolt and turn to violence. The fear of crime, muggings, rape, abuse, or gang-violence destroys inner peace and freedom.

Within the search for security there is temptation. Whether subtle or obvious, we can be tempted. Initially we desire a reasonable share of the world's goods. We want a good job. We want to support our families and help them achieve a good life. We enjoy doing caring things for friends. We want to help in supporting the Church or paying off the mortgage on the house. A second job becomes important just to make ends meet. Societal demands continue to motivate us to move up the financial ladder. If possible, we move away from places that are dangerous. If we are forced to stay, we barricade our homes and lives to avoid being scarred by the violence around us. Fear and worry become daily companions.

As we move up the social ladder, we seek something a little better — a finer car, a better wardrobe, season tickets to sporting events or the symphony. We develop management skills and find ourselves doing well. We develop a power base. People like our style and creativity. Each step offers opportunities for career growth. We grow accustomed to the "good things of life." Our wealth grows. We can afford more luxury items.

Expensive things need to be protected. Alarms, security systems, and insurance policies meet that need. Each step on this path seems natural and right. We participate in programs to aid the poor. "Everyone should do something for society." A lifestyle of luxury develops quite naturally.

Few people walk this path with devious and devilish ideas in mind. As we go up the social-success ladder, each step seems to "happen." As we look back, we create a myth about how we "pulled ourselves up by the bootstraps." (A nonsensical statement: Pulling on bootstraps lands you on your rear end or your face — hardly a place of success!) Undaunted, we believe in our false myth.

There is still a nagging fear it may all fall apart. Things over which we have no control can deprive us of what we have earned. If such threats worry us, we try harder. We work more hours. We hedge our investments more carefully. We rely on new techniques and seek new inventions to maintain our place at the top. It may even be necessary to bend the rules a bit. What's more, we may enjoy every minute of it! (Or — we may begin to feel tied to a task that is deadening!)

Jesus calls this a trap! Success-oriented-people begin to feel invincible. Everything they possess is important to maintain and develop. There is never enough. Jesus says that people relying on these idols find his view of people and the world hard to accept. Jesus' point of view seems foolish to these folks. They find it difficult to let go of what they have and put their trust in God. They domesticate God so that their ''god'' gives approval to their actions and lifestyle. They want God in their lives, but on their terms. They seek to maintain control — even of God. A call to surrender to God is politely rebuffed. How difficult it is to get the camel through the eye of the needle! ''Enter through the narrow gate; for the gate is wide and the road is easy that leads to destruction, and there are many who take it. For the gate is narrow and the road is hard that leads to life, and there are few who find it!'' (Matt 7:13-14).

We are talented enough to rationalize about our lifestyle, to find ways to maintain it without guilt. We find experts to support us. A little creativity allows us to turn criticism back onto the critic. We find ways of discrediting critics with innuendo and rumor about their personal lives. Nothing that needs proof. Just ''items'' that get passed around. We have invested in the system. We don't want it changed. We want to conserve and preserve it. It is our security. Any talk of change and conversion is subversive. It must come from people who are ignorant of reality. Maybe they are radicals out to destroy us!

As I typed these words, I remembered some words I had written during a reflective moment in 1987:

> When God comes by, all boundaries are split and walls fall down. Infinite love cannot be contained and there are no boundaries to hold it.

Boundaries come when only self is served, when the "me" is always first, when no light is reflected to brothers and sisters who walk in the dark. When that happens, my own darkness is deep indeed.

Joy is not mirth, but the rebound of love freely given and not withheld. Mirth is passing, small, shallow, and easily lost. Joy lasts. For love, freely given, lasts. It grows and blossoms like the bounding leap of a deer in flight. To have joy, pressed down and running over, is to have loved without check or holding back.

Gospel people face tough choices. It is a fact that we will die. What we possess will pass to others. Material things will not offer support when we are dying. As Dolly sings in the musical *Hello, Dolly:* "On those cold winter nights, Horace, you can snuggle up to your cash register! It's a little lumpy, but it rings!"

Things we feel and see and touch are most susceptible to being lost. Accident, fire, hurricane, theft can deprive us of things. What we see and touch is least reliable for creating security. The gospel alternative does not deny that our world offers beautiful things and experiences. Gospel people *love* this planet of ours. They delight in beautiful music and gorgeous sunsets. They enjoy climbing mountains and hiking through quiet forests. Gospel people recognize and appreciate human creativity. They use products with a sense of gratitude. Gospel people own cars and eat at restaurants. They own a home and have TV's. Gospel people have bank accounts. They work hard to prepare a good future for their children. From the outside they look like everyone else climbing the ladder of success.

The difference lies in their hearts. Accumulation and acquisition are not a first priority. Relating to people and sharing resources are fundamental for them. They believe the earth is for all people — not just a few. They need food and clothing and shelter, but other people need them too. They avoid the accumulation or waste of resources that would deprive others of human needs. It doesn't matter if the "others" live in

America or Somalia. They are not overly concerned whether folks are "worthy" of help. That is a tough judgment to make. The gospel calls us to help our neighbor as a sign of love. Tough love or gentle love or anything in between will be shown. "*How*" we help will take wisdom. But we will help!

> "There was once a rich man, who used to dress in purple and the finest linen, and feasted sumptuously every day. At his gate lay a poor man covered with sores. He would have been glad to satisfy his hunger with the scraps from the rich man's table. Dogs used to come and lick his sores. One day the poor man died and was carried away by the angels to be with Abraham. The rich man also died and was buried. In Hades, where he was in torment, he looked up and there, far away, was Abraham with Lazarus close beside him. 'Abraham, my father,' he called out, 'take pity on me. Send Lazarus to dip the tip of his finger in water, to cool my tongue, for I am in agony in this fire!' But Abraham said: 'My child, remember that the good things fell to you in your lifetime, and the bad to Lazarus. Now he has his consolation here and it is you who are in agony' " (Luke 16:19-25 — REB).

Gospel people try to avoid possessiveness. Less dependent on things for happiness, they spend less time and energy protecting what they own. They spend more time with people they love. Since relationships survive death, they have a rich treasure-lode laid up for themselves.

Gospel people with this attitude do not lose the need for security, food, shelter, and friends. What we lose (i.e., deliberately surrender) is the power "things" have to dictate our lifestyle. When we must choose between buying or helping, we lean to helping. When we must choose between sharing and keeping, we lean toward sharing. When we must select what we need or what we want, we lean toward what we need. When we must decide between family values or a move up the corporate ladder, we lean toward family values. If we must choose between convenience for ourselves or meeting the need of a neighbor, we lean toward our neighbor. If a national policy is detrimental to the poor but makes money for the rich, we lean toward supporting a policy that helps the poor. If national budgetary priorities provide for a more surgical ability to kill people or provide services for people, we lean toward using our resources to serve people. If we must choose between negotiations or war, we choose negotiations. If we must choose between forgiveness or revenge, we choose forgiveness. The list could be expanded. But we always lean toward the gospel alternative. We trust God's word as the way to life. Such things may sound foolish to practical-minded Americans.

It makes sense to us because we believe in Jesus Christ. We believe his presence on earth shows God's desire to be with us. Since Jesus came among us, the power of evil is not the dominant force on earth. The gospel shows a Jesus who successfully defeated the power of evil. When he seemed to fail and was put to death, God raised Jesus from the dead! No longer confined by human limitations, Jesus is present with us and among us. Jesus gives us power to choose gospel ''leanings.'' The Spirit of Jesus helps us make choices that give light and life.

Jesus does not abandon us. But neither does he solve all our problems or cure all our ills. He is *with* us! Relationship with him gives us a new point of view. As friendship grows, his values and vision grow within us. Jesus' influence shows itself in the way we live. We recognize the need to change many of our perceptions. Jesus offers insights that move beyond our small perceptions. The power and ability to be faithful to the gospel come from Jesus. The Spirit of the risen Jesus enables us to trust the gospel word.

On the last day of the festival, the great day, while Jesus was standing there, he cried out: ''Let anyone who is thirsty come to me, and let the one who believes in me drink. As the scripture has said: 'Out of the believer's heart shall flow rivers of living water.' '' Now he said this about the spirit, which believers in him were to receive (John 7:37-39).

''Why do you call me: 'Lord, Lord' — and never do what I tell you? Everyone who comes to me and hears my words and acts on them — I will show you what he is like. He is like a man building a house, who dug deep and laid the foundations on rock. When the river was in flood, it burst upon that house, but could not shift it, because it had been soundly built. But he who hears and does not act is like a man who built his house on soil without foundations. As soon as the river burst upon it, the house collapsed, and fell with a great crash'' (Luke 6:46-49 — REB).

Reflection

Is money more important to me than God? Do I feel more secure when I have more material goods or a deeper faith? Is the gospel nice stuff for Sundays but not practical for work? How would I describe my attitude toward possessions? How would I describe a gospel-attitude toward possessions? How can riches be a problem for being a gospel-person? Are tax-deductible donations enough to fulfill the gospel ideal of sharing resources? What is the connection between the national budget (how money is spent) and Jesus' call for sharing resources? If I increase expenditures for security, will I be more secure? What are my most nightmarish fears about? When I *must* make a choice, do I lean toward acquisition or sharing? Which do I serve most faithfully — God or Money? Do I have solid relationships that give me a sense of security? Do I feel isolated and alone? How does faith in God offer security? Who/what is the source of security in my life? What criteria do I use to judge what/who is the source of my security? How often do I take quiet time to nourish my spirit? What criteria do I use to evaluate policies, people, groups? How biblical are these criteria? On what do I expend my energy? What does this tell me about my values and/or commitment to the gospel?

Prayer had confronted me with many weaknesses. My life was dusted with failures. I was being called to a new ministry. I knew the right things to do, but my heart was resisting.

Looking back, my fears were foolish. But at that time, in that place, they seemed real — and overwhelming. At that crossroads in my life I wrote the following:

> Would I dare to be a fool? Would I dare to see written in bold letters the word "Fool" as clear as a fly walking across a window? (Chesterton) What good does the whole world do if one has no spirit, no dream? How can a person purchase soul and spirit? How can one buy spirit from the Lord? Certainly not by denying the dream! Somewhere, in the deep recesses of my heart, there is a longing to be possessed by the Lord. So taken hold of that there would be no release. So loved that love would never cease. So full of joy that no sadness could destroy it. So convinced of the Truth, that no one could turn me from him. So intimate with Life that I would be one with him. Free, because Divine Love would lead me to be myself!

> I am afraid. I have not yet embraced the pearl of great price. Many things I call "mine" keep me down on my farm, unwilling to sell this land for the sake of the pearl. The Lord keeps trying to pry me loose, but I insistently cling to "my farm."

> Change me, Lord. Say to me as you did to Lazarus' friends: "Unbind him — let him go free!" (John 11:44).

CHAPTER FOUR

The Real Thing

What is more important: to "understand" our faith or to "sense and feel" it? Is it better to be well-informed about dogma or deeply committed to Jesus? Is a conflict between these ideas real or not? Let's explore these elements of faith.

The intellectual tradition of the Church is a rich one. I am proud of people like Irenaeus, Cyprian, Basil, Catherine of Siena, Thomas Aquinas, Francis de Sales, Bonaventure, Benedict, Julian of Norwich, Ignatius, Teresa of Avila, John of the Cross, Cardinal Newman, and a host of others. They offer insights into the nature of God and Christian spirituality. Their writings open many doors to theological and spiritual knowledge and development.

Modern writers and theologians continue the tradition. Without such continuing tradition we would be a feeble people. Knowledgeable people of faith offer stability and strength to the Church. We need their insights in the arena of faith. Much is lost if we ignore the wisdom of tradition, past and present. Modern theologians continue to push out the horizons of understanding. They follow in the footsteps of a host of writers on theology. They continue the development of Church tradition. They blend new and old ideas into a fresh vision for the present. As Bernard of Clairvaux put it: "We are like dwarfs, seated on the shoulders of giants; perhaps we see more things than the Ancients . . . but this is due neither to the sharpness of our sight nor to the greatness of our own stature, but because we are raised and borne aloft on that giant mass.''

On the other hand, there is a dimension of faith not so easily expressed or explained by theologians and scholars. I speak of the *experience* of God. I speak of the awareness of God's presence that is "real" to me but not provable to you. There may be intellectual explanations for this. But intellectual explanations are unnecessary to those who have such experiences. They simply "are." No explanation is needed. Jesus is our friend. We "know" that the Spirit of Jesus dwells in us. The Spirit enables us to face difficulties, even death, with a tranquil heart. *Religious experience* is another way of knowing God. It is not so much a planned happening as a gifted experience. It comes from within rather than being absorbed from the outside. It teaches us to value who we are even as we bow in awe before the God who is revealed. We speak of it in poetry and symbol because words are too fragile to contain its majesty.

There can be problems in this way of "knowing." Religious experiences can lead to purely subjective ideas. We can meander on a self-induced or self-centered "God-spoke-to-me" trip. We can refuse to listen to healthy guidance. But it need not be so.

The "knowing" of religious experience can be joined to intellectual knowing. Together they add richness to our faith-life. Together they invite us to new horizons in gospel living. Together they use the gifts of both head and heart to know God.

> Hear, LORD, when I cry aloud;
>> be gracious to me and answer me!
> "Come," my heart says, "seek his face!"
>> Your face, LORD, do I seek.
>> Do not hide your face from me. . . .
> I believe that I shall see the goodness of the Lord
>> in the land of the living.
> Wait for the LORD;
>> be strong, and let your heart take courage;
>> wait for the Lord (Ps 27:7-9, 13-14).

Consider what a genuine religious experience can do. When I hurt, I am not impressed by an analysis of my problem. Neither do I seek an explanation of doctrine. I am not concerned about explanations of the Trinity when someone I love is dying of cancer or a friend has AIDS. I find dogma almost irrelevant when a friend is accused of sexual abuse. I need God to be with me in my pain and confusion; to weep with me when I feel helpless; to hug me gently when I am alone with my unanswerable questions. I need to *experience* loving presence when I am lonely. When life is drowning in sorrow, I need to experience the gentle presence of Jesus through the compassion of a friend. Books, dogmas, and theological insights are precious. But sometimes they are insufficient to meet my needs. I need a God "with skin on" to treat me tenderly. The religious experience of God's presence is a gift for such times. The gift is given freely whenever God wishes.

We will have to deal with potholes in the road. There is danger of deception in the interpretation of my experience of faith. We humans are imperfect. We can create problems for ourselves.

I remember a story told about Jacoba. She had experienced a strong sense of the presence of God. It seemed to her that she was being called to give away her considerable wealth and work among the poor. The Scripture texts seemed absolute. She was ready to respond by giving away her fortune and becoming "poor." But Jacoba was a wise woman. She sought advice from a good spiritual guide. Her guide asked some clarifying questions. "Did the experience actually demand that you give away your money?" Quite honestly she replied: "No. But it seemed to me a pre-condition if I was going to work with the poor. After all, the gospel says 'sell what you have and give to the poor.'" Her guide persisted: "But if you become poor, how will that help the poor? As soon as the money is gone, there will simply be one more poor person. Is it possible to put your wealth to work for the poor?" Continued dialogue led to the decision to establish an organization to help the poor. Jacoba's skills in business management enabled her to help hundreds of poor people. Her initial experience was real. Her interpretation could have led her to disaster. Good guidance helped her come to a healthy interpretation of the religious experience.

My own search for understanding is helped by good reading. I love reading good books. I am stimulated by the challenge of creative ideas. I am excited by contemporary discoveries that are echoed in the Bible and tradition. I am delighted with Bible studies that break open new meanings for God's word. Fresh insights bolster faith. They bring me closer to God's world, to God's people, and to God! Reading helps me interpret my religious experiences. Seeking competent guidance is another way that is helpful. It is dangerous to remain isolated and righteous about religious experiences. Isolation and self-divinization is the way of cults. We can avoid such dangers with the help of a wise community of faith.

New ideas do not have equal value. Every novel idea is not a gift. Some ideas are foolish and ridiculous. Some ideas are quickly replaced by others in a cycle of novelty. But it is foolish to reject ideas and experiences out of hand without exploring their value.

We need the community of faith known as Church. In sorting treasure from trash we are blessed with the creative conflict of discussion and dialogue within the Church. No one person can decipher the difference between good and bad ideas in every case. Right and wrong, valuable and useless intertwine in our religious experiences. New insights and theological expression need time for common reflection. We would be the losers if we abruptly dismissed them without dialogue. The community of faith need not fear them. Prayerful and respectful interaction will draw out the truth. Institutions need not fear the healthy and truthful discoveries that religious experience can offer. Individuals need to trust the wisdom of the faith-community. Trust and listening to competent people will help us avoid misreading our religious experiences.

Good as this sounds, it is difficult to implement. I find that if a new idea or experience threatens my mindset, I resist it. My resistance springs from being threatened (fear) rather than from thoughtful reflection. Some new insights make me uneasy. Sometimes they disturb me. They invite me to a change of behavior when I don't want to change! Perhaps institutions experience the same fears.

I think: "Either the idea is wrong or I am wrong." I *presume* that I am right. The idea and/or its author must be rejected. My resistance comes from fear of being inadequate in my knowledge. Fear keeps me from having an open mind and heart. I become a doctrinal purist. I am afraid that my "truth" is too weak to stand a challenge. I energetically defend "my truth" against all threats. I dedicate myself to the task of disposing of "bad" ideas, experiences or "disruptive" theologians.

A healthy, reflective attitude might lead in a different direction. I might begin a search to discover the values in these "new" truths. Instead of closing my mind, I might open it. I could accept my limited understanding and see possibilities for learning. Such honesty would allow me the freedom to discover more of the truth. I may be cautious but I won't be close-minded. I will make an honest effort to search for a richer understanding of my faith. I will do some serious reflection rather than become an "infallible" protector of the faith. There is so much to learn. With an open mind I will move past the fear of change that binds me.

If the faith-community and I look at ideas fairly and honestly, we can learn. Through respectful dialogue we can discover new insights. That takes time. Dialogue requires readiness to listen without prejudice. It permits a fresh look, without fear, at another portion of the truth. Otherwise, I rely on a personal infallibility that is an illusion. Any institution that uses power to crush this search for truth is standing on tenuous ground. Too often it is fear that hinders faith development. Fear that cannot tolerate dissent often locks us in a rigidity that has little joy. Real truth is not threatened by dialogue. Rather, it opens the door to new life and understanding. Truth has no need to fear new insights. It is not so fragile that it feels threatened.

Many early Jewish Christians faced tough issues. They quarreled about accepting Gentiles into the Church unless they were circumcised. They had a long religious tradition that required circumcision. The arguments were serious. The combatants spoke eloquently for their positions. It was not easy to break with the experience of centuries. A new way of doing things did not seem appropriate. Listen to Peter as he addressed this issue:

> After there had been much debate, Peter stood up and said to them, "My brothers, you know that in the early days God made a choice among you, that I should be the one through whom the Gentiles would hear the message of the good news and become believers. And God, who knows the human heart, testified to them by giving them the Holy Spirit, just as he did to us; and in cleansing their hearts by faith he has made no distinction between them and us. Now therefore why are you putting God to the test by placing on the neck of the disciples a yoke that neither our ancestors nor we have been able to bear? On the contrary, we believe that we will be saved through the grace of the Lord Jesus, just as they will" (Acts 15:7-11).

These Christians struggled with changes that threatened long-held ideas. Their religious experience did not include these new ideas and practices. When it became clear God was asking for something new, they surrendered to God's new call. God calls, we respond. To do otherwise is to cling to security based on human knowledge rather than God's continuing revelation. The challenge can be painful. But it is important to listen to God's fresh revelation. The *truth* need not fear such fresh understanding. It is strong enough to stand and, with delight, embrace fresh insights into its meaning.

St. Paul struggled with this conflict in his ministry. He did not know Jesus when Jesus walked on earth. His experience of Jesus was a faith-experience. Its power moved him from being a persecutor to a follower, from a protector of the law to a proclaimer of the gospel. The lesson of his conversion was not lost on Paul. Jesus is the center. The law, in all its beauty and power, could not match what is given through Jesus Christ: "Rather, a person is a Jew who is one inwardly, and real circumcision is a matter of the heart — it is spiritual and not literal'' (Rom 2:29). ''There is therefore now no condemnation for those who are in Christ Jesus. For the law of the Spirit of life in Christ Jesus has set you free from the law of sin and death'' (Rom 8:1-2).

Human learning cannot provide everything we need to know. It is in Jesus that God reveals a ''gospel of life.'' God invites us to trust Jesus. Trust grows as intimacy with Jesus grows. We listen, with openness, to the word of the Bible. Biblical words call us to conversion. Security comes through Jesus, not doctrines about Jesus.

We will not find security in wealth or power, but in Jesus. He calls us to be a forgiving people, unwilling to tolerate division and violence. He calls us to search, eager for more learning about the gospel. He calls us to an alternative to the lifestyle the world offers. We give unashamed witness, confronting a society whose values come into conflict with the way of Jesus. Our conviction to follow the gospel is supported both by religious experience and intellectual knowledge of Jesus. ''I am the true vine, and my Father is the vinegrower. He removes every branch in me that bears no fruit. Every branch that bears fruit he prunes to make it bear more fruit. You have already been cleansed by the word I have spoken to you. Abide in me as I abide in you. Just as the branch cannot bear fruit unless it abides in the vine, neither can you unless you abide in me'' (John 15:1-4).

If we refuse to change, concerned only with doctrinal purity, we remain dormant. If we succumb to individualism with no concern for the faith-community or its leaders, we remain dormant. If we refuse to show justice to our neighbor, we remain dormant. If we refuse to relinquish things that burden us, we lose the gift of new life and remain dormant. If we refuse to widen our understanding of the truth, we remain dormant. If we shut out the gospel words that call for personal conversion, we remain dormant. If we choose the path of doctrinal rigidity, refusing to accept growth in understanding our faith, we remain dormant. If we cringe in our little world of understanding, fearful of any fresh insights, we remain dormant. Such actions are obstacles to healthy faith development.

One cost of following the gospel is "insecurity." One consequence of discipleship is trust in Jesus without clear blueprints for life. It seems dangerous to walk without such assurance. We feel insecure. Yet it is the way of faith. Our security is Jesus Christ. He is with us. Our faith is in God, who "put on skin" and walked among us. Security is built on a faith relationship, not on knowledge of doctrine. As we walk with one another in the faith-community, we delight in common new discoveries. Sharing our religious experiences and ideas widens the horizons of our faith. "I was overjoyed when some of the friends arrived and testified to your faithfulness to the truth, namely how you walk in the truth. I have no greater joy than this, to hear that my children are walking in the truth" (3 John 1:3-4).

The gospel journey is not a vacation planned by a celestial travel agency. The gospel journey invites us to abandon whatever would burden us: hatred, unforgiveness, anger; weapons of destruction, desire for revenge; violence, vanity, fear, self-doubt; physical, sexual, or psychological abuse; prejudice and racist and sexist attitudes — must all be surrendered. They weigh us down. Rid of them, the journey is less burdened. We experience new freedom. We experience God's presence. Religious experience of God is free to go beyond what we can put into words. The flexibility to learn of God in many ways allows us to grow more intimate with God.

Gospel living may bring conflict and confusion. The effort may seem too costly and demanding. This is not a one-time "I'm saved" approach to life. It is not satisfied with a one-time "born-again" experience. The experience of God moves us to embrace the whole gospel. It is a lifetime commitment. Religious experience can be a powerful motivator in following the gospel of Jesus. Without Jesus, it is impossible to be faithful to the gospel. With Jesus (and a healthy experience of his presence), all things are possible. Our choices reflect the level of our commitment to Jesus and the gospel.

The kingdom of heaven is like a treasure hidden in a field, which someone found and hid; then in his joy he goes and sells all that he has and buys that field. Again, the kingdom of heaven is like a merchant in search of fine pearls; on finding one pearl of great value, he went and sold all that he had and bought it (Matt 13:44-46).

The gospel speaks of selling everything to possess the treasure or the pearl. We need to experience the "treasure" of God's presence in Jesus before deciding to sell everything. The joy of "selling everything" makes sense when we experience the value of the pearl/treasure. We embrace this pearl/treasure. Nothing else seems very important. This positive experience attracts us and is not imposed on us. "Letting go" seems a normal way of faith. The name of this treasure and pearl is Jesus.

"Again, the kingdom of heaven is like a net that was thrown into the sea and caught fish of every kind; when it was full, they drew ashore, sat down, and put the good into baskets but threw out the bad. . . .
"Have you understood all this?" he asked; and they answered: "Yes." So he said to them, "When, therefore, a teacher of the law has become a learner in the kingdom of heaven, he is like a householder who can produce from his store things new and old" (Matt 13:47-48, 51-52 — REB).

When the net is pulled to shore, it contains all kinds of things. There are good and bad fish in the net. Weeds, algae, and dirt clog the net. We have to throw out the inedible fish in order to get good fish to eat. We cannot use the net again until we clean out the junk.

Sorting things out is part of life. If we want to eat good fish, we discard the inedible ones. This is not punishment for fishing — it is reality. Real life requires that we make choices.

Many useless things cling to the net of life. We are not asked to discard the net. Neither are we told never to fish again. We are not required to complain to the Fish and Game Department about the condition of the water. Quite simply, we learn that we are imperfect. Life has both good and bad elements.

Some things in life nourish us. Some things in life debilitate us. It helps to know the difference. For Christians, the gospel of Jesus teaches us the difference! The experience of responding to the gospel helps us establish criteria for making good choices.

I remember when Vatican II brought changes to our community life. For a number of years after ordination, I regularly said my "own" private Mass at the seminary. I grew to love this time for "my Mass." When the community began to have concelebrated Masses, I refused to participate. I wanted my "own Mass" and this new stuff made no sense to me. But little by little I began to feel that I was missing something. I felt isolated from the community's worship when I was saying my "own Mass." I did some reading on the theology of concelebration. I began to understand the power of the community gathered at worship.

Then I allowed myself the experience of joining the rest of the community at Mass. The gathering of the community became more precious to me. Having my "own Mass" gradually became less attractive. It took time for this change to take place. It was not a loss but a gain for me. I think many Catholics feel the same way about devotions and practices that were important to them. It is not easy for me to sell my "treasures" in order to possess the pearl offered by Jesus. Many people have found this surrender very traumatic. For some it seems impossible.

Jesus offers a way to evaluate things. We go to the Bible to learn what is life-giving and what is not. Without gospel criteria our sorting-out would be a waste of time. We might discard treasure and keep trash. We need help and a willingness to learn. If I am a "know-it-all," or think that I'm already "saved," I am closed to the word of the Lord. I am to be pitied in my self-righteousness! Once again, a healthy experience of responding to the gospel helps me to grow. The gospel values become a pearl. Surrender is less difficult.

Jesus says that when a teacher of the law has become a learner, he can then draw good things from the storehouse.

I can choose to be a learner. It is opportunity for discovery. People who presume infallibility for themselves miss many life-giving possibilities. People who acknowledge the limitations of their understanding continue the search. Wisdom is God's gift. As the writer of Proverbs says: ''Get wisdom. . . . get insight. . . . The beginning of wisdom is this: Get wisdom, and whatever else you get, get insight. Prize her highly, and she will exalt you; she will honor you if you embrace her'' (Prov 4:5, 7-8).

Imperfection is a part of reality. I am imperfect. I see imperfection in the faith-community. I see imperfection in folks who claim to be infallible. I see imperfection in people in authority. It is not depressing to acknowledge reality. Rather, it helps me deal with the imperfection. In other words, it calls for conversion ''across the board.'' My experience of Jesus allows me to move ahead without the need to have things work my way. Awareness of my imperfection helps me avoid perfectionism. Another obstacle now has less power to hinder my spirit. Knowing of Jesus' presence through experience gives me strength to remain faithful.

> Rid yourselves, therefore, of all malice, and all guile, insincerity, envy and all slander. Like newborn infants, long for the pure, spiritual milk, so that by it you may grow into salvation — if indeed you have tasted that the Lord is good. Come to him, a living stone . . . like living stones, let yourselves be built into a spiritual house, to be a holy priesthood, to offer spiritual sacrifices acceptable to God through Jesus Christ (1 Pet 2:1-5).

> This is the message we have heard from him and proclaim to you, that God is light and in him there is no darkness at all (1 John 1:5).

Reflection

Are society's values my only impetus for action? If I choose to follow the gospel, will I persevere when it gets tough? Can I go it alone? How healthy is it for a Christian (me) to straddle the fence and keep things comfortable? How do I know which ideas to listen to? . . . which ideas to reject? . . . which ideas to integrate with others? . . . which ideas should replace others? What motivates me if I close my ears to gospel values? How do daily decisions affect my ability to live a gospel lifestyle? How can I achieve consistent joy? Can I be joyful if I ignore the gospel? Why should I listen to an imperfect faith-community? What's so important about knowing Jesus? Are catechism answers totally sufficient for living a good life? What do I fear about the gospel way of life? Have I managed to ignore or deny my fears? How? Is open-mindedness a virtue or a vice? Explain! How do I develop strong faith convictions? How can I blend tradition with the treasures of the present? How can the need for security keep me from living the gospel? What are some religious experiences in my life? Did I trust them? What did they mean for me? What role does a faith-community play in understanding religious experiences? How do I feel about personal change? How do religious experiences help me follow the gospel? What are some consequences if I live the gospel wherever I go? What is most disturbing about my faith-life right now? How does my reading material help (or hinder) my faith growth?

Who will separate us from the love of Christ? Will hardship, or distress, or persecution, or famine, or nakedness, or peril, or sword? . . . For I am convinced that neither death, nor life, nor angels, nor rulers, nor things present, nor things to come, nor powers, nor height, nor depth, nor anything else in all creation, will be able to separate us from the love of God in Christ Jesus our Lord (Romans 8:35, 38-39).

CHAPTER FIVE

A Second Look

Ideas and opinions often influence us without our awareness. We accept many ideas and opinions uncritically. We depend on family and friends as resources. We rely on a trusted news magazine or TV commentator. We accept information from professional religious people for religious beliefs. The art of critical reflection is not a common skill among us.

Ideas about God and gospel are frequent victims to this lack of critical reflection. We accept without question much of what we hear or read about God or Church. Busy with living, we have precious little time for the "luxury" of reflection. We do our job. We are good citizens. We have neither space nor time to critique all the ideas and opinions that bombard us.

Gospel People and Their Needs

Gospel people need more than survival skills. "Getting along" in life is not sufficient for them. A *personal* response to Jesus and his gospel is vital. We need ways to link life's everyday events to the perspective offered by Jesus. Whatever time it takes, we recognize the importance of reflection. It belongs to the rhythm of a gospel lifestyle. A personal response to Jesus includes a commitment to the gospel of Jesus Christ. Gospel people accept this as part of genuine gospel living. Daily life is where the gospel "takes flesh." Faith in Jesus requires us to interpret life from the perspective of the gospel. A *reflective attitude* is one way to facilitate this integration of Bible and life.

There are numerous ways to explain our faith. Insights from many sources nourish our understanding of faith. In Catholic tradition there are divergent theological opinions. Theologians may hold a common belief with differing ways to explain that belief. An attitude of openness offers possibilities of growth in understanding our faith. Very often the divergent opinions create new insights that coalesce into a richer understanding of the faith.

Theologians stretch our understanding of the faith. They offer perspectives that come from searching and re-searching, from prayer and reflection, from contemplation and study. Though their ideas are not infallible, they generate fresh ways of understanding the gospel. Their ideas offer insights for exploring and understanding our faith. In the interchange of ideas, the disagreements, the restating of ideas, the process of understanding the faith develops. The freedom to search offers possibilities for deepening our knowledge of God and God's revelation. To cut off such exploration would leave us in a sorry state. Ultimately, as history attests, the faith-community assesses and accepts the results of such dialogue. Conclusions may take centuries to form. In an atmosphere of freedom, the Spirit offers fresh and invigorating insights into God's revelation.

For example: Theological viewpoints about spirituality offer a variety of insights about the spiritual life. Note the differing viewpoints in the following opinions about spirituality:

1) God is "out there." We do what we can to let God into our hearts. We clean the "rooms" of our lives. Only then will we be worthy to have God dwell within us. Personal prayer, penance, and attempts to be a better person assist this process of growth. Spiritual growth is important. As we overcome sin and weakness, the Holy Spirit can operate more freely in our lives. We busily clean

up our lives so God can live there. We are personally responsible for such an achievement.

We believe God may not act until we make our lives as holy as possible. There is a subtle feeling that God is handcuffed if we aren't good enough.

2) We believe that God loves us. Even when we are unfaithful, God continues to love and forgive us. God dwells within us and gives us rootedness. As we abandon sin and weakness, God can act more freely in our lives. God does this from within. Even before we "clean up our act" God dwells with us. God is not indifferent to unfaithfulness. God expects us to be responsive and faithful to the covenant. God's gracious power works to transform us. God remains faithful even when we renege on the covenant. Our performance is not God's criteria for being faithful to us. Neither do our sins have power over God. God acts freely and is not controlled by us. Our sins keep us from being awake to God's love.

Acknowledgement of God's presence frees us. God's power works from within to achieve our conversion. The Holy Spirit dwells at the core of our being. As we surrender to God, our intimacy with Jesus grows. This in turn plunges us into the gospel and the gospel way of life. Conversion happens as we implement the gospel in daily life. The loving power of God (Holy Spirit) is at work throughout this process. We gradually "wake up" to God's presence as conversion continues.

3) Another approach has God speaking through the Church. Our primary task is to listen to the Church. We accept responsibility to be obedient to the regulations and teaching of the Church. There is a sense that our role is simply to listen to the Pope and the hierarchy and follow their lead.

It does not require a great deal of personal reflection. It does ask for unquestioning obedience. There is less need to reflect on "how" to implement the gospel. Our role is simply to listen to the hierarchy of the Church and obey. Obedience to the hierarchy is our way to conversion. This model has a simplicity in bringing us to God.

Each viewpoint has a *portion* of the truth. There are consequences flowing from each viewpoint:

Re 1. God enters our lives from "out there" somewhere. I must work hard to prepare a place worthy of God. I struggle to overcome sin and clean up "my act." Only then will I be able to host God in my life. There is a serious responsibility to "be good" *before* God can enter my life. There is a focus on what "I do" in this process of spiritual growth. I retain control of the timing of God's entry into my life. It is possible for perfectionism to creep into my attitude and cause me difficulty. Sometimes I feel that I will never be good enough!

Re 2. I am a temple of the Holy Spirit. I develop a respect for my whole person, body and spirit. I am aware of God's presence within me and respect that presence. There is no limit to what God may ask of me. The gospel calls for a lifestyle that reflects the dignity I and others have received from God. I learn to surrender control to God. There can be a danger of thinking that I can do anything and it's okay with God. Sometimes I may be too passive, thinking that God will do it all.

Re 3. I need only listen to the Church and follow the rules. I can readily assess how well I am keeping the rules. My personal responsibility is simply to obey. There is no need to pursue a deep personal understanding of my faith other than what catechisms may give me. I know the limits of responsibility and need not move beyond them. God's control is mediated through Church authority. The danger here may be in not taking personal responsibility for my actions. I can always blame the Church or someone in the Church.

Though the end results look similar, each viewpoint creates a different atmosphere. Guilt and responsibility are seen differently. Personal worth and self-denial take on different perspectives. God's role is seen with different eyes. There is a difference in our image of God. We may live in an atmosphere of fear of a judging God or rejoice in the presence of a compassionate God. We may prepare for salvation by "housecleaning" our soul or by depending on a saving God made present in Jesus Christ. The Church may be more a "them" than an "us." Our role is seen differently in the various theologies. No matter which theology we follow we can get to heaven. But the journey has a different flavor depending on the theology that points the way.

Exploring Some Theological Problems

Exploring these topics gives an idea of differing ways of understanding our faith. There is a wide spectrum of explanations for the things we believe.

Christology, i.e., the way we answer the question: "Who is Jesus?" Is he a victim appeasing an angry God in order to save us? Is he a person whose faithfulness and obedience gain salvation for us? Is Jesus' shedding of blood the only way of salvation? Is the faithful love of Jesus for his Father the source of our redemption? Is the death of Jesus a punishment endured for our sinfulness . . . *or* . . . is it the final act of loving faithfulness to the will of the Father? Is salvation achieved by healing the breach between God and the human race . . . *or* . . . is it achieved by the faithful response of Jesus to the will of the Father? Or is salvation explained through some combination of the above? These questions touch our relationship with God. God may alternately be an angry God to be appeased or a loving Father to be obeyed. God may be our "Abba" or a God out to "get us." God may be a merciful God reconciling people through the life and death of Jesus. God may be a demanding God imposing the cross as the way of reconciliation. Our perception offers a clue to our image of God and our understanding of Jesus. Our answers offer clues

about the "flavor" of our faith. It does not change the basic
fact that Jesus saves us.

The revelation offered by Jesus may be seen as a message
from "above." It may focus on the divinity of Jesus and find
its starting point there. Or it may focus on the humanity of
Jesus and reflect the incarnational aspects of Jesus' life and
teaching. In this instance, the humanity of Jesus gives an
"earthly" dimension to revelation. Christology offers ways of
perceiving and knowing Jesus Christ from both perspectives.

Church . . . a term with many meanings. Church can mean
the building where we worship. Church can mean the people
who worship. Church can mean the hierarchical structure that
governs the people. Church can mean the place where we get
baptized and confirmed, married and buried. Church can mean
the local community called parish. It can be identified with the
local pastor or pastoral assistant or anyone in authority. It can
mean the local chancery. It can mean the Pope and anything
he says or does. Church can mean bingo and May processions,
festivals and novenas. It can mean mornings at Mass and at-
tendance at religion classes.

The word "church" stimulates a variety of responses. If
"church" is a lifeless place for us, we may want to look more
deeply at the mystery called "church." If we have never
thought about the subject, we may need to give some time to
reflection. Church is many things to many people. We ought
to be in touch with our understanding of Church. The flavor
of church life is different if church is "them" or "us." If we
identify church with hierarchy we respond differently than if
the church is all of God's people joined by the Spirit. The community of believers will exist in any case. What differs are our
feelings and perspectives about church.

Penance . . . has its own set of images. It may mean the
struggle to make a complete confession. It can mean turning
our lives around and becoming more gospel-oriented. It can
mean doing penances like fasting and almsgiving or other
"hard" things. It is associated with giving up things in Lent.

It may surface in the tales of the gross penances of some saints. It may have negative connotations and be quite unattractive. We may do penance because the gospel demands it!

The negatives and positives of penance/reconciliation roam the rooms of our mind. Words are connected with penance. Words like conversion, metanoia, reconciliation, forgiveness, sackcloth and ashes, Lent, the Cross, fasting, giving up things, doing hard things for God! Everyone does not have the same image of penance. We need to search for beauty and value in penance. A non-reflective attitude is not much help in discovering its value. As richer images of penance grow in us we are changed by their positive influence. Pruning the vine is for growth, not for pain. Real conversion brings a fresh sense of our worth. Living a gospel life brings the happiness Jesus promised. Fasting and alms-giving offer positive ways of learning how to surrender to God. Penance can give new direction to our lives or conjure up images of what we must ''endure'' in order to please God.

Native American people see penance as a service to the people. I engage in sacrifice so that my negative actions (*against* the people) may be changed to light *for* the people. Transformation is for the sake of the people and not for my own sake. My penance is not viewed as a way of personal perfection but to free my gifts for use by the people. Self-centeredness is abandoned for the sake of other-centeredness. Compassion replaces selfishness. Concern for others replaces concern only for self.

If we never ask any questions, we can remain naively ignorant. Such ignorance is not bliss. Jesus invites us to listen and understand as fully as we can. We cannot be satisfied with either the interpreted ''facts'' of an ultraconservative newspaper or the ''opinions'' of a liberal journal.

It may seem easier and safer to do nothing. When *nothing* is what we do, *nothing* is what we get! We allow editors and writers to do our thinking for us. We may accept everything that TV evangelists tell us. It seems easier to accept such input than to think for ourselves. We allow others to create our con-

victions. "Come, let us go up to the mountain of the LORD /
to the house of the God of Jacob / that he may teach us his
ways / and that we may walk in his paths" (Mic 4:2).

Commitment requires knowledge. A gospel commitment
requires a personal relationship with Jesus and a knowledge
of the gospel. Lacking either keeps our faith from achieving
its full potential. We are not all we can be. When faith influences only a part of life, we are undernourished. God has
much more to offer. God's passionate desire for intimacy will
use every possible means to draw us to deeper commitment.
God cares too much to leave us alone. What we interpret as
punishment or guilt may be God's attempt to get our attention. How sad to wallow in guilt and punishment when God
desires intimacy and love. Jesus wants us to know the length,
the height and the breadth of God's love for us, which surpasses all understanding.

When we fail to commune with God (Jesus), we know little
of God. When we lack communication, it is hard to know the
"other." Without the dialogue of prayerfulness, we are ambiguous about committing ourselves. God is a mystery of vast
proportions. Our learning will not dilute the mystery. It will
give us glimpses of the mystery without exhausting it. Our continuing education will reveal the depth of the mystery of God.
Wonder blossoms in the presence of this awesome God. God
will capture our imagination. As knowledge grows, we will
make a deeper commitment to this God-made-flesh in Jesus.

We can reject God's call and still live. God will continue
to seek our friendship. God considers the covenant to be
sacred. God will remain faithful, not diverted from being God
by our unfaithfulness. Rather, God uses creative ways of love
to continue calling us to faithfulness and to the experience of
God's love.

> Where can I go from your spirit?
>   Or where can I flee from your presence? . . .
> If I say, "Surely darkness shall cover me,
>   and the light around me become night,"

even darkness is not dark to you;
    the night is as bright as the day,
    for darkness is as light to you (Ps 139:7, 11-12).

He [God] gives power to the faint,
    and strengthens the powerless.
Even youths will faint and be weary,
    and the young will fall exhausted;
but those who wait for the LORD shall renew their
      strength,
    they shall mount up with wings like eagles,
they shall run and not be weary,
    they shall walk and not faint (Isa 40:29-31).

God speaks a powerful and demanding word. It invites us to trust this God of ours. No matter what our ideas on spirituality or religion, God empowers us with the Holy Spirit. With such "graced power" we can live the gospel. Gospel living depends on God and the gracious gift of the Holy Spirit.

We will interpret God and God's gifts according to our theological understanding. We will interpret the events of life according to our theological perspective. Our view of life will flow from the manner in which we understand our faith. It is helpful *to know* what we believe and why. It calms our fears to know that there are many ways to understand and respond to Jesus and the gospel.

We *do choose* what to believe. Our choice gives color and meaning to our attempt to be holy. To remain ignorant is to miss some of the "spice" of faith. Prayerful theological exploration is one way to improve our wisdom.

> For we do not proclaim ourselves; we proclaim Jesus Christ as Lord and ourselves as your slaves for Jesus' sake. For it is the God who said, "Let light shine out of darkness," who has shone in our hearts to give the light of the knowledge of the glory of God in the face of Jesus Christ (2 Cor 4:5-6).

The light of insight invites us to change. Change is not always a welcome guest. Many ideas about faith have become part of life. It is difficult to spend years understanding our faith one way, only to discover that it is not the *only* way. It is unsettling and fearful. If my older ideas are being questioned, what assurance is there that the new ones won't be questioned? Is it so smart to listen to these new ideas? Perhaps it is better to stick with the tried and true. After all, many folks lived good lives without these new ideas. Why should I change my mind now?

I remember listening to a 72-year-old woman tell me of her fears. She had a deep devotion to the Blessed Virgin Mary. She said her rosary each day. She was finding it hard to complete the rosary. She would get caught up in the mysteries of the rosary and she'd never finish the decades. It bothered her that she seemed to be reneging on her promise to say the rosary each day. Puzzled and confused, she wondered why this was happening to her. Gently we explored her experience of what was happening. We concluded that she was being invited to a more contemplative form of prayer. The mysteries of the rosary became the invitation to ''rest with the Lord'' rather than saying the Hail Marys. Mary was leading her to Jesus in a way that was new to her. The newness surprised and confused her until she gently accepted this new form of prayer as a sign of progress. With the decision to allow herself to go with this new form, she found peace. Reflecting together had helped both of us discover God's creative way of inviting us to change. Read the gospel. Listen to what it says. Let the Scriptures speak to your heart. Reflection on God's word may open new doors in your life. It can be exciting. The call to conversion is God's to make. If my words have a part in that, I rejoice. It is not my task to convert you. You and God will deal with your conversion. The gift I offer is my own experience and delight in discovering God in fresh ways. ''Pray for us, so that the word of the Lord may spread rapidly and be glorified everywhere. . . . But the Lord is faithful; he will strengthen you and guard you from the evil one'' (2 Thess 3:1, 3).

Reflection Tools

Personal reflection is our attempt to understand the inner meaning of our experiences. We examine experience in the light of the Scripture and tradition of the Church. The interchange brings new insights as well as fresh ways of acting in response to our reflection. It may confirm previous understanding of experience or critique it. It may bring new understanding or challenge us to change the way we act. Personal reflection is *not* simply faith-sharing or problem-solving. It brings a fresh wisdom to our experiences and perspectives. It is wisdom honed from linking life with Scripture, tradition, theology, and experience. This, in turn, leads to a change in our way of responding to life situations.

There are many methods of doing personal reflection. We will take a brief look at how we might do such reflection.

1) In this method we gather information about a particular personal situation. Explore theology or tradition, personal experiences or cultural factors related to the situation. When we do this with others, it is important to *listen* to the information they offer.

For example: A political campaign is in progress. Campaign literature and advertising is abusing the truth with innuendo and highly selective quotes from the opposition. The Bible forbids the use of deceit and lies to destroy someone's reputation. Experience says that political campaigns often indulge in such practices. On a personal level, I acknowledge that I do this when I discuss people I don't like. What do these events/situations teach me about life and reality? Personal experience/practice may conflict with biblical teaching. Biblical stories of Jesus dealing with prejudice may enter the reflection. In the process of my personal reflection, I discover hidden prejudices I had previously ignored. Now I must determine what to do about this new information. I need to change in order to have greater integrity between my life and biblical values.

Summary: *Attend* to the situation (facts), whether from tradition (the Bible or tradition), experience (personal and communal), or culture (philosophy/politics/social sciences, etc). *Assert* the relative value of each, comparing it with personal experiences or communal values. *Decide* what to do about this new input. Then *do something!*

What values do I now apply to life? If I realize my own mischief in this regard, what will I choose to do? If I am a politician, what decisions will I change to maintain Christian integrity? What value(s) would I follow to integrate scriptural principles into real-life situations.

2) Another form of personal reflection joins stories from Scripture with personal experiences. Listen both to the Scripture and your own stories with a heart yearning for discovery.

For example: I read the story of a woman doctor who was tortured because she treated a guerrilla (anti-government person). The government accused her of treason. After torture and imprisonment, she was released. She spoke of her suffering in terms of the scriptural call to forgive those who persecute you. She stated her belief that all people were legitimate subjects of her healing power as a doctor. (Bible stories show Jesus caring for outcasts like lepers.) For her beliefs, the doctor suffered.

I might reflect on this woman's reasons for acting as she did. Her personal reflection led her to forgive those who tortured her. I reflect on the way she dealt with injustice and pain. How does her story (or a scriptural story) reflect God's faithfulness and care? What does the story call me to do? Are there people that I refuse to forgive? What does the Bible require of me?

How does this insight affect a tough situation in my life? Our stories can connect to God's word revealed in Jesus.

This method calls for some imaginative skills. Life experiences need to be linked to gospel stories. Not everyone feels competent and comfortable here. We need to *do something* about what we learn. The woman doctor forgave those who tortured her. Reflection led to action. Story-telling helps link personal stories to the gospel story. It awakens us to the human dimension of people in Bible stories. Good reflection leads us to act on what we learn.

Reflection frees us from standard solutions (conditioned responses?) and allows creative powers to blossom. Good reflection can help people in ministry from falling into routine ways of interacting with people. We avoid clinging to preconceived notions about how things should be ("We always did it this way!").

Various forms of personal reflection are not mutually exclusive. You may readily mix and match them. Use different forms at different times and in differing situations. Don't worry about "doing it right." Focus on using this "tool" to integrate life experiences with the gospel, tradition, and theology. Let it transform your perceptions and perspectives on living the gospel.

Personal reflection is not an esoteric discipline but a healthy way to keep life in touch with God and gospel. Your own reading and experience may have given you other useful methods of personal reflection. Use methods best suited to your spiritual growth.

My favorite reflective model uses the Scriptures as a mirror held up to life. There is a gentle process that can be used.

Reflect on some incident in your life. Think it through. What happened to you? What effect did it have on you? How did you feel about it? What did it teach you? Find a Scripture story/text that reflects your experience. Think it through. What happened in the Scripture story? How were people affected?

What changes occurred in their lives? Then see how your experience and the Scripture experience are similar or dissimilar. How does the Scripture story speak to you in dealing with your own experience? If you like, you can reverse the process. Look first at a Scripture story. Then find a personal experience that reflects the Scripture story. Use the same process as before.

Joining Scripture, tradition, theology, and life is a continuing process. When you listen to the Scripture proclaimed, let it soak into your experiences. Listen to tradition. See how it might nourish your life. Listen to tradition that is being formed today. Let it enhance your intimacy with Jesus. Reflection is an ongoing way of listening to God speak in daily life.

Here are some personal reflections on Scripture and life. I hope they open the door for your own reflection.

Reflections on Jonah

I suppose you have heard of the prophet Jonah. Most people remember the Jonah story as connected with a whale. If you read the story in the Bible, the large fish ("whale" is not mentioned) plays a small part. Jonah is *not* a fish story. It is not a tale about somebody whom God saves from drowning. It is not essential to believe that Jonah was swallowed by a large fish or that a fish could swallow a man. The story is richer than that. It is a story about God. It is a story about God's dealing with people (Jonah/Ninevites). It is about Jonah's attitudes about people and God. It speaks of ideas and attitudes that were being threatened. It speaks of Jonah's struggle to accept God's freedom to be God. Jonah struggles with God's love that is more universal than Jonah would like it to be. Jonah is a conversion story, a partial conversion story.

These background "notes" may help in understanding Jonah's story:

1. **The sea** is often considered the place where evil and chaos reign. To be tossed into the sea is to be plunged

into chaos and disorder. For example, when Jesus teaches from a boat, he is literally "on top of" (overcoming) chaos and evil.

2. **Nineveh** is the capital of Assyria. For 150 years the Assyrians had oppressed the Near Eastern world. The Ninevites were not popular with the Jews. Any punishment Ninevites received was fine with the Jews and with Jonah. Compassion for the Ninevites was not a common feeling for Jonah.

3. **Jonah's ideas** about God are revealed in this book. They were not always in accord with God's ideas about God. Jonah had some partial ideas about how God ought to act. Like ourselves, Jonah's partial ideas were not enough to bring him to a healthy response to God. Even his accurate ideas of God's generous forgiveness were of no help in dealing with his "crisis." Death seemed preferable to accepting God's way of doing things — especially when it did not agree with Jonah's ideas of how things should be settled.

4. **Jonah's response** is the result of his prejudice both about Nineveh and about God. Jonah finds it hard to understand why God acts with compassion toward the Ninevites. In fact, Jonah is downright angry about it. Jonah felt God had made a fool of him by allowing the people of Nineveh to live. The problem of understanding God is our problem as well as Jonah's.

This sharing of the "Jonah" story comes from personal reflection. It is not an official interpretation! The story of Jonah fits many of my responses to God. My "personal reflection" sees me in the Jonah story! I am challenged by what Jonah reveals about Lester!

> Now the word of the Lord came to Jonah, son of Ammittai, saying, "Go at once to Nineveh, that great city, and cry out against it; for their wickedness has come up before me." But Jonah set out to flee to Tarshish from the presence of the Lord. He went

down to Joppa and found a ship going to Tarshish; so he paid
his fare and went on board, to go with them to Tarshish, away
from the presence of the Lord (Jonah 1:1-3).

Jonah obviously understands the message of the Lord.
Jonah obviously does not wish to go to Nineveh. Jonah obviously chooses to get away by doing a disappearing act. Tarshish is the opposite direction from Nineveh. Jonah buys a
ticket, i.e., invests in his escape. This is not an unwitting man.
He boards a boat that is headed away from God and Nineveh.
This is conscious escapism. Jonah wants nothing to do with
people who have been oppressors for over a century. He cares
little whether their wickedness touches God or not. He simply
wants to avoid the whole issue by running away. Does this
sound familiar to you? I find that I often do exactly such "running from God's way" of doing things.

Jonah goes aboard the ship, finds a place to rest, and falls
asleep. But the boat runs into a storm that threatens to sink
it. The pagan sailors believe that someone has stirred up the
evil powers of the sea. They try to figure out how to appease
the sea-gods or rain-gods or any god needing to be appeased.
The captain finds Jonah sleeping and grows angry. He demands that Jonah pray or do something! Angry questions are
asked. Finally, Jonah admits he is running from the God of
heaven and earth. The sailors are astounded that Jonah would
risk the anger of such a great god. Caught in his escapism,
Jonah offers himself as a sacrifice to save the others. (I sometimes think he had a victim-complex.) Since he is caught, he
might as well get it over with and die. In any case, his attempt
at escape didn't work. Reality is setting in. Does Jonah fit
anything in your life yet? I really play my victim role to the
hilt. Often the "poor me" approach is my response when
confronted by my escapism. We co-dependents find this to be
a normal way of life!

At his own request, Jonah is tossed overboard and the ship
is saved. Jonah thought that it was all over. But he is swallowed by a great fish sent by God. In the belly of this fish,

Jonah finally decides to pray. He is pretty good at it, and his prayer reflects his need for God (chapter 2). Conversion is going on in Jonah — at least in some ways. Three days of wet darkness wear Jonah down a bit. He may have had time to do some personal reflection on his relationship with God. Then the fish spews him back onto the shore.

> The word of the LORD came to Jonah a second time, saying, "Get up, go to Nineveh, that great city, and proclaim to it the message that I tell you." So Jonah set out and went to Nineveh, according to the word of the LORD. Now Nineveh was an exceedingly large city, a three days' walk across. Jonah began to go into the city, going a day's walk. And he cried out, "Forty days more, and Nineveh shall be overthrown!" (Jonah 3:1-4).

After Jonah's experience in the sea, he was wise enough to obey orders. This time he hears and he goes. At least he changes his behavior even if his heart is still resisting. God is intent on dealing with the Ninevites. Jonah is willing to give it a try. So he does his job. He prophesies to the city of Nineveh. Then he leaves the city and waits for it to be destroyed by God. At least something worthwhile will happen now! God will give those Ninevites what they deserve!

The Ninevites spoil Jonah's dream. Everyone in the city, from the king down to the lowest servant, puts on sackcloth and ashes. ". . . they shall cry mightily to God. All shall turn from their evil ways and from the violence that is in their hands. Who knows? God may relent and change his mind; he may turn from his fierce anger, so that we do not perish" (Jonah 3:8-9).

Wouldn't you know it! God relents. God does not destroy the city because the people listened and changed. Jonah was not happy at all. He was so angry he was willing to die. He couldn't stand the way God was acting. Even worse, the things he had said to the people of Nineveh didn't come true. He felt like a fool. Quite rightly, he was angry with God! Is the story beginning to sound anything like your own story? Jonah's "bitching" is not unknown in my life!

But this was very displeasing to Jonah, and he became angry. He prayed to the Lord and said, "O LORD! Is not this what I said while I was still in my own country? That is why I fled to Tarshish at the beginning; for I knew that you are a gracious God and merciful, slow to anger, and abounding in steadfast love, and ready to relent from punishing. And now, O LORD, please take my life from me, for it is better for me to die than to live!" (Jonah 4:1-3).

Jonah's confusion and anger sound like my reaction when God doesn't follow my script. Of course, God is wrong, not I. If God would stop being compassionate and gracious . . . but that's also what I like about God! What a fool I am to question the way God works. Jonah's story is so like mine that I am embarrassed when I read it.

I love finding escape routes from God. Whether it is my intellectual acumen or simple intuition, I find a reason why some demand of the gospel is not meant for me. However, I do know someone who could use the Bible a bit more! There are people who ought to listen to the gospel better than they do! I have no trouble offering gospel advice to others. "They" really need it! But I hate being transported by big fish in order to do a job the Lord wants of me.

Jonah's story is my story over and over again. It is my refusal to walk the gospel way — always for good reasons, of course! It is my anger when God chooses a way that doesn't fit my plans. It is my grousing when I don't like the way things turn out. It is my readiness to try to escape when I realize what God really wants. God's compassion for "them" makes no sense to me! Stay away from Jonah if you want to have peace and quiet. Read Jonah and it is hard to stay with the "status quo" simply because it is more comfortable.

Even more important is what the book of Jonah tells me about God. I think the last words of the book are the most important. These words tell us how God sees the situation:

Then the Lord said, "You are concerned about the bush, for which you did not labor and which you did not grow; it came into being in a night and perished in a night. *And should I not be concerned about Nineveh* [italics mine], that great city, in which there are more than a hundred and twenty thousand persons who do not know their right hand from their left, and also many animals?'' (Jonah 4:10-11).

God's generosity to people I label as ''nobodies'' does not sit well with me. But God knows me inside out. God invites me to stop using labels to put people in their place. Conservative and liberal, progressive and traditional, left and right, all are useless in God's eyes. Labeling the Ninevites did little for Jonah's conversion process. It is unwise to think that any one of us has the *whole* truth. Too often I fulfill this definition of a fanatic: ''A fanatic is someone with a passionate dedication to a portion of the truth.''

Religious fanatics (Jonah/me?) have a passionate devotion to a *portion* of God's truth. The problem is not passionate devotion. The problem is the conviction that I possess the *whole* truth when I do not! A portion of the truth is easier to handle. It is easier to enforce. It requires no more searching or doubt. It means that no more growth or change is required. It is being ''Jonah'' before God. Solid personal reflection moves me to face Jonah's problem in myself — trying to understand God's generosity toward people I dislike.

Review

Good *personal reflection* links God's word and daily life. It invites us to look at the structures and attitudes of our life. It does not allow us to hide indifference or ignorance under the rug of unreflective living. Personal reflection pushes us to see the linkage between theology, Scripture, tradition, and daily life. It pokes itself into the corners of our presumptions. It challenges half-baked ideas that have gone unexamined. It permits us to face the needs of maturity in being a faith-filled people. It creates an atmosphere of openness to creative change in my life. In short, good personal reflection clarifies the way *I live the gospel*. It invites me to get in touch with how my ''self'' relates to God, to people, to the world, and to the events of life.

> If you love to listen you will gain knowledge,
>   and if you pay attention you will become
>   wise. . . .
> Reflect on the statutes of the Lord,
>   and meditate at all times on his commandments.
> It is he who will give insight to your mind,
>   and your desire for wisdom will be granted (Sir
> 6:33, 37).

Reflection

Do I avoid conversion by ignoring anything that challenges me? Do I act as though I am infallible? Am I a fanatic? Does the gospel affect my life or is it just nice reading? How am I at labeling people? Do new ideas frighten me? . . . excite me? . . . bore me? What (who) is the source of my understanding of my beliefs? Do I believe that the understanding of faith cannot change? Do I feel trapped by religion? How much time do I spend expanding my understanding of the faith? Am I satisfied with catechism answers to faith or do I want more? What do theologians offer me for life? Are theologians helpers or enemies for me? How does my Christian reading support my search for fresh understanding of faith? How life-giving is my faith for my friends? If it is not, why not? If so, how so? How do I feel about my personal conversion process? How does my life reflect my faith? What do the words *Church, Penance,* and *Christ* mean to me? How can good personal reflection help my faith-life? What form of personal reflection is most attractive to me? What is the title of the last book I've read on the faith? When did I read it? Do I share my faith-experiences with others? . . . often? . . . occasionally? . . . rarely? . . . never? What keeps my faith alive? Does the story of Jonah touch any area of my life? What ways do I use to escape from God? Am I just a Sunday Catholic? How deep is my commitment to a gospel lifestyle? What changes will such a lifestyle require? What area of my faith-life gives me the most difficulty and worry? How could personal reflectiveness help my spiritual growth?

————————————

God invites us to walk beyond fear, confident of God's faithfulness.

> I called on God, and the spirit of
>   wisdom came to me. . . .
> I loved her more than health and beauty,
> and I chose her rather than light,
>   because her radiance never ceases.
> All good things came to me along with her,
> and in her hands uncounted wealth. . . .
> I learned both what is secret and what is manifest,
> for wisdom, the fashioner of all things, taught me
> (Wis 7:7, 10, 21).

CHAPTER SIX

Does It Really Make the World Go 'Round?

Love — a beautiful, honorable, and abused word. It describes the concern of caring people. It is used to identify romance. It describes people who care about animals. It can be used in reference to sexual intercourse. It describes all degrees of relationship from puppy love to the deepest intimacy. It is used to describe gospel people in Paul's letter (1 Cor 13:1-7). Love is patient and kind, not arrogant or rude. It endures all things and hopes for all things. With such a variety of meanings, understanding the meaning of love is no easy task.

There are languages in the Middle East that have over sixty words to identify varying degrees of love. English uses one word. This single word bears the burden of hundreds of "love" actions. It defines everything from infatuation to the deepest kind of intimacy. Not surprisingly, one word cannot bear the burden. Love is frequently misunderstood and its meaning unintelligible.

Think about it! I say: "I love you." You have to guess what I mean. Do I like your company and love you for that? Do I like your beauty and love you for that? Do I like your conversation and love you for that? Am I happy that you help me and love you for that? Do you fill the lonely gaps in life, and I love you for that? Do we have good sex together, and I love you for that? Do you like my friends, and I love you for that?

Do you cook good meals, and I love you for that? Do I feel accepted when you're around, and I love you for that? Do you fill my need for affection, and I love you for that? Do I like your bank account and love you for that? Do I like your sense of humor and love you for that? Do I love you because you are so beautiful or handsome? Do I love you because of your charming personality? Does "I love you" mean simply that I love *you*? Or is love a combination of all of the above?

If human love words seem confusing, imagine what we understand when we say: "God loves me." Frequently the same confusion exists. We need to dig deeper to sort out our understanding of this word.

Individual definitions of love have built-in limitations. Manipulating people or using people for personal satisfaction is not very loving. Romantic ("puppy love") love is fun. But it has little staying power. It is wise not to invest too heavily in its promise. A "snuggly love" that finds ultimate joy only in sex is incomplete. Definitions offer some insight into the meaning of love. But they lack the richness needed for a full understanding of the wonder that is love.

Love has another face. It is a *relationship-love (intimacy)* that requires commitment from the people involved. It is sought not simply for personal pleasure, though that is not rejected. It does not merely seek to satisfy one's own desires and needs, though that is not neglected. It is not arbitrary, depending on feelings, though feelings are not ignored. It is a relationship that loves the person. The goal of love is to bring joy to the beloved. There is delight in seeing joy in the eyes of the loved one. There is awareness of the moods and needs of the other. There is a desire to respond to such needs. This love transforms the people involved. Such love respects the dignity of the other person. It also acknowledges and respects personal dignity.

Not all loving relationships are exclusive. It is possible to relate to many friends. It is possible to respond to the needs of many people who are loved. Mothers and fathers do it all the time. Love is tailored to the person who is loved. It responds to particular needs. It shares skills and gifts so that the other may grow and live. It is not overly concerned about self. In the process of loving, it finds personal satisfaction. It is not neglectful of self-needs but can put them aside for the sake of the ''Beloved.''

This love is common among maturing people. It does not ignore personal growth and development. On the contrary, its outgoing attitude brings fresh things to ''life'' in the individual. As love responds to the needs of others, personal gifts seem to blossom. We trust that the loved one will respond to our personal needs. Real love does not hide needs and feelings. There is honesty in the relationship. It is *not* a demanding, tit-for-tat favor-giving. As knowledge of one another grows, so does love. Weaknesses in the beloved do not stifle love. The ''common sense'' of love deals with weakness in a life-giving way. The deeper our knowledge of the other and the better our communication of self, the richer is the quality of love. Love is neither naive nor ignorant. It does not ignore tough issues and disagreements. The commitment of love is faithful. It is not easily brushed aside when strong, persistent action and faithfulness are called for. Love is a knowledgeable commitment. Once made, it builds on a solid foundation of communication and caring. Love *is* a knowledgeable, caring, direct response to the ''other.''

Love creates an atmosphere of acceptance. This allows the beloved to deal with tough issues without falling apart. Acceptance is a normal part of the relationship. It is not something that must be earned. Neither is acceptance a doormat allowing the beloved to destroy self or others. Real love confronts. It succeeds in confronting because it confronts from an accepting love, not a ''gotcha'' spirit. Real love has a price that is willingly paid. Acceptance of person can exist even when we disapprove of the attitudes of the beloved.

The joy of love may be touched and tempered by loss. In the sixties, I had a good friend. Clare's friendship enriched me, and her presence challenged me. I believe I did the same for her. She was full of life and always concerned about people in need of help. She often involved her friends in projects to aid others. It was delightful to be with Clare. I pictured her as a woman full of life and in touch with the wonders of life.

One day she called and wanted to see me. I was busy that day and invited her to come "tomorrow." I didn't hear the plea in her voice. My picture of her did not include personal problems. She didn't come "tomorrow." I didn't respond for a few days. I finally phoned her. I was informed that Clare had been buried that morning. She had killed herself the night after she called me. Though I never feared for Clare's salvation, since God is so gracious, I did not get off so easily. The pain of the loss and my own "not hearing" were a traumatic experience. I wrote these words at that time about my feelings: "I don't know if you can understand the pain and grief of a person who has failed to be aware. I don't know if you can begin to realize how deeply I have felt failure. 'Tomorrow.' Tomorrow is no time to do it if it can be done now. Can you understand what I am saying? Can you realize that all the excuses are just words? Someone needed a listening heart — and I missed the urgency in her voice?"

I didn't wallow in guilt, but I learned much about the price of loving someone. The hills and valleys of love are often unknown when we make our commitment. Love stays with the beloved even when the cost is great — and somehow it offers life in the midst of loss.

Scripture and Love

Walter Brueggemann shared ideas about God's love at a convention some years ago. He spoke about God's love as found in the Hebrew Testament. These ideas are from notes I took while listening to the tapes of his talks.

1. God's love is *public*. God establishes a relationship with liberated slaves from Egypt. God goes public with it. God openly declares love for the poor and those without power. God uses divine power on behalf of the

"chosen people." Real love respectfully expresses itself publicly. It doesn't "have to" do this. It comes quite naturally. True friendship offers such a respectful, public relationship.

2. God's love is *transformative,* i.e., it refuses to leave things as they are when they can be better. There is an expectation in this love that the beloved will *change,* and change often. It is not a love that stands still or allows things to remain stagnant. It is a love alive with the desire to enhance life rather than merely to preserve life. This love presumes that the relationship will bring about change. It does not *force* change. It does not manipulate people in order to change them. Rather, it provides an atmosphere where change seems normal and fear of change is diminished by the presence of love.

3. God's love is *countercultural,* i.e., it goes counter to many of the values and ideas that society proclaims. It seeks reconciliation, while others seek revenge. It listens, when others turn away. It will walk an extra mile, when others would break the relationship. This love is not a mushy, sentimental approach to people. It requires a maturity and self-acceptance that is part of its strength. It does not attempt to control or dominate, but neither is it afraid to deal directly with behaviors that need to change.

Since it seeks life, it will not compromise with forces that bring death. It is a love that death cannot destroy. It will not allow false values to overwhelm it nor fall victim to "everyone's doing it" rationalizations. It is strong and clear-sighted. It is a love that is realistic in a gospel way.

4. God's love is *concerned with justice.* It cannot tolerate oppression or injustice in any form. It opposes the psychological oppression of sexism and racism. It opposes the violent oppression of war and weapons of destruc-

tion. It opposes economic oppression that keeps people powerless and under the control of others. It is concerned about abuse, whether sexual, physical, or psychological. It seeks to offer God the worship that is due to God.

It looks for ways to bring freedom and dignity to people. It looks for ways to heal abusive parents. It looks for ways to stop psychological abuse. It looks for ways of security that do not include inhumanity to others. It looks for ways to share resources so that all people can live in dignity. It proclaims the dignity of life from the womb to the tomb. It will do "band-aid" things that people need to stay alive. It will engage in the long-term work to change oppressive systems. It is not depressed by failure. It hangs tough and persists in seeking creative ways to do justice. It does not use power to achieve personal "perks" or positions of control. As far as possible, it uses power for the good of all. It joins justice and charity to create an atmosphere where mercy can grow. Love delights in the joys of others. Love celebrates with a sort of reckless abandon. Love brings joy by its presence. Peace follows in its wake. Love can be quiet or exuberant as the situation requires. It is sensitive to the need of the beloved to be listened to or to be hugged. Love realizes that sharing truth lovingly can bring new life. If one way of dealing with a problem does not work, love creatively seeks other ways.

Having come this far, you may say that such love is impossible. We are only human. No one can consistently maintain such a love! If this *is* gospel love, we don't think we can fulfill its demands!

Something needs to be added to the equation. God is love. Love describes God and God's way of dealing with us. *Union with God* enables us to do what we cannot accomplish by ourselves. When we add this element of faith, we touch a power that *enables us* to love. ''A new heart I will give you, and a new spirit I will put within you; and I will remove from your body the heart of stone and give you a heart of flesh. I will put my spirit within you'' (Ezek 36:26-27).

''You are not lacking in any spiritual gift as you wait for the revealing of our Lord Jesus Christ. He will also strengthen you to the end, so that you may be blameless on the day of our Lord Jesus Christ. God is faithful'' (1 Cor 1:7-9).

History tells of people whose love is based on faith in God. St. Francis of Assisi's embrace of poverty is an impossible lifestyle without faith. St. Peter Claver's willingness to take the place of slaves makes no sense unless we recognize his faith in Jesus. St. Clare of Assisi's bold confrontation of invading soldiers makes sense when viewed with the eyes of faith. The persistence of Sts. Teresa of Avila and John of the Cross, despite problems within their own religious communities, can be explained when viewed with the eyes of faith. The demands of Jesus make sense when faith reveals the presence and power of the Holy Spirit.

We *can* love publicly, allow for transformation, be counter-cultural and sensitive to justice when we believe in Jesus. It *is* the way of gospel people. With God, all things are possible. Everyone will know who we are by our gospel love.

The Struggle

Love as shown by Jesus is not saccharine or indifferent. Jesus was intimately identified with his Father. The things the Father wanted, Jesus wanted. Whatever countered the Father's way was anathema to Jesus. His anger at the abuses in the Temple moved him to drive out the profit-making money changers. When he taught and people closed their minds, he was deeply grieved by the hardness of heart that refused to see things in the Father's way. Jesus showed the compassion his Father showed. In short, Jesus completely identified with the agenda of the Father. No matter what price had to be paid, Jesus' love for his Father moved him to be faithful to all the Father asked of him.

In our case, if we wish to be Christian, we develop the same kind of commitment to Jesus. Our love for Jesus moves us to implement the gospel in all situations of life. No matter what the price, we will not be separated from our love of Jesus. The intimacy of a loving relationship will color all we do (cf. Acts 6:8-10).

> With all wisdom and insight he has made known to us the mystery of his will, according to his good pleasure that he set forth in Christ, as a plan for the fullness of time, to gather up all things in him, things in heaven and things on earth. . . . In him you also, when you had heard the word of truth, the gospel of your salvation, and had believed in him, were marked with the seal of the promised Holy Spirit (Eph 1:8-10, 13).

But . . . it is easier to remain an intellectual Catholic. It is simpler to be an unreflective and obedient Catholic. It is comfortable to let others decide what we should do and believe. It is more enjoyable to be an excited Catholic, running from one religious experience to another. Being a "real," loving gospel person is no easy task. "No one can serve two masters; for a slave will either hate the one and love the other, or be devoted to the one and despise the other. You cannot serve God and wealth" (Matt 6:24).

Trying to do dual service brings us to exhaustion. We are tired. We refuse to choose whom/what we will serve. The worship of idols has not disappeared. We call it progress, climbing the corporate ladder, building the economy. We call it business-as-usual or portfolio needs. We are "providing for our future" or developing a nest egg for a rainy day. If we choose the idol of *money*, we try to appease God by Sunday worship, dutifully attended! We show generosity to charities with money from our idol-god. An honest look at where we expend most of our energy reveals that the gospel often takes second place!

Avoidance tactics leave us uncommitted and confused. We choose both God and Money. But real love requires that we prefer one or the other. When the choice is made, life reflects that choice. Life is touched by our choice. If we choose love of money, it shows in our lifestyle and attitudes. If God is the choice, it shows in our lifestyle and attitudes. If we try to choose both, confusion and lack of conviction and consistency are reflective of our indecision. We cannot serve both and expect to be at peace.

Straddling the fence is *not* what gospel love requires. Our refusal to choose one or the other leaves us unsatisfied. The opportunity to be gospel people of integrity is lost. Headed in two directions, we are satisfied with neither. It may appear good on the outside, but the heart realizes the hypocrisy. Bodily sickness sometimes gives an indication of the stress such "un-decision" brings.

> "You have seen what I did to the Egyptians, and how I bore you on eagle's wings and brought you to myself. Now therefore, if you obey my voice and keep my covenant, you shall be my treasured possession out of all the peoples" (Exod 19:4-5).
>
> "*Hear,* O my people, while I admonish you;
>   O Israel, if you would but listen to me!
> There shall be no strange god among you;
>   you shall not bow down to a foreign god.
> I am the LORD your God. . . .
> But my people did not *listen* to my voice;
>   Israel would not submit to me.
> So I gave them over to their stubborn hearts,
>   to follow their own counsels.
> O that my people would *listen* to me,
>   that Israel would walk in my ways! . . .
> I would feed you with the finest of the wheat,
>   and with honey from the rock I would satisfy you"
> (Ps 81:8-10, 11-13, 16 — italics mine).

God's word is sharp and clear. The word reveals a passionate desire for intimacy. God's anger does not seek to destroy the beloved but to point them in the right direction. God wants wholeness of life for the loved ones. God clearly desires to be acknowledged as God. God nowhere indicates that other gods should replace the true God in our lives. God uses every possible means to keep our faith relationship strong and clear-sighted. It is a healthy decision to have no other god. It is a wise decision. With the help of God we can do whatever is asked of us. *Listen* to some of the ways to recognize people who faithfully love God.

> "Let your light shine before others, so that they may see your good works and give glory to your Father in heaven. . . . Love your enemies and pray for those who persecute you, so that you may be children of your Father in heaven; for he makes his sun rise on the evil and the good, and sends rain on the righteous and on the unrighteous" (Matt 5:16, 44-45).

> "Not everyone who says to me 'Lord, Lord,' will enter the kingdom of heaven, but only the one who does the will of my Father in heaven" (Matt 7:21).

> And he said, "It is what comes out of a person that defiles. For it is from within, from the human heart, that evil intentions come: fornication, theft, murder, adultery, avarice, wickedness, deceit, licentiousness, envy, slander, pride, folly. All these evil things come from within, and they defile a person" (Mark 7:20-23).

The texts could be multiplied. A serious reading of Scripture finds clear evidence of a demanding God who loves us passionately. The life and teaching of Jesus reveal a deep desire for intimacy with us. Our response to this desire does not always match the passion of God. We are not always passionately dedicated to the gospel. Personal, consistent reflection on the gospel will prompt a response — to radical conversion.

We have many models — people who committed themselves to integrity in following Jesus. Saints, canonized and uncanonized, give us models to follow. Alcoholics who turn from liquor to an alcohol-free existence. Business people with the courage to be honest and fair even if profits diminish. Women who fearlessly stand before violence and confront its stupidity. Look around you! See people who invest their lives in the struggle for justice throughout the world. They offer proof that a gospel lifestyle and real love are not outdated or impossible. When we commit ourselves to Jesus, integrity requires us to *both listen to and do* the gospel. No two masters for us! We have but one master — God. Propaganda and opposition from society will not deter us from the integrity of gospel living.

> "I have come as light into the world, so that everyone who believes in me should not remain in the darkness. I do not judge anyone who hears my words and does not keep them, for I came not to judge the world, but to save the world. The one who rejects me and does not receive my word has a judge; on the last day the word that I have spoken will serve as judge" (John 12:46-48).

> "If you abide in me, and my words abide in you, ask for whatever you wish, and it will be done for you. My Father is glorified by this, that you bear much fruit and become my disciples. As the Father has loved me, so I have loved you; abide in my love" (John 15:7-9).

Love — that many-splendored thing. Love fills postcards and greeting cards. Love is the subject of movies and TV shows. Love, we are told, makes the world go 'round. Love means never having to say you're sorry [*sic*]! Love overlooks everything and is a pushover for real strength (Oh?)! Love is linked with sexual encounters. In the name of love, foolish things are done and called "okay." Listen to the lyrics of some love songs and hear about a mushy love. Country music often sings of the problems of love — from loneliness to "My honey doesn't love me any more" — without giving an answer to the problem.

This four-letter word has so many meanings as to be meaningless. We Christians want to give it meaning, and practice it with integrity. We return to the gospel again and again. There we find love given "flesh" in Jesus, our model. There we see the consequences of real love. There we discover God willing to risk life itself by entering our world. There we find attitudes that will be our attitudes as gospel people in love with Jesus.

Every generation learns the ways of love. Part of our task is to live in such a way as to model love for others. It is not enough to talk about love. It is insufficient to sing melodies of love. It evades the issue if all we do is write about love. Love is learned in the crucible of everyday life. Gospel love takes on flesh in living people who care for others. It finds expression in groups who gather to worship God with loving hearts. It shows continued forgiveness when persistent hurt comes from others. It struggles with how to deal with annoying people or people who always cause trouble. It works mightily to deal with family members who choose behaviors and values that counter everything in which we believe. Gospel love cannot choose evasive tactics to avoid tough decisions. It intervenes when people are trapped in addictions. It walks with people who can no longer remember the simplest things.

God chose to become human and walk among us. Part of the reason was to offer a clear example of the power and life-giving qualities of love.

> But now, dear lady, I ask you, not as though I were writing you a new commandment, but one we have had from the beginning, let us love one another. And this is love, that we walk according to his commandments; this is the commandment just as you have heard it from the beginning — you must walk in it (2 John 1:5-6).

A Listing About Love

I had the good fortune to give a program at John XXIII Centre in Windsor, Ontario. While I was there, I picked up a brochure they had used for a marriage program. There was no note about who wrote it, so I freely pass it on to you — with thanks to its author(s).

What Love Does	**What Love Doesn't Do**
Love accepts you wherever you are	Love doesn't abuse you or take you for granted

Love affirms your goodness
and giftedness

Love cares about you, wants
to know that you're okay

Love challenges you to be all
you can be

Love empathizes — knows what
it is like to be you

Love encourages you to believe
in yourself

Love is gentle in its way of
dealing with you

Love keeps confidences — your
secrets are safe

Love is kind — is always for
you

Love laughs a lot, always with,
never at you

Love looks for goodness in you
and finds it

Love makes you feel glad that
you're you

Love overlooks your foolish
vanities, human weakness

Love prays for your needs
and your growth

Love sees good things in you
that others never noticed

Love shares itself with you
by self-disclosure

Love speaks up when you need
someone to defend you

Love is tactful even when
confronting you

Love takes responsibility for
its own behavior

Love tells you the truth always
and honestly — trying to be
sensitive to your ability to
hear it

Love thinks about you and your
needs

Love doesn't ask you to march
to a different drummer

Love doesn't blame you or
carry angry grudges

Love doesn't bully you by
anger, a loud voice, or tears

Love doesn't get you into
win-lose arguments

Love doesn't give you
unsolicited advice

Love doesn't judge you or
tell you "what your whole
trouble is"

Love doesn't just tolerate
you as a condescending favor

Love doesn't make you prove
yourself again and again

Love doesn't need to be
always right, to have all the
answers

Love doesn't pout or refuse
to talk to you

Love doesn't punish you
vindictively for being wrong

Love doesn't remember all the
things you have done
wrong

Love doesn't seek and call
attention to itself

Love doesn't show off, just
to let you know where you
stand

Love doesn't undermine your
confidence in yourself

Love doesn't use you for its
purposes and then discard you

Love doesn't ventilate its
emotions on you as a garbage
dump

Love doesn't write you off
because you didn't meet its
demands

Love is tough or tender,
  depending on your needs
Love understands your ups and
  downs, allows you ''bad days''

Reflection

What ideas/values most often influence my decisions? How passionate am I in my response to the gospel? Does God make any difference in my life? How would I describe my ''love'' of friends? What love-idols can I identify in my life right now? When push comes to shove, which way do I lean — gospel values or me-first values? Am I a dictator to my family, but excuse it because I ''love'' them? How do others describe my response to them? . . . Caring? . . . Impersonal? . . . Cold? . . . Warm? . . . Always seeking to escape responsibility? . . . Too busy to bother? Does getting *my* needs met dominate my relationships? Do I lack self-esteem and bow and kow-tow to everyone in an attempt to gain acceptance? Do I like myself? Love myself? Who (What) gets me angry most often? How do I deal with feelings of anger/hatred? How do I contribute to a spirit of community in my parish? What effect does fence-straddling have on my ability to love? How do I help others to strengthen their faith? How healthy is my way of showing love? Do I become possessive (clinging) when I love someone? Do I try to force people to change in the name of ''love''? How well do I communicate my love to people close to me? How do I show love where I work? What does love look like in a supermarket? How would love be shown in a beauty parlor? How would love treat the neighborhood gossip? How would love deal with ornery neighbors? How can love deal with drug dealers? Murderers? Rapists? Unrepentant criminals? What would love do about government policies that hurt people? How would love respond to policies or governmental actions that oppress people or deny them dignity? How do I practice love with my friends? How do love and justice come together in my life?

_____

These questions support good reflection. They are *not* asked in an effort to create guilt. *We are good but imperfect* people. It is not surprising that we do not have perfect love for one another. One of my spiritual guides told me: ''Fear not, Lester, you are inadequate!'' I am a good person, but I can do better. Statements about my imperfection and inadequacy will always be true of me. I don't anticipate becoming *perfect* in this life. Awareness of my inadequacy keeps the door of my life open to change, challenge, and conversion! God passionately loves me. God continues to transform me. *Love* offers me daily opportunities for new life!

> Love is patient; love is kind; love is not envious or boastful or arrogant or rude. It does not insist on its own way; it is not irritable or resentful; it does not rejoice in wrongdoing, but rejoices in the truth. It bears all things, believes all things, hopes all things, endures all things. . . . And now faith, hope, and love abide, these three; and the greatest of these is love (1 Cor 13:4-7, 13).

CHAPTER SEVEN

A Nine-letter Word

Our society has a fixation about sex(uality). The dictionary defines sexuality as: *1. the state or quality of being sexual. 2. a) an interest in or concern with sex. b) sexual drive or activity.* TV talk shows spend a lot of time talking about sex. Listening to the kids outside my window when I lived in Chicago, I heard the "F" word used indiscriminately. When arguments got heated on the street corner, sexual language boomed from human voice-boxes. All this talk gives the false impression that people are experts on the subject of sexuality. People certainly know the language of sex. Graffiti throughout our cities or in the rest rooms of public buildings make that graphically clear. Word-knowledge is often touted as real knowledge.

Much of the talk is about "sex" and not sexuality. It is a limited conversation about genital activity of various sorts. It is language that is geared to minimal understanding of sexuality and lots of verbalism about sex. It is sad that we have banished sexuality and focused on sex. Sex is body; sexuality is person. Sex is intercourse; sexuality is relationship. Sex is pleasure for fun; sexuality is pleasure that deepens mutuality in relationship. Sex is penis/clitoris; sexuality is loving self-disclosure. Sex permits others to be used; sexuality brings respect to the other. Sex does what it wants to enjoy itself; sexuality has an attitude of respect and responsibility.

A chasm exists between knowing sex words and understanding sexuality. Pregnancy among the young, casual intercourse between people despite the spread of sex-related diseases, the AIDS epidemic and talk of "safe sex" indicate some ignorance of the beauty of sexuality. Fear may make people more careful. But fear and carefulness do not prove the presence of sound knowledge about sexuality.

We need attitudes about sexuality that move from a merely genital performance to an enriching human experience. Sexuality honors both the spirit and the body of oneself and others. It senses the wholeness of the human person. It avoids any form of addictive sex that isolates sexual activity from the rest of life.

Sex As a Proving Ground

Some people use sexual intercourse and pregnancy in an effort to prove their maturity. A baby proves that I am someone. This infant needs me. I am important for this child's welfare. The baby satisfies my need to be someone. Sometimes sex is used to solve problems unrelated to sex. A marriage in trouble because of a communications breakdown will not be healed by having sex. Neither can an abusive relationship be healed by intercourse.

A baby may be abused or rejected when it interferes with *my* freedom. Selfishness is not uprooted by pregnancy. Both father and mother will be challenged by the presence of this "new person." If the discovery of personal selfishness and self-centeredness is not dealt with, the baby ceases to be a magical solution. The child becomes the problem. Father and mother face the demands of reality. Both discover what kind of people they are. The demands of generous, unselfish parent-love require a healthy measure of maturity. Selfish and/or immature people will find such responsibilities too much to handle. Healthy sexuality requires respect, responsibility, and restraint.

Some Considerations

People with mature and healthy attitudes about sex and relationships are too few. The process of developing mature, loving relationships requires fidelity and persistence. It requires an ability to develop intimacy. Healthy relationships require more than the physical actions of sex. Healthy relationships need more than intellectual understanding of the psychology of sex. Spiritual idealism, by itself, is insufficient for building healthy attitudes about sex and long-term relationships. Building sound relationships requires both a sense of one's own dignity and respect for the dignity of others. In a society where "instant" is the key word, many people lack the willingness and persistence needed for building long-term relationships.

Long-lasting relationships require the integration of spiritual, psychological, and sexual knowledge/attitudes. A maturing person knows that the process of maturation is the process of a lifetime. It calls for a person with self-respect, healthy self-love, and an attitude of respect for others. It does not happen instantly. Claudia Black says that it requires honest *communication*, i.e., "Getting to know you." As knowledge grows, *caring* follows in its wake. Knowing and caring allow us to make an informed *commitment* to the other person. Very often a commitment is made before communication has revealed who the other person really is.

Jerry Kafer, O.F.M. Cap., shared these reflections about sex(uality) at a workshop (my notes):

> 1. We can *fake* sexuality — i.e., give the impression of great knowledge, lots of experience, and deep understanding — when we actually have meager knowledge or experience of sexuality. Here is where the language of sex serves the "faker" very well.

> 2. We can *fear* sexuality, i.e., remain in ignorance, fearing the reality of sexuality and avoiding opportunities for gaining sound knowledge about this "awful" subject. We can avoid thinking about the consequences if we did "it!"

We can avoid taking responsibility for the consequences of sexual activity. Many people deny any ignorance. A dual fear of appearing stupid and fearing the implications of sex often paralyzes people. This fear may also torpedo healthy programs that could help the younger generation understand sexuality.

3. We can *faith* it, i.e., put it in a healthy, realistic, holistic framework. This would include body and spirit awareness, sexuality, and intimacy, pleasure and joy. Developing healthy attitudes and values about sexuality gives us healthy people and joyful sex. Failure to do so brings manipulation, loneliness, selfishness, and alienation. Faith requires us to develop a realistic attitude toward sexuality. Faith invites us to share a healthy understanding of sexuality, one that gives it a meaning beyond instant gratification.

Our sexuality (not just "sex") serves well when it is part of a committed relationship. It offers life when it is a sign of concern for the other. It brings light when it supports growth in oneself and others. It is beautiful when it fulfills the gospel design for relationships. In good relationships, dominance disappears. Respectful response grows in good relationships. Loving relationships recognize both the "feelings" of sexuality and the need for limits in their expression. "Or do you not know that your body is a temple of the Holy Spirit within you, which you have from God, and that you are not your own? For you were bought with a price; therefore glorify God in your body" (1 Cor 6:19-20).

When we make an idol of sex, we wind up disappointed. In its extremes, unhealthy sex is destructive. People addicted to such an idol lose touch with life and compassion. Sex becomes an idol that ultimately destroys. The awful accounts of sexual abuse by relatives and trusted people bombard us. The after effects are devastating! Sirach speaks wisely about the attitudes that true wisdom brings: "Never speak against the truth, but be ashamed of your ignorance. Do not be ashamed to confess your sins. . . . Fight to the death for truth, and the Lord God will fight for you" (Sir 4:25-26, 28).

Intimacy

It is risky to reveal oneself. To show one's body can be embarrassing or emotionally problematic, but it is easy to do. Simply remove your clothes in the presence of the other. No special relationship is needed. No special commitment need be made. It does not demand a brilliant understanding of sex.

Revealing our inner self — our fears, our dreams, our needs, our vulnerability, our confusion, our hopes, our innermost feelings and ideas — that is demanding! It presumes healthy self-knowledge. It requires trust in the other person. It leaves us without hiding places. It opens our real self to the "other." It demands honest attempts to understand how the other person "understands."

There is need for dialogue between people. Each may hear and understand the same information in different ways. Understanding the differing ways of hearing and responding as men and women requires unprejudiced listening. Men and women hear differently. The same situations and words can be interpreted differently. No one does this unless the friend is trustworthy. A committed and healthy friendship makes it easier to accomplish.

Intimacy calls for a revelation of self to the other. In friendships that are not exclusive, there are obvious limitations. We reveal ourselves to friends in ways that fit the friendship. Self-revelation is a part of our intimacy with them. Acceptance by a good friend gives us a sense of security. If we have only superficial and shallow friendships, feelings of loneliness and isolation result. Intimacy is a gift not easily given. It is reserved for people whom we can trust with our whole self. Choose carefully those who hold your life in their hands and heart.

Such intimacy is given to only a few. Their friendship is a continuing support on life's journey. "Do not abandon old friends, for new ones cannot equal them. A new friend is like new wine; when it has aged, you can drink it with pleasure" (Sir 9:10).

Consider . . .

If sexuality means only pleasure and is merely functional, there need be no commitment. It is a possibility for anyone whose body is mature enough to achieve intercourse. However, healthy sexuality is richer than that. It requires psychological/ emotional maturity. It joins knowledge, faith, and sound attitudes. Reflection on human sexuality brings us face-to-face with our "good but imperfect" human nature. Sexuality and intimacy belong together in healthy people. We need healthy values and attitudes to guide its development. Reflection on the gospel of Jesus provides such values and attitudes. Gospel values make sexuality and intimacy a gift rather than a problem.

> "We do not live to ourselves, and we do not die to ourselves. If we live, we live to the Lord, and if we die, we die to the Lord; so then, whether we live or whether we die, we are the Lord's" (Rom 14:7-8).

> "But I have called you friends, because I have made known to you everything that I have heard from my Father" (John 15:15).

Difficulties

The philosophy of some people is a sex-for-pleasure philosophy. These people claim that men and women have only a temporary and functional need for one another. The demands of permanence are out of the question for "modern" people. Relationships are disposed of as easily as old clothes. Sex is kept on the recreational level!

As people live longer, dedication to a friend for a longer time takes hard work. Pleasure alone cannot sustain it. To offer freedom to a good friend, allowing them other relationships, may not be tolerated. At the level of physical sex, there is no problem in this philosophy. "Sleep with anyone you like!" Since there is no committed relationship, there is no call for fidelity. Possessiveness and personal neediness may pose as signs of a relationship. But if the relationship is fragile or artificial, it cannot endure the long haul. Ultimately, we recognize the relationship as a hollow shell. If all of our relationships are shallow, terminal loneliness enters.

Society flaunts sex as a solution for many problems. It uses sex as a sales tool for products. It taps our fear of rejection by offering a "sexy" person as the life of the party. Whether it is beer, cars, cosmetics, clothes, or a host of other products, "sexy" folks always seem to have the most fun. Only blindness could block the images created by ads that surround us. Constant repetition subtly convinces us that being sexy is the only way to go. It creates tempting problems for gospel people. We are not immune to such pervasive influences.

Because sexuality is such an intimate part of who we are, it touches many areas of life. Fragile marriages sometimes rely on sex as a way of healing the relationship. People with a strong sexual urge find it difficult to discipline these powerful feelings. Sexual addiction is a possibility for many people. Like alcohol or work addictions, it cannot ordinarily be handled alone. Like Alcoholics Anonymous, support groups like Sexual Addicts Anonymous offer help for people with sexual addictions. Both men and women are prone to this addiction. Sex can begin to run one's life and make it unmanageable.

Our world is filled with the cries of people who are addicted. They, in turn, often hurt the very people they love. Sexual abuse of children by friends and relatives is a world-wide problem. Spousal abuse and family violence is a growing problem. Anyone caught in the web of sexual addiction lives a limited and limiting lifestyle. No strata of society is exempt from the problem. No amount of denial will make the problem go away.

Some people estimate that one in four women are sexually abused and about one in six or eight men suffer the same indignity. The prolonged suffering and psychological problems are innumerable. We dare not hide our heads in the sand with so much pain around us and within us! These kinds of sicknesses must be exposed and dealt with fairly and promptly. The problem shows no favorites. It can strike any family or community.

We do not want to give sex such power to dominate our lives. Sex, by itself, is not proof that someone loves us. Neither does it prove that we love the person who has sex with us. Sex cannot save a marriage in trouble. It does not prove that we are attractive to other people. It doesn't solve problems, nor does it do away with loneliness. Being terrific in bed is no guarantee of a good relationship. Being able to seduce someone doesn't mean that the person accepts us. Neither does it make us important to people. Sex is sex and no more. It is part of a good relationship. But it is not the only tie that binds. It cannot satisfy the deepest longings of the human heart and spirit. It does not have such power!

When sexuality is seen as a *part* of a fulfilling, loving relationship, it adds to intimacy. Our sexuality offers not just bodily functions but a person who is sexual — and more. In exclusive relationships it colors and adds vibrancy to the relationship. It offers much more to the "other" than just "having sex." The acknowledgement of both the wonder and limitations of sexuality provides a firm foundation for relating to others.

Maturing

Growth in maturity is not a ready-made product. Maturity is not a magic moment. It is a lifetime process. The process of growth faces many struggles. Feelings of insecurity may move us to act foolishly. A controlling desire to be accepted may crumple our values. Lack of a vision to give meaning to life can leave us drifting aimlessly. If we lack any kind of faith, we may find it difficult to deal with the reality of sexuality. "Eat, drink, and be merry" can be our vision for life. Somewhere along the line we will *choose* to believe in someone or something. That vision will direct our life.

It is unfair to expect humans to avoid mistakes. But it is despicable to do nothing about healthy sexual development. To make no choices, to seek no learning, is unwise. To develop no values, to have no good models to follow leaves us subject to every whim of pleasure and self-seeking. To listen to no one, to presume that maturity will "just happen" is to condemn us to mediocrity. We are people with dignity, not animals operating on instinct. Our choices ought to reflect our human dignity. A "me-first-last-always" approach destroys any hope for meaningful and satisfying relationships. Letting growth "just happen" is unlikely to achieve sound human maturity. For Christians, isolating sexuality from gospel values is destructive of our integrity.

Self-acceptance is one important ingredient of maturity. A sense of worth helps us have a healthy response to the demands of sexual maturity. Personal decisions not controlled by an addictive need for acceptance will be more realistic. If I am controlled by others, I allow them to manipulate me. I am angry at myself when I act this way. But I am trapped in a vicious cycle. I try to please others, yet I get angry as I feel manipulated by them.

An open, accepting atmosphere about sexuality in the family and among friends is important. It allows me to deal with ignorance and fear about sexuality in constructive ways. Acceptance from friends/family enables me to address sexual issues in my life.

On the other hand, domineering, prudish families or demanding and indifferent friends force me to conform rather than grow. Inner loneliness becomes a regular companion. If loneliness and alienation seem overwhelming, depression appears. If the darkness of depression is great, suicide seems a viable option. Loneliness, depression, self-hatred, and the feeling that no one cares can lead to the use of drugs and alcohol as a means of escape. Some people become workaholics rather than face their inner emptiness. For others, aggressive behavior or becoming "religious" covers up their fear and insecurity.

Our society has far too many dysfunctional families, families where there is little or no modeling of healthy relationships. Divorce, physical, psychological, and sexual abuse create shame that can last a lifetime. It can make us feel that we are bad persons. Even when we suppress such feelings, their influence continues. We can spend a lifetime trying to "prove" ourselves to others. Misuse and abuse of sexuality can be one of our escape mechanisms. It is an odd way of trying to prove oneself and punish oneself at the same time. Shame is learned early. It tells us we are bad. Not just that we do bad things but that we are bad persons. "What does it matter what I do? I deserve misery because I am so bad." Abuse may seem normal to such people. In this person's life situation, sexuality has no value. It means nothing more than momentary pleasure or legitimate abuse by another. Such death-dealing attitudes and ideas need to be dealt with in the presence of someone who is competent and cares. Otherwise, life will have neither light nor life.

Some victims of abuse withdraw into feelings of inferiority. They accept personal guilt for what has happened. Children often know no other recourse. Other victims use their victim-power to "get" the abuser. The oppressed become the oppressors, laying burdens on the abusers. Neither role solves the inner need for acceptance. Gentle, competent, and compassionate people can help heal the wounds of abuse.

Reflection shows the value of healthy intimacy. We need it! When relationships are shallow, life seems shallow. We use work as an escape. We use pleasure as an escape. We use violence as an escape. We withdraw into our dream world as an escape. We may use drugs and alcohol as an escape. We may become "religious" as an escape. When we do not develop healthy, intimate relationships, life holds little joy. We lose touch with reality. We lose touch with God.

> When you were slaves of sin, you were free in regard to right-eousness. So what advantage did you then get from the things of which you are now ashamed? The end of those things is death. . . . For the wages of sin is death, but the free gift of God is eternal life in Christ Jesus our Lord (Rom 6:20-21, 23).

Idols

Our thinking may follow this pattern: This world is ours to use as we like. Money is a tool to buy happiness for ourselves. Success is the key to fulfillment. Getting power is the way to happiness. No matter how we phrase it, no matter what idol we worship, the idol ultimately disappoints us. What initially seems vital grows dull. What was exciting in its beginning, grows boring. The thrill of pleasure may gradually fade as it becomes apparent that no one cares for us.

We can ''use'' religion as a source of escape. We escape into a ''cultish'' discipline to keep from taking responsibility for our decisions. We hand over responsibility for our lives to others — the boss, the Church, the spouse, the job, ''everybody's doing it,'' etc. We become childish people in grown-up bodies. We are walking around, but our spirit is dead. Failure to deal with our sexuality is but one sign of immaturity. God asks us to deal with our immaturity rather than give up hope.

> Then he said to me, ''Mortal, these bones are the whole house of Israel. They say, 'Our bones are dried up, and our hope is lost; we are cut off completely.' Therefore prophesy, and say to them, Thus says the Lord God; I am going to open your graves, and bring you up from your graves . . . O my people. I will put my spirit within you, and you shall live'' (Ezek 37:12, 14).

Ezekiel addresses people who had lost hope. Things had gone badly. Life was not worth living. It seemed there was no way out. Idol worship and attempts to accommodate to another culture had not brought the expected results. Hope had disappeared. God had forgotten them. The end seemed imminent. Such feelings haunt all who fall into the pit of hopelessness. We describe it in various ways. But doing our own "thing" instead of God's does not bring new life. It seems exciting and energizing for a while. But then it no longer supplies what we need. When we sacrifice relationships to the idol of personal success and pleasure, we reap loneliness. When we wander in the clutch of the latest fad, it passes, and we are left with ashes instead of roses.

Intimacy Again

Intimacy is not a luxury for the elite, but a necessity for all. We need intimacy. Intimacy includes healthy sexuality, but is not exhausted by it. It includes revelation of self, but is not exhausted by it. It includes forgiveness and reconciliation, but is not exhausted by it. It includes acceptance of another, but is not exhausted by it. Intimacy includes self-acceptance, but requires more. Intimacy requires the revelation of self; forgiveness and reconciliation; acceptance of both self and the "other"; healthy sexuality and the final gift — faith. We choose to believe in Jesus. We derive strength for fidelity from the power of faith. God fills the inner space we call "heart and spirit." Intimacy with God brings wholeness to relationships between people.

> "Righteous Father, the world does not know you, but I know you; and these know that you have sent me. I made your name known to them, and I will make it known, so that the love with which you have loved me may be in them, and I in them" (John 17:25-26).

There are no exceptions to gospel love. No one can be left out because they are "different" or hard to deal with. Jesus reveals the dignity of all people in his commandment of love. This difficult, universal love requires the gift of power that comes from the Spirit of Jesus. It is obvious to me that many people I know stretch my ability to love them. Temptations test my ability to be faithful to a healthy sexuality. Only with Jesus are all things possible.

I remember having good friends who were a source of joy to me. I felt a healthy sense of intimacy with them. A break in that friendship led to conflict, misunderstandings, and ultimately to angry separation. I found ways and means to "get" them. No tool seemed too outlandish to win battles with former friends. It was an awful time. It took years for me to allow healing to enter my life. The gospel injunction to "love my enemy" seemed impossible for me. But the gospel demand would not let go. Whenever it was read, I felt a twinge of guilt even while I resisted. After all, I was "right"! Let "them" come crawling to me! Then we can do something about the situation. As I was able to let go of anger and begin the journey of forgiveness, I began to be free again.

The command to love my enemy was no easy thing. Neither is it easy to be wise in my decisions about sexual matters. I am powerless to do it without Jesus. Intellectual knowledge is not enough. *Doing* it, i.e., relying on Jesus, is essential!

It took almost ten years to mend things with friends who had become my enemies. The friendship did not (could not?) return to its former intimacy. Dealing with problems of sexuality can likewise take a long time. Love is a very demanding commandment.

The ability to know *how* to love is the tough part. Jesus is the way to discover intimacy and love. He is the truth who gives direction to our choices. He is life. He gives life to those who believe in him. Persistence in listening to the gospel leads to penetration by the word of God. Walking with Jesus leads to healthy perspectives on life. Surrendering to Jesus leads to freedom in life. Then the *how* of loving becomes a bit more clear. At least we know the general direction to take. Choose the things that bring *light and life* to ourselves and others. My fear of "losing too much" often holds me back. Death to self seems a strange way to life. As Jesus put it: "For those who want to save their life will lose it, and who lose their life for my sake will save it'' (Luke 9:24).

The life and words of Jesus offer a model for developing intimacy. His words about his Father bear marks of what intimacy means. ''If you know me, you will know my Father also. . . . Believe me that I am in the Father and the Father in me'' (John 14:7, 11).

What has this to do with sexuality? Simply this: Our bodies, our sexuality, the feelings that touch us, are gifts. These gifts come from God and are good. We choose how to use these gifts. We can make poor choices and use gifts unwisely. We can use them in a destructive manner. Such misuse of God's gifts is all around us. Pornography, prostitution, sexual abuse, physical abuse, bodily masochism, violence against people, sex without love, torture, rape, pedophilia, and abortion, to name a few. We misuse the good gifts of God. But misuse does not make the gift bad. Rather, it shows a lack of wisdom on our part.

The Lord calls for an intimacy that is respectful and loving. Jesus Christ says that Christian love is essential for joy. It is found not in self-seeking but in self-giving. It counters many practices of society. It is the way of gospel people. If we treasure sexuality, we give it the dignity it deserves. We experience and enjoy the pleasure that intimate relationships can bring. But we do not isolate pleasure and make an idol of it. We do not ignore the gospel to follow the ways of our own satisfaction.

Interpersonal relationships are important to us. We come together as friends without manipulation. We both struggle with and enjoy feelings. We try to direct them in ways that are life-giving. We do not let them become dictators of our behavior. Discipline is needed, but it is needed in many areas of life. We may fail, but failure does not diminish our respect for the beauty of sexuality. The gospel teaches us to love and respect our body and its feelings. It teaches us to love and respect our inner spirit and its needs. We try to nurture both — in ourselves and in others! The goal is a ''wholeness'' that brings dignity in its wake.

As relationships grow, love, respect, tenderness, and faithfulness grow. Intimacy allows us to reveal our feelings to one another. Intimacy creates an atmosphere that allows others to share with us. Intimacy allows us quiet presence in grief as well as exuberant joy in celebrations. Intimacy listens intently and speaks in loving honesty. Intimacy reveals body and spirit in a sensitive and respectful way.

Intimacy senses the needs of the "other" and responds with love. Intimacy is real rather than artificial. Intimacy respects confidences and invites openness. Christians see intimacy within the context of gospel values. Intimate friends are a great treasure, a gift beyond measure!

> For a brief moment I abandoned you, but with great compassion I will gather you. In overflowing wrath for a moment I hid my face from you, but with everlasting love I will have compassion on you, says the Lord, your redeemer. . . . For the mountains may depart and the hills be removed, but my steadfast love shall not depart from you and my covenant of peace shall not be removed, says the Lord who has compassion on you (Isa 54:7-8, 10).

People of the gospel choose the way of love and intimacy. We know the demands of such a choice. It is not a simplistic choice. Temptations abound and attractions multiply as we walk this way. We are aware of our need for God. We are not always successful in following the gospel. Nevertheless, we do not sulk in failure but rise to try again. Jesus is with us and enables us to do what we cannot do alone. Powered by the Spirit, we make choices that are filled with life. Jesus himself prays for us: "Holy Father, protect them in your name that you have given me, so that they may be one as we are one. . . . I am not asking you to take them out of the world, but I ask you to protect them from the evil one" (John 17:11, 15).

Reflection

How do I feel about my body? How do I deal with feelings, sexual or otherwise? Do I have negative ideas of sexuality? How do I deal with guilt feelings about sex? Do I feel that sex is just for pleasure, or does it have more to offer? Do I talk honestly with competent people about sexual problems? Is masturbation a problem for me? How do I deal with it? How do I handle relationships with other men and women? How do I live Christian values in my sexual life? What do I understand by the term "intimacy"? How do I feel about intimate relationships? How do I handle rejection? How would I evaluate my living of gospel values in my sexuality-life? . . . in my relational life? Do I feel "finished" in my growth or still "on the way"? How do I judge others who are sexually promiscuous? What do I do to develop healthy intimacy with others? How do I help others understand sexuality? How do I deal with sexual fantasies? Where did I get my information about sex? How do I handle feeling "horny"? Is my marital relationship an intimate one, only a sexual one, or "none of the above"? How does sexuality contribute to holiness? How would I critique my sexuality values in the light of gospel values?

It is important to wrestle with these questions and sharpen the ability to live a healthy and holy life. Jesus calls us to wholeness. He will not abandon us. God is faithful. God desires faithfulness from us. God made a covenant of intimacy and faithful love with us. The Spirit of the risen Jesus enables us to respond with faithful love. With God's help all things are possible.

> Now this I affirm and insist on in the Lord; you must no longer live as the Gentiles live, in the futility of their minds. They are darkened in their understanding, alienated from the life of God because of their ignorance and hardness of heart. They have lost all sensitivity and have abandoned themselves to licentious-

ness, greedy to practice every kind of impurity. This is not the way you learned Christ! . . . You were taught to put away your former way of life, your old self, corrupt and deluded by its lusts, and to be renewed in the spirit of your minds, and to clothe yourselves with the new self, created according to the likeness of God in true righteousness and holiness. . . . Put away from you all bitterness and wrath and anger and wrangling and slander, together with all malice, and be kind to one another, tenderhearted, forgiving one another, as God in Christ has forgiven you (Eph 4:17-20, 22-24, 31-32).

CHAPTER EIGHT

A Little Hope, By Gum!

Hope, that delightful and demanding virtue. Hope — fragile enough to be devastated by rejection. Hope — strong enough to face the threat of death and live. Charles Péguy wrote about hope in a poem called "Abandonment." He writes as though God were speaking.

> I know man well. It is I who made him. A funny creature. . . .
> You can ask a lot of him. He is not too bad. You can't say that
> he is bad. . . .
>
> You can ask a lot of kindness of him, a lot of charity, a lot of
> sacrifice. He has much faith and much charity.
>
> But what you can't ask of him, by gum, is a little hope. A little
> confidence, don't you know, a little relaxation. A little yield-
> ing, a little abandonment into my hands, a little giving in. He
> is always so stiff![1]

Hope is the ability to surrender to a loved one without fear. Hope is the confidence of a child in the strength of her parents. Hope is the ability to trust that promises will be kept. Hope accepts the vision long before it is accomplished. Hope believes that things can be different. Hope persists in reaching for the stars when others have given up. Hope dreams of flowers when snow covers the ground. Hope is light when we

---

[1]Charles Péguy, *Basic Verities*, trans. Ann/Julian Green (New York: Pantheon Books, 1943) 217–219.

are surrounded by darkness. Hope is salt when things seem tasteless. Hope is the supporting arm when another step seems impossible. Hope listens expectantly to gospel truth when life drives us to despair. Hope awaits celebrations with eager anticipation. Hope has the ability to stand back, survey life, and keep it in perspective.

Hope knows that the world does not spin around my personal axis. Hope is aware of the power of the gospel to change lives.

Hope is hope because Jesus is trustworthy. Hope is hope because God enables us to do what the gospel calls us to do. Hope is hope because Jesus has made us heirs of the gospel promises. Hope is hope because Jesus seeks oneness with us as he is one with his Father. Hope sleeps peacefully because tomorrow is a gift. Hope can face death because death leads to intimacy with our beloved God. Hope thankfully uses its personal gifts and gives God praise for them.

> "Believe in God, believe also in me. . . . I am the way, and the truth, and the life. No one comes to the Father except through me. If you know me, you will know my Father also. From now on you do know him and have seen him" (John 14:1, 6-7).

When we are without hope, things are quite different. Once again Péguy's words are fitting:

> Let the gentleman consent, let him yield a little to me. Let him stretch out his poor weary limbs on a bed of rest. Let him ease his aching heart a little on a bed of rest.
>
> Above all, let his head stop working. It works only too much, his head does. And he thinks it is work, when his head goes that way.
>
> And his thoughts . . . Did you ever . . . What he calls his thoughts! Let his thoughts stop moving about and struggling inside his head and rattling like calabash seeds. Like a little bell in an empty gourd. When you see what they are all about, those ideas of his, as he calls them!

Poor Creature. I don't care for the man who doesn't sleep.[2]

One reason why hope is difficult is that it requires a surrender of control. We have many reasons for maintaining control. Even our use of the word touches much of life. Self-control, arms control, control the economy, control the class, control the parish council, control crime, control our emotions and our anger, control the children, the car, the production line, control our words. Control, control, control! With our many efforts to control life, it is little wonder that hope is often an orphan. Though control is not evil, when it becomes an idol it rarely brings lasting joy. People who control are not known for their sense of humor.

Hope asks us to let go of attempts at total control. Not simply letting go and that's it. But letting go and giving control to God. Hope surrenders control because it trusts God. We trust God to keep promises made to us. We trust in God's support when we are fragile. We trust in God's surprises when life grows dull. Surrender to God is not irrational, but faithful. We believe in God's faithfulness to the covenant God has made with us. Hope is a gift, given when we least expect it. Hope enjoys the freedom of a trusting spirit. Trusting God brings light and fullness of life.

> Who is a God like you, pardoning iniquity and passing over the transgression of the remnant of your possession? He does not retain his anger forever, because he delights in showing clemency. He will again have compassion on us; he will tread our iniquities under foot (Mic 7:18-19).

The poor in spirit understand hope. People who rely only on what they see have trouble understanding. People who rely on accumulating goods as the way to security find it hard to practice hope. When a system works well for us, hope is an unneeded extra. If we get too practical, hope seems naive and foolish. If we are doing fine because we're successful, we feel

[2]Ibid., 219.

no need for hope. Our "hope" relies on what we can touch and feel.

Real hope knows the present situation is precarious and fragile. Houses burn down. People die in accidents. Black Mondays on the stock market wipe out fortunes. Sickness bankrupts our savings. Rape destroys peace of mind and violates our person. One nuclear explosion could end our world. People we know and love get arrested for drug use. Banks fail and our savings are wiped out with them. Con artists steal life-savings in get-rich-quick schemes. Mental illness may destroy our ability to deal with living. Terminal illness leaves us helpless no matter how intelligent, rich, and successful we may be. It doesn't take much to upset reliance on the "practical." Hope acknowledges this fact. It refuses to put all its trust in the basket of the practical. It is not seduced into believing that our present economic, political, or intellectual systems will last forever.

Hope is realistic. It has the wisdom and audacity to believe that things can change. Hope believes they can change for the better. It keeps dreams alive, because dreams are a guide for walking into the future. Hope does not take material things too seriously. It realizes they do not have staying power. "For in hope we were saved. Now hope that is seen is not hope. For who hopes for what is seen? But if we hope for what we do not see, we wait for it with patience" (Rom 8:24-25).

Consequences

Hope is a radical idea, especially when we see the consequences. We live only in the present moment. Hope reminds us of the fragility of life. However, hopeful people are not passive dreamers waiting for an unknown future. That would be ridiculous! Hope invites us to take the gospel vision seriously. Hope allows us to be independent of the present systems. It allows us to view reality in the light of the gospel vision. We can step back and critique present events in the light of the gospel vision. Hope allows us the liberty of dealing with death without fear. Our God is present both to our "now" and to our "hereafter."

Listen to Jesus. Discover the hope in his heart. Jesus was present to and aware of what went on around him. His critique of "reality" flowed from the perspective of his Father. Much of what he saw did not fit his Father's vision. Jesus, with courtesy or with anger, offered his criticism in the light of the vision.

He could respect law as coming from his Father. But he could not tolerate law that became oppressive. He could support authority because it is God-given. But he would not tolerate the abuse of authority that burdened people instead of freeing them. Jesus could understand weakness in others and still challenge them to be strong with the power of the Spirit. He loved the temple as a place of prayer. But he could envision a time when worship would be in spirit and truth. He enjoyed the beauty of creation. He loved the generosity of the rich young man. But he knew how difficult it is to be a gospel person when people rely on riches instead of his Father. Jesus could experience a sense of abandonment on the cross and still trustingly hand his spirit over to the Father.

The quality of Jesus' hope is clear. He trusted his heavenly Father to build the reign of God. Even when he was in the grasp of the political system, as he stood before Pilate, Jesus was confident of his Father's power and care:

> Pilate therefore said to him, "Do you refuse to speak to me? Do you not know that I have power to release you, and power to crucify you?" Jesus answered him, "You would have no power over me unless it had been given you from above" (John 19:10-11).

People with vision are able to survive most anything. They are considered a nuisance by the reigning system. They prick the bubble of absoluteness flaunted by the system. Dictators are hard-pressed to tolerate anyone with gospel vision. If you remain passive and shut up, you are tolerated. But when you offer a vision other than the system's vision, you are a troublemaker. You must be silenced! Look at the people put in prison by dictatorships. (Calling them "Radicals" or similar demeaning names is a common ploy of dictators and other folks.) Christians who challenge the system or propose an alternate system are a threat. They dare assert that the existing system is flawed. Powerful folks hate to hear that. People of hope are persecuted.

People who put absolute trust in the existing system of things are carrying an albatross. When the system begins to decay, collapse, or break down, it has little hope to offer. People who trust only what they see and touch are the first to feel hopelessness. Jesus knew that people need a vision to maintain hope.

> So if you have been raised with Christ, seek the things that are above, where Christ is, seated at the right hand of God. Set your minds on things that are above, not on things that are on earth, for you have died, and your life is hidden with Christ in God (Col 3:1-3).

Hope dwells naturally among the poor in spirit. They do not put their hope in an economic system or political power, but in God. Economic and political systems often oppress the poor. The poor are not tricked into putting their trust in such systems. However, should the poor develop a victim-complex and quietly suffer the oppression of a system, they too become hopeless. What would have happened to the blind man if he had allowed himself to be silenced by the crowd?

> They came to Jericho. As he and his disciples and a large crowd were leaving Jericho, Bartimaeus son of Timaeus, a blind beggar, was sitting by the roadside. When he heard that it was Jesus of Nazareth, he began to shout out and say: "Jesus, Son of David, have mercy on me!" Many sternly ordered him to be quiet, but he cried out even more loudly, "Son of David, have mercy on me!" Jesus stood still and said, "Call him here." And they called the blind man, saying to him, "Take heart; get up, he is calling you." So throwing off his cloak, he sprang up and came to Jesus. Then Jesus said to him, "What do you want me

to do for you?'' The blind man said to him, ''My teacher, let me see again.'' Jesus said to him, ''Go; your faith has made you well.'' Immediately he regained his sight and followed him on the way (Mark 10:46-52).

Hope is not silent. Hope speaks out and proclaims the truth. It offers a vision that confronts unjust situations. As they grieve over their situation, hopeful people speak up and declare that oppression is not right; that destitution is not right; that war against the poor is not right; that rat-infested housing is not right; that sexual discrimination is not right; that racial prejudice is not right. In short, their grieving becomes public. It springs from a hope that things *will be* different. Guided by the gospel vision, hopeful Christians speak loudly against injustice.

> ''Woe to you, scribes and Pharisees, hypocrites! For you clean the outside of the cup and plate, but inside they are full of greed and self-indulgence. You blind Pharisee! First clean the inside of the cup, so that the outside also may become clean'' (Matt 23:25-26).

Jesus confronts unjust situations and people. He was free to critique because he was not tied to the system. He could view it honestly from a position free from the system. His vision cut through rationalization and legal double-talk that is used to justify injustice. He would not be free if he had been co-opted by the system. Hopeful people are helpful for clearing the air. But they pose a threat to people in power. People tied to the system wonder: ''Will I retain my position if things change?'' Hopeful people who confront the status quo face stiff resistance from those entrenched in existing power structures.

People of hope, accepted for their gifts, can help society. A leader who desires the common good will find hopeful people a precious gift. They offer clearsighted ideas, unencumbered by vested interests.

There is another enemy of hope. It has various names. It is revealed by exploring the trust we put in machines and technology. Until the Challenger manned space rocket exploded, we felt that space travel was commonplace. We had conquered all the problems. Scientific instruments gained a reputation for infallibility. Then it exploded before our eyes and seven people died. We began to question scientific infallibility. Reliance on computers and technology as tools to deal with crises continues. When we put too much reliance on such tools, hope has meager impact on our lives.

Machines are manageable. We can control them. With them we can control other things. The greater our reliance on this form of control, the less hope we need. No matter how much the tools of technology proliferate, they are not easily available to everyone. Rosy prattling about a "trickle down" theory does little to help the poor. Hope is a victim in this scenario. Reliance on technology diminishes reliance on a faithful God. Without the vision of a society created by a passionate and loving God, we create *our* kind of society. Our small vision does not always meet human needs nor draw us together in unity. The "left-out" people in human society remain lost in hopelessness.

Within the community of faith, hope may pose a threat. When the vision of the gospel calls us to an unfamiliar future it can be frightening. If we want to control our faith-life through study and learning, we may fall into an intellectual contentment. We know our faith. We are good people who don't hurt anyone. We go to Mass each Sunday. We raise our kids right. We don't jump on peace and justice bandwagons or go around criticizing the government. Social-justice folks are rabble-rousers who create problems in the Church (*sic*). I feel fine about my faith-life. I have it in good shape and under control. I know who God is and try to live a good life. Let me alone! Social action is outside my notion of religion! I want to stabilize things so that life is predictable. I am not anxious to discover a God who cannot be domesticated. Too much mystery and wonder makes me uneasy. In short, please do not upset my applecart with this talk about hope.

On another occasion when he went to synagogue, there was a man in the congregation who had a withered arm; and they were watching to see whether Jesus would heal him on the sabbath, so that they could bring a charge against him. He said to the man with the withered arm: "Come and stand out here." Then he turned to them: "Is it permitted to do good or to do evil on the sabbath, to save life or to kill?" They had nothing to say; and, looking round at them with anger and sorrow at their obstinate stupidity, he said to the man, "Stretch out your arm." He stretched it out and his arm was restored. Then the Pharisees, on leaving the synagogue, at once began plotting with the men of Herod's party to bring about Jesus' death (Mark 3:1-6 — REB).

"You have a fine way of rejecting the commandment of God in order to keep your tradition!" (Mark 7:9).

Jesus spoke strongly in these situations. He was angered by people who control religion through man-made traditions. Jesus wants people to let God be in charge; God to have the controlling interest; God to give direction to life. If the gospel calls us to proclaim justice, we do well to proclaim justice. If the gospel calls us to serve one another, we do well to serve one another. If the gospel calls us not to lord it over others, we do well not to lord it over others. If the gospel calls us to love our enemies, we do well to love our enemies. If the gospel calls us to examine our heart's treasure, we do well to examine the treasure we have in our hearts. If the gospel invites us to conversion, we do well to convert. If the gospel requires us to put our trust in a faithful Father, we do well to trust the Father of Jesus. The gospel vision does not allow us to remain passive before God. We walk with hope, knowing that Jesus is with us as we mature in faith.

Each day of life offers fresh possibilities for living the gospel. People who want religion neatly wrapped and packaged or want to control the gospel journey will be hard-pressed to be a hopeful people. People who have it "all together" will have little need for hope.

There is mystery here. We try to promote the reign of God while we know it will not find completion here on earth.

Glimpses of the dream-in-action are a powerful incentive to persist. We will not be passive before God. We do not presume that God will do everything while we wait. God reveals the wide dimensions of truth. "But as for you, return to your God, hold fast to love and justice, and wait continually for your God" (Hos 12:6) is only one part of the word. "Go therefore and make disciples of all nations . . . teaching them to obey everything that I have commanded you. And remember, I am with you always, to the end of the age" (Matt 28:19, 20) is of equal importance. Our vision may not always be clear. Though the light of God is present, we can still walk in darkness. The light may be so bright that we are momentarily blinded. But God never withdraws the light. Listen to the call of God and follow it with hope.

Hopeful people do not abandon the vision. Our lifetime is short. We work persistently to create room for the vision in our short time on earth. We do all we can to pass on the vision of hope that the gospel offers. We keep on keeping on!

> So we do not lose heart. Even though our outer nature is wasting away, our inner nature is being renewed day by day. . . . for what can be seen is temporary, but what cannot be seen is eternal (2 Cor 4:16, 18).

And yet . . . we easily abandon hope for what is seeable and touchable. We are not bad people, but this hope business is hard. Our training has not prepared us for the mystery of God's love. We think if we work harder (the all-American way) we will accomplish more. It works in business, why not in religion! Little wonder that we put such trust in techniques, technologies and processes that work so well (*sic*)!

Consistent prayer and reflection will be needed to develop a spirit of hope. Working harder may not be the way to grow in hope. Re-doubling our workload means that we are relying on "our" power. George Santayana put it this way: "Fanaticism consists in re-doubling your efforts when you have forgotten your aim!"

Sometimes we throw money at the problem. Money may help, but it doesn't make the problem go away. Folks who mismanage money will need to change their ways of managing money. Personal problems change only when we change. We often blame other people for our problems. "They" are the cause of our despair, our sadness, our problem! Hope does not tolerate such "junk-thinking."

Hope asks us to envision what we want and seek it. Hope, as a gospel virtue, looks to the vision of Jesus and seeks to implement that vision. When it seems out of reach, we stretch ourselves to achieve what we can. Hope gives us courage to embrace the vision and see things as they can be. Hope tells us that we can influence others and be influenced by them. We are careful about how people influence us. We use the gospel as a yardstick to measure the hope that is in us. We can make a difference!

At one of the parish missions I was giving with a laywoman, Emily, we were delighted by a lady who translated our talks in sign language. Each evening, this lady would translate our message for the hearing impaired. Each evening, Emily and I would tell her of our appreciation. Each evening, it was received with silence. Our "sign-lady" had little or no hope. She evidently felt that no one really cared. Two strangers who affirmed her could hardly be believed. On the Sunday after our mission she had planned to take her own life. She went through with the beginnings of her plan.

But a concerned parishioner discovered her plan. This parishioner sought out our sign-lady. In the end, persistent and loving concern made the difference. It moved our sign-lady to seek help rather than commit suicide. A gentle, persistent, caring person brought hope and new life. As usual, someone who loves makes the difference. Hope entered into our sign-lady. She chose to face her life issues rather than evade them through suicide. The caring person walked with our sign-lady as she struggled to rediscover hope. Hope demands such persistent love.

Hope brings anticipation to life. Hope offers an alternative to the present order of things. Hope pushes us beyond present goodness to a bigger and wider vision. Hope allows us to discover what Jung calls our "shadow" side and integrate it into our lives. Hope is fearless because it relies on One who is faithful. Hope knows that all problems will not be solved. But it finds improved ways to deal with and/or live with the problem. Inner resources are discovered that give us strength for the journey.

Sarah and Abraham

The story of Abraham is a story of hope. Old Abraham put his trust in God's promise. That's all he had when he left Ur — God's promise of a place to settle down. Abraham and Sarah were too old to have children, but hope dwelled in Abraham, and God gave him a son. Abraham saw little sense in sacrificing his son, the sign of the promise-come-true. But hope led him up the mountain. The story wends its way through events that only hope can explain. Listen to the human response when a son is promised to old Abraham and Sarah:

> Then one [of the men] said, "I will surely return to you in due season, and your wife Sarah shall have a son." . . . Sarah laughed to herself, saying, "After I have grown old, and my husband is old, shall I have pleasure?" The Lord said to Abraham, "Why did Sarah laugh, and say, 'Shall I indeed bear a child, now that I am old?' Is anything too wonderful for the Lord?" (Gen 18:10, 12-14).

Of course, the child came. The promise was fulfilled. With a bit of humor, Abraham and Sarah named the child Isaac, i.e., "He laughs." This human response to the message of hope is quite understandable. Sarah's response makes sense to me. God's promise seems a bit wild. Little wonder that hope is often homeless. Scripture puts the fulfillment of the promise to Abraham in a few words:

> The Lord dealt with Sarah as he had said, and the Lord did
> for Sarah as he had promised. Sarah conceived and bore Abra-
> ham a son in his old age. . . . Now Sarah said, "God has
> brought laughter for me; everyone who hears will laugh with
> me." And she said, "Who would ever have said to Abraham
> that Sarah would nurse children? Yet I have borne him a son
> in his old age" (Gen 21:1-2, 6-7).

Hope brought joy to this old couple. Though they found
it hard to believe, the promise of God is kept. Reading this
story gives me hope because I often doubt whether God will
really come through. I dabble in hope rather than practice it.
The vision of the gospel can seem ridiculous. It can't happen!
It doesn't fit my human equations and experience. I walk
gingerly into the neighborhood of hope. I think I am being
naive or simplistic. I have a hundred reasons why God will
not do something great in my life. Hope dies little deaths over
and over again before I put my hope in the power of God.

> But God, who is rich in mercy, out of the great love with which
> he loved us even when we were dead through our trespasses,
> made us alive together with Christ — by grace you have been
> saved — and raised us up with him and seated us with him
> in the heavenly places in Christ Jesus, so that in the ages to
> come he might show the immeasurable riches of his grace in
> kindness toward us in Christ Jesus. For by grace you have been
> saved through faith, and this is not your own doing; it is the
> gift of God — not the result of works, so that no one may boast
> (Eph 2:4-9).

The scriptural word of hope is clear. We want to make our
response equally clear. It takes us out of a control mode and
puts us in a hope mode. Control and direction pass over to
God, our "Abba." The revelation of God through Jesus Christ
is the way we choose to follow. The vision is there for those
who "take and read." Gospel people perceive reality as Jesus
proclaims it. Acceptance of the gospel leads to daily conversion. We move to the place to which the vision calls us. It is
a call to intimacy with Jesus.

As intimacy grows, we continue the life of Jesus by our presence in the world. We are leaven and seed; we are salt and light; we are candle and proclamation. Since we are not yet perfect, we live in hope. We rely on God's power to help us build a gospel society. Hope continues to bring us to conversion. Without hope, we would stagnate and die.

Reflection

What does hope mean to me? How do I show that hope dwells in me? Right now, what gives me hope that things will get better? Why do I feel that things can't get better? To whom or what do I give power over me? Can hope live without faith and love? Vice versa? What is the foundation of my hope? What Scripture texts strengthen my hope? What experiences in my life have diminished my hope? How can I deal with them? How can I bring hope to the world? What kind of world does God want me to build? Must I do everything? Can I do anything? What is a possible way to do better? Why do people feel hopeless? How can I help them in a positive way? What does Jesus say about hope? Is hope in touch with reality — or — is what the world calls "reality" more real? Where do my ideas of "reality" come from? Do I put my trust only in what I can feel and touch? What about the fact that things I touch and feel may not always be there for me? What then? How can I develop a deeper trust in God? What keeps me from hope in my future? Do I have more trust in techniques than in God? Does our society need hope? need God? Why? How can I illustrate my desire for control? How do I feel about letting go of control? Is this the same as "losing control" or is there a difference? What is the difference? How does the poetry of Charles Péguy help me understand hope? Do I trust only what I can understand? What role does mystery play in my life? Is my God gentle, demanding, or both? Does my God offer hope or only condemnation? How personal is my relationship with

Jesus? How can a personal relationship with Jesus bring me greater hope?

"Now to him who by the power at work within us is able to accomplish abundantly far more than all we can ask or imagine, to him be glory in the church and in Christ Jesus to all generations" (Eph 3:20-21).

CHAPTER NINE

How's Your Vision?

The dictionary defines vision as "the ability to perceive something not actually visible, as through mental acuteness or keen foresight (a project made possible by one person's vision)." Our topic in the next chapters is the "project made possible" by the *vision* of Jesus Christ. Our source book is the Bible. Our goal is to explore and develop ideas relating to the gospel vision.

The scriptural word is a continuing revelation. Our generation is gifted with fresh insights in theology and Scripture. Bible study books and programs are available in great abundance. People are discovering the riches of the Bible for both knowledge and prayer. Books, workshops, tapes, talks, study groups, scriptural prayer groups, and video programs offer help for Bible study.

If all we ever do is *talk* about the Bible, however, we may feel good but never actually live the gospel vision. If we do not implement the gospel, letting it influence our lives, we are easy prey for biblical con artists. We need to understand and live the gospel-vision. Otherwise we can dilute the gospel or fall into the magic-gospel of some persuasive preachers. We may fall for slickly written pamphlets offering simplistic biblical solutions for every human problem. Prophets of doom can frighten us with "end-time" predictions. The desire for security may make us gullible listeners. We can attempt to avoid confusion by refusing to search for truth. If we choose such "safe" ways, we may never experience the gospel vision of Jesus.

There *is* another way. People who believe in Jesus and follow the gospel vision are willing to walk with us. Such companions can guide us. Their presence diminishes the fear we feel. Hand in hand we can learn ways of living the gospel vision. People with solid and healthy gospel lifestyles help us grow in genuine gospel living. Our biblical heritage offers a rich resource in our search, and biblical material is readily available to us. Reflection on the Bible offers a panorama of possibilities for gospel living.

The Bible

The Bible offers information on how God and people interact. The stories, the history, the wisdom, the prayers, the interaction of God and God's people fill the Bible. When God became human, the community recorded Jesus' life, teaching, passion, death, and resurrection. The letters of Paul, Peter, James, John, and Jude reflect the vision of Jesus. The Bible reveals much about God and people's response to God. It is inspirational as well as informative.

The Bible carries its own set of difficulties. Most of us read translations of the original languages. Translations are never totally accurate. Modern linguistic studies lead to more accurate translations. The English language continues to change. Translations take such changes into account. New translations are published regularly. It is a natural, human phenomenon. It will continue as long as learning continues. Biblical translations obviously bear the mark of human limitations. God is not confined by such limitations. God's Spirit guides the faith-community as it seeks to understand the Bible.

Catholics recognize the Bible as a library of books. It was written over many centuries by people from many social situations and cultural backgrounds. Isaiah and Peter are quite different people. The writer of Proverbs is certainly different from Paul. Prophets writing from exile experienced life differently than King David writing psalms. Knowledge of such data helps us read the Bible more intelligently. The cultural and historical situations influence the way a certain book was written. When we get a "feel" for the scriptural writers and the influences that moved them, their words are more easily understood.

Biblical events took place in settings quite different from our own. The language, the traditions of the time, the culture of the people, and the social milieu flavor the telling of the message. As we walk in the shoes of biblical people we get a clearer understanding of biblical words and ideas. It does not determine God's message. It does help our understanding of the message.

For example: Luke's story about the prodigal son (Luke 15:11-32). The father in the story acts counter to the customs of his community. For the son to demand his inheritance is equivalent to wishing his father were dead. Under these circumstances, when the son leaves home, the community considers him dead. The separation from family and community is total.

When the son returns, the father again goes counter to community traditions. Those traditions demanded a long process before the son could again be accepted as "son." But the father in the story runs to meet the prodigal son. He accepts him back into the family immediately. He returns family authority to the son by putting a ring on his finger. This father acts in countercultural ways. He ignores the human traditions because of his delight at the return of his son.

The portrait of Jesus' Father takes on new vibrancy through this story. This prodigal father is a worthy image of "Abba." If an earthly father shows such astounding love, consider what our heavenly Father might do! Good background knowledge enhances this word of God.

We may not have time and resources to study these things. We benefit from the work of scholars. Sound scholarship enhances the "word." One truth (cultural) will not destroy another truth (biblical). We need not fear the work of reputable scholars.

Inspired

We believe that the Bible is inspired by God. But every word is not of equal importance. Words describing the passion and death of Jesus have greater impact for faith than the words that talk about bird-droppings that blinded Tobit (Tobit 2:10). Both are in the Bible, but they are not equally important for faith. If every (translated) word has equal value; if every word can be understood in only *one* way; if every word requires total acceptance for salvation, we face much confusion when words come into conflict with one another. Thank goodness such is not the case!

Some biblical writers spoke the truth through the stories they told. The power of the story of Jonah does not come from its actually having happened as told. Its power comes from the way it reflects the human condition. The truth of the Book of Jonah is powerful. But the Book of Jonah is not in the same category as a reporter writing ''facts'' about what happened at a political convention. Both can report the truth, but each uses a different literary form to communicate it. When I allow for these differences, I hear the truth without being trapped into making the Bible a scientific textbook. The Bible proclaims truth that is spiritual, not scientific. If we were to deny this form of truth-telling, we would scuttle much of biblical truth. We would trap ourselves in a false protectionism of the Bible.

If science proves that there was no universal flood, the story of Noah and the ark would be threatened. If science proves that humankind is older than the sum of the years mentioned in the Bible, Bible numbers would be questioned. If science proves that creation was a big bang and not as it is described in Genesis, we would be forced to defend a false creationism to protect God. In short, if we deny the Bible its creative variety of ways to proclaim truth, we would waste time and energy on non-problems. If, however, we listen for God's message in scriptural stories, we will let the words reveal the truth God chooses to share with us. Wonder and reverence for the Bible grows. It takes us far beyond the limited ideas offered by a literalism that confines the truth.

Can I be certain that this English translation is totally accurate and faithful to the meaning of the original language? Probably not. But a translated word need not bear such a burden. *Context* can help determine word meanings. We listen to a whole text or story to get the meaning of scriptural words.

For example: Gospel parables often contain a moral. We can grasp the moral without analyzing every word in the story. Jesus tells a story about a man who built bigger barns to house an abundant crop (Luke 12:16-21). Jesus called him foolish. The farmer would die and his "great" possessions would pass to others.

We don't have to know everything about barns to understand the message of Jesus. The "truth" is clear: *Don't rely on bigness/wealth for salvation!* Material possessions do not guarantee salvation. They pass away and we are left empty-handed before God. There may be other meanings in this story. But every word does not have equal importance. The content and context of the story give a clear meaning. God chooses to communicate through our human language. We listen in a way that allows the text to teach us.

Listen for the full impact of the message of Scripture. Listen with reverence and expectation. Then implement the word in daily life. *Living the "word"* is the best way to reverence it.

Apocalyptic Writings

God's word includes a form of writing known as apocalyptic writing. For some groups, these sections of Scripture become the whole Bible. Some people proclaim an imminent second coming of Jesus based on an interpretation of apocalyptic writings. Some speak about the "rapture" that is soon to take place

(1 Thess 4:13-18). They warn us to be prepared because time is running short. Such "doomsday" interpretations, isolated from the rest of Scripture, are misleading. When we read apocalyptic literature in the Bible we need to link it to the rest of Scripture. Otherwise we easily misinterpret it.

Some people worry about the rapture, the millennium, and the end-time. Their concern develops because of "end-of-the-world" interpretations of apocalyptic writings. A book like "Revelation" is a book of hope. God's people are cared for when they suffer persecution and crises. The Book of Revelation shows God's faithfulness and power repeatedly. God overpowers the "beasts" that threaten God's people. God's constancy offers hope in situations of personal powerlessness.

Ordinarily, apocalyptic literature is not a prophecy of the future. Frequently it is an interpretation of past events with a call to be faithful. It shows God as victor over the power of evil. God deserves faithfulness from us in return. Sometimes apocalyptic writings use "code" words so the persecutors cannot understand. If the writings were to fall into enemy hands they would be unable to interpret them. Images from tradition, symbols from Greek mythology, and stories from other cultures are rewritten by the apocalyptic writer. This was a common practice among writers of biblical times.

Some interpreters of apocalyptic literature are pessimistic about world history. They tend to be passive in the face of evil. They claim that there is no hope for transforming the world. Rather, the world needs to be destroyed. Then God will create a new world. Don't waste time trying to change anything! Be quiet! Don't complain about your misery! Suffer patiently. God will overcome!

Passivity is counter to much of the gospel message. Such passivity is based on changes accomplished by God with no human cooperation. It ignores Scripture texts that invite gospel people to actively participate in God's work. "Very truly, I tell you, the one who believes in me will also do the works that I do and, in fact, will do greater works than these, because I am going to the Father" (John 14:12).

Passivity is *not* an accurate reading of apocalyptic writings! Many doomsayers ignore the injustice that touches so many people (Matt 25:31-46). To ignore the words of Matthew 25:40, ". . . just as you did it to one of the least of those who are members of my family, you did it to me," is to live a diminished gospel life. Unbalanced concentration on the rapture and end-time diminishes concern for social justice. "Be good and wait for the end. No more is required of you. Bear your misery in silence. God will take care of everything!" If you are caught in such passivity, reexamine your understanding of the Bible.

The person who is absorbed with concern about future events tends to miss the present. Such limiting interpretation may be non-Christian as well. Passivity in the face of evil is *not* recommended by the gospel. However, if you are anxious for the end-time to get here; if you fear that God's world is so evil that it requires destruction, it would seem reasonable to support nuclear armaments. Such power can hasten the coming of the end-time. Forget about any responsibility to build a gospel-oriented society in this world. Hope is useless. Evil has triumphed! Before the "saved" have to suffer, Christ will take them home in the "rapture." Oh, happy day!(?) How contrary to God's word: "The Lord's love is surely not exhausted, nor has his compassion failed; they are new every morning, so great is his constancy" (Lam 3:22-23 — REB).

Most apocalyptic writings follow a common pattern.

1. God's faithful people are persecuted.
2. God is faithful to the people and shows compassion for them.
3. God succeeds in saving the people.
4. God's people are called to be faithful to this gracious God.

Writers of apocalyptic literature write during crisis situations. It may be war, evil governments, cultural dominance by another country, or similar crises. God has a distinct preference for those who are powerless. God's preference shows itself by using power on their behalf. God works among these "poor ones" to overcome the threatened evil or offer strength and insight in the midst of suffering.

Evil seems so powerful. People are so weak. God enters the situation. God's presence brings hope to people who face the awesome power of evil. As we address the apocalyptic issue, remember that *the victory of Jesus is the resurrection,* not the second coming. What we need in order to face evil is available to us through the *risen Jesus.*

The resurrection of Jesus is not just a resuscitation of a dead body. It is the transformation of Jesus into a whole new mode of existence. No longer confined by human limitations, Jesus is freely present wherever he wishes. Thus, Jesus remains present among us. If resurrection means only that the human body of Jesus is revived, then when Jesus ascends to heaven he is gone. Then he is *not* present among us. We can only hope for the second coming to get in touch with him. Such a belief would nullify any sacramental presence of Jesus. But the contrary is true. The Scriptures proclaim Jesus as one who is truly transformed through the resurrection. Jesus is free to be everywhere and with all people. No limitations bind him. His care, compassion, and love are present to everyone. That is *good news* indeed!

The Vision of Jesus

Much of Scripture, especially the Gospels, modifies apocalyptic writings. Jesus invites us to deal with our present reality. He invites us to respond to oppression and injustice. He calls us to the quiet places where he speaks to our heart. Action and contemplation are partners in the vision of Jesus. He paints a vision of the reign of God that differs from what we see around us. No one is excluded. Citizenship does not require political, economic, or social power. Consider some qualities of the reign of God found in the Bible:

1. In this society there are no "nobodies." Dignity is the right of all people.
2. God shows a preferential love for the poor.
3. Forgiveness is a vital ingredient in the lives of gospel people.
4. "Love of riches" is an obstacle to living the gospel vision.
5. Gospel people respect and reverence the earth.
6. Economic, political, psychological, or religious oppression is opposed by people of the gospel.
7. In a gospel community, no one needs to walk alone. A community of caring and believing people creates an atmosphere of acceptance and companionship on the journey.
8. Individualism is replaced by a personalism that is concerned about the larger community more than oneself.
9. False idols of power, prestige, and possessions are recognized as idols by people of the gospel vision.
10. Gospel people place their hope in Jesus, the Christ.
11. Gospel people discover the pearl (Jesus). Everything else pales into insignificance when we possess the pearl.
12. Personal integrity in living the gospel brings us a peace that the world cannot give.
13. Gospel people recognize the primacy of God in their lives.
14. Jesus is Emmanuel, "God-with-us." We listen to his word and follow it. We observe his example and imitate it.
15. At the heart of gospel life is the Holy Spirit, whose power makes it possible to implement the gospel vision.
16. Communication and communion with Jesus, in prayerful union, keeps us on the road to intimacy with Jesus and one another.

Apocalyptic writings are *part* of the whole story. Our understanding of apocalyptic writings will improve with a better understanding of the whole Bible. A balanced reading of Scripture will lead us to develop the gentle strength and strong compassion of a gospel lifestyle.

What to Do in the Meantime

The "end-time" view of gospel writers is placed in the larger context of the *vision* of Jesus. In Matthew 24:45–25:30, there are three parables. They propose some ways of acting while waiting for the end-time. Some scholars speak of this period of waiting as the "meantime," i.e., the time between Jesus' first coming and his second coming at the end of the world. How are we to live in the "meantime"? What attitudes are we expected to have in the "meantime"?

> "Who then is the faithful and wise slave, whom his master has put in charge of his household, to give the other slaves their allowance of food at the proper time? . . . But if that slave says to himself, 'My master is delayed,' and begins to beat his fellow slaves, and eats and drinks with drunkards, the master of that slave will come on a day when he does not expect him. . . . He will cut him to pieces and put him with the hypocrites" (Matt 24:45, 48-51).

This parable deals with a proper use of authority. The servant is given responsibility by his master who goes on vacation. When the master is slow in returning, the servant abuses his authority. He gets drunk. He abuses his fellow-servants. He parties till all hours. When the master returns unexpectedly, he is punished.

One message for the "meantime": Don't misuse and abuse authority.

The story of the ten wise and foolish bridesmaids gives another message for us as we await the end-time. At its conclusion we read:

But at midnight there was a shout, "Look! Here is the bridegroom! Come out to meet him." . . . The foolish said to the wise, "Give us some of your oil, for our lamps are going out." But the wise replied, "No! . . . you had better go to the dealers and buy some for yourselves." . . . Later the other bridesmaids came also, saying, "Lord, Lord, open to us." But he replied, "Truly I tell you, I do not know you." Keep awake therefore, for you know neither the day nor the hour (Matt 25:6, 8-9, 11-13).

The foolish bridesmaids *presume* that they will have enough oil. But when the bridegroom returns, they are left outside because they did not plan ahead. The ones who acted wisely and prepared for the long haul entered the wedding feast. Being attentive (awake) to the task at hand is important.

One message for the "meantime": Do not presume that someone else will take care of you if you lack foresight. Don't doze! Stay awake and alert to life!

The third story speaks of a man entrusting three employees with varied amounts of money. The man then left the country. On his return he asked for an accounting. Two of the men have invested the money and bring the profit from the investment to the employer. He rewards them by giving them better jobs. The third man was not so enterprising:

"Then the one who had received the one talent came forward, saying, 'Master, I knew that you were a harsh man, reaping where you did not sow, and gathering where you did not scatter seed; so I was afraid, and I went and hid your talent in the ground. Here you have what is yours.' But his master replied, 'You wicked and lazy slave! You knew, did you, that I reap where I did not sow, and gather where I did not scatter? Then you ought to have invested my money with the bankers, and on my return I would have received what was my own with interest. . . . Throw him into the outer darkness, where there will be weeping and gnashing of teeth' " (Matt 25:24-27, 30).

Each man works with the capital given to him. Two servants make the money grow through sound investments. One does not! He was too frightened to take any risks. He buried his capital so that no one could steal it. This last man is condemned when the master returns. Timidity and fear had kept him from acting wisely with the money.

One message for the "meantime": Don't let fear and timidity dictate your decisions and rule your life.

The parable that follows (Matt 25:31-46) gives us the story of the last judgment. People who ignore their neighbor are condemned.

One message for the "meantime": Care for one another as you wait for the end-time.

None of these parables tolerates passive do-nothingism. The gospel calls for active involvement with others while awaiting the end-time. The time of waiting is a time of concern. It is the opposite of the passivity proclaimed by some interpreters of apocalyptic writings.

Unlike some apocalyptic groups who call for killing the enemy, Jesus calls for loving the enemy. Unlike apocalyptic groups who call for a form of "ritual purity," Jesus eats with sinners and tax collectors, ritually impure people. Repeatedly, the gospel says: Even though the end may be near, be faithful to the gospel! Don't sit around and wait for God to do everything! Faithfulness will bring greater clarity to the *gospel vision*.

Jesus is with us. He does not expect us to conquer every existing evil. But neither should we allow evil to paralyze us. We confront evil with the power of our faithful God. We are not helpless. Faith in Jesus (and his *vision*) gives us power to overcome evil. Good scriptural reflection enables us to deal with injustice and evil *now!* We may not succeed, but we will try. A friend wrote these words in a book he gave me: "It is not incumbent upon you to complete the task — but neither are you free to desist from it."

Some Elements of the Gospel Vision

The Bible speaks about the coming of the reign of God. We live within the "meantime" between Jesus' first coming and the end-time. We are not competent to determine when the end-time will come. We look to the gospel for direction in living the gospel vision. Here are some biblical guidelines:

1. The Bible recognizes that suffering and conflict are an inevitable part of the Christian experience. ''Whoever does not carry the cross and follow me cannot be my disciple'' (Luke 14:27).

A good friend, Barbara Campbell, died of liver failure on August 14, 1991. She wrote these words in 1988. They reflect an inner response to powerlessness in the face of terminal illness. Very often our woundedness and pain is a window to our inner spirit. The ''cross'' becomes a place of insight.

Pain cuts deeply into the body like a knife and passes on into the soul, penetrating in a way that nothing else can . . . exposing parts of us that we don't like to see or claim as our own.

That small child within us, crouched and cowering in a corner, clutching a disheveled rag doll, an image of herself . . . terrified . . . alone . . . hurting and broken . . . afraid of the unknown and future pains, afraid to speak up, lest a cure be found that would be more excruciating than the existing pain.

Wondering if, when, it will go away and how that will happen. She doesn't even ask the question *why?*, because in her childlike wisdom she knows it must be so.

Alone, because she knows that for this part of the journey she must walk by herself through the darkness;
no one can do it for her.

It triggers faded and dulled memories of other times when she was hurting and alone.
She knows, too, that only from the inside can anyone share the experience.
On the outside there are the sympathetic looks and touches that often lead others on their own journey to and through their own pain.
Then — alone again, yes, it must be so.
Hurting, outside and inside, dreading the darkness and loneliness of this time. Just being in that room — knowing it and owning it — it must be so.

It's hard to come in touch with brokenness while in the midst
of pain, especially for the small child; and yet — it must be so.
Hurting outside and inside, dreading the darkness and loneliness of this time,
Just being in that room, knowing and owning it, it must be so.

Hard though it is, clearer it becomes . . . She notices: "I am
a little better this time, not as hopelessly terrified as I once was;
not as lonely, nor as hurting or broken as the last time, or the
time before . . ."
And though she is still afraid a voice resounds in her heart:
"Don't be afraid . . ."

And though she still feels lonely, she knows she isn't alone as
she hears that same voice in her heart: "I am with you always."
Even in the midst of the worst, the voice proclaims: "When you
pass through roaring fires, you shall not be harmed."

Broken . . . dismembered . . . paradoxically she experiences
being re-membered, made whole, put back together again, and
in those broken places she has been made strong, renewed and
transformed.
And the little girl looks up as the light fills the room . . . and
she begins to dance.

2. There are a variety of ways to deal with suffering
and conflict. Do not rely on just one way. The Bible is
pluralistic in its response to conflict and suffering. "So
we do not lose heart. Even though our outer nature is
wasting away, our inner nature is being renewed day by
day . . . So we are always confident . . . for we walk
by faith, not by sight" (2 Cor 4:16; 5:6-7).

3. Evil is powerful and aggressive. It comes into conflict with the *vision* of the gospel. Be prepared to confront
this enemy. "Discipline yourselves, keep alert. Like a
roaring lion your adversary the devil prowls around, looking for someone to devour. Resist him, steadfast in your
faith, for you know that your brothers and sisters in all
the world are undergoing the same kinds of suffering"
(1 Pet 5:8-9).

4. Jesus has risen from the dead to a new life, no longer
hindered by earthly limitations. The power that raised

Jesus from the dead is the power with which we face the threat of evil. We need not tremble before the power of evil. God's power overcomes even death itself. "If Christ has not been raised, then our proclamation has been in vain and your faith has been in vain. . . . But in fact Christ has been raised from the dead, the first fruits of those who have died" (1 Cor 15:14, 20).

5. Jesus expects us to be alive and awake, sensitive to what is going on around us. The gospel helps us form our ethics and our stance on issues in the world as well as in our personal lives. "Truly I tell you, just as you did it to one of the least of these who are members of my family, you did it to me. . . . Truly I tell you, just as you did *not* do it to one of the least of these, you did not do it to me" (Matt 25:40, 45). "There must be *no limit* to your goodness, as your heavenly Father's goodness knows no bounds" (Matt 5:48 — REB — italics mine).

6. In the Beatitudes (Matt 5:3-12; Luke 6:20-26), Jesus offers a *vision* of what a Christian looks like. It calls for an active response to the world around us. Making peace, hungering for justice, showing mercy and knowing our need for God are not passive responses. The Beatitudes declare war on passivity and a "let God do it" approach to the Christian life.

7. Each Christian is gifted by God. We use our gifts for the good of the community. Self-seeking and isolationism are not gospel virtues. "So let us not grow weary in doing what is right, for we will reap at harvest-time if we do not give up. So then, whenever we have an opportunity, let us work for the good of all, and especially for those of the family of faith" (Gal 6:9-10).

8. Communication with Jesus and the Father of Jesus are life-giving. We become undernourished and weak without such communication. The Holy Spirit teaches us the ways of communication when we do not know how to speak. Prayerfulness is our way to communion with

God, self, and others. "I pray that the God of our Lord Jesus Christ, the Father of glory, may give you a spirit of wisdom and revelation as you come to know him, so that, with the eyes of your heart enlightened, you may know what is the hope to which he has called you, what are the riches of his glorious inheritance among the saints, and what is the immeasurable greatness of his power for us who believe" (Eph 1:17-19).

9. Forgiveness and reconciliation will be needed because humans hurt each other and separate from one another. We fail to maintain the unity for which Jesus prays. When that happens the vision calls us to seek ways of healing, forgiveness, and reconciliation. "All this is from God, who reconciled us to himself through Christ, and has given us the ministry of reconciliation; that is, in Christ God was reconciling the world to himself . . . entrusting the message of reconciliation to us. So we are ambassadors for Christ, since God is making his appeal through us; we entreat you on behalf of Christ, be reconciled to God" (2 Cor 5:18-20).

10. Gospel people need Jesus. They establish a firm relationship with Jesus. Such a relationship requires regular communication. Hence, gospel people are prayerful people.

"This is how you should pray:
Our Father in heaven,
may your name be hallowed;
your kingdom come,
your will be done,
on earth as in heaven.
Give us today our daily bread.
Forgive us the wrong we have done,
as we have forgiven those who have wronged us.
And do not put us to the test,
but save us from the evil one" (Matt 6:9-13 — REB).

11. When we share the vision with others, not everyone will be receptive. Gospel people will be persecuted

in a variety of ways. We remain strong so long as we are united with Jesus and are supported by a faith-community of dedicated people. "When we cry 'Abba! Father!' it is that very Spirit bearing witness with our spirit that we are children of God, and if children, then heirs, heirs of God and joint heirs with Christ — if, in fact, we suffer with him so that we may also be glorified with him" (Rom 8:15-17).

Dealing with Each Other

People interpret the vision of faith in many different ways. People who accept a fundamentalist interpretation of the Bible are good people. They do not have horns nor do they desire evil for others. Yet the atmosphere in which they share the faith can be judgmental. It may condemn others who believe differently. Catholics are often singled out as the great "unwashed" of Christendom. We will rarely, if ever, convince strict fundamentalists through scriptural arguments. Die-hard fundamentalists are already convinced about what the Bible says and means. No argument is going to change that. This applies to "Catholic" fundamentalists as well. Arguments are useless when people are convinced that their interpretation of the Bible is the only right one. Sometimes they become infallible interpreters of other writings as well. They find "errors," i.e., points of view that disagree with their infallible opinions.

There are sincere fundamentalists who truly believe that only literal interpretation can give them biblical truth. They seek to be honest to the Bible as they interpret it. For other fundamentalists, this infallible, literal approach is fed by an insecurity that needs reassurance. Sometimes the rigidity of a fundamentalist masks a fear that they may be wrong. Sometimes fundamentalism develops from a simple and honest desire to do what is right by "tuning out" any conflicting ideas. Sometimes the generosity of a fundamentalist group attracts us to them. It is natural to accept their doctrine when they have graciously accepted us.

Whatever it is that makes fundamentalism attractive, ridicule and anger will get nowhere in our dialogue with them. Rather, affirm the good they do. Support the good. Join them in doing good things. Doctrinal differences need not keep us separate. There is too much to be done in our world to use our energy fighting one another. Join hands in doing good. Gently let grow a spirit that listens to the gospel with an open heart. Share a firm faith that brings you joy and offers hope. Love one another and allow your faith and hope to penetrate where arguments could never walk. Allow the gentle Spirit of Jesus to touch your heart and theirs!

> It is he [Christ] whom we proclaim, warning everyone and teaching everyone in all wisdom, so that we may present everyone mature in Christ. . . . I want their hearts to be encouraged and united in love, so that they may have all the riches of assured understanding and have the knowledge of God's mystery, that is, Christ himself, in whom are hidden all the treasures of wisdom and knowledge (Col 1:28, 2:2-3).

> "Do not judge, and you will not be judged; do not condemn, and you will not be condemned. Forgive, and you will be forgiven; give, and it will be given to you" (Luke 6:37-38).

A sensitive and gentle spirit will enable us to touch one another with love. We will share our "seeing" with others. We will not condemn people but confront the issues that diminish faith and life. We will try to reach people's hearts through a mature Christian love. Growth in faith, hope, and love is a never-ending journey. We embark on it confidently. When faith touches people, it shows in their lives.

Creating an atmosphere of acceptance opens doors to dialogue. Dialogue requires us to listen as well as speak. We share our portion of the truth (as we know it at this point) with others who may possess another portion of the truth. From respectful dialogue comes a deepening acceptance as well as a richer understanding of the truth. This is what a gospel pilgrim experiences along the way. Some years ago, I wrote about being a pilgrim:

Can a pilgrim forget the way?
Does the person who chooses Jesus always know the way to go?
Ah, the mystery of the pilgrim.
So very clearly on the move,
but often not clear about the way to go.

Struggling with an inner need
to have things settled once and for all,
yet caught in the uncertainty of being a pilgrim
for whom things are not settled.

There is something romantic about the pilgrim.
It overshadows the difficulty of being a pilgrim.
The romantic ideas sound so right and attractive
and still allow for so much ambiguity.
It is strange that I can talk about it so much
and do so little to make it a reality in my life.

'Tis a puzzlement that Christians are called to be pilgrims
and then try to settle into little ruts.
The rut can be anything from total solitude
to harried social action. It can mean being "stuck" in one
place or refusing to become "unstuck" from memorized
answers.

We get rooted in the wrong soil.
We plant our seeds and want to push them up
to grow into what *we* want them to be.
We hate waiting or traveling or letting *our* work alone.

Real pilgrims move on
and reflect . . . to appreciate what *God* has done.
How often we poke our sticks into the soil
to see what is happening to *our* seed.

How wonderful is our God who not only
tolerates such nonsense, but smiles at it.
A God who sees our stumbling around and is
more amused than angered.

For God knows what will happen sooner or later.
What we will experience when God's presence is felt.
God delights in waiting for that moment,
standing at the door of our hearts,
waiting for the moment when
we discover the God who was always present.

When the discovery comes, God holds us
and begins to waltz with us in celebration.

Being a pilgrim is a stumbling business at best.
We are free to recognize our foolishness
and know the God who never leaves us.
That's why pilgrims are always at home —
because of Jesus and the Spirit who
dwell in our hearts. Amen

We have begun our search into Jesus' vision. The Bible is
our sourcebook. Read on! Another dimension of the *vision* of
Jesus awaits us.

Reflection

How do I feel about fundamentalism? About fundamentalists?
How does the Bible unveil its message to me? Is a literal interpretation of the Bible the only way to understand it? Why
is it important for me to know about the writers of the Bible?
. . . about the cultural setting of the Bible stories? . . . about
the way writers use words in the Bible? Can praying the Bible
give me an insight that may not be true for everyone? How
can I pray with the Bible? How good is my knowledge of the
Bible? How will I develop a better knowledge of the Bible? Do
I pick arguments about religion rather than share insights with
others? Why do people cling to a fundamentalist stance? What
does Jesus expect of me while waiting for the "end-time"?
What kind of questions will Jesus ask me when I stand before
him after death? How do I feel about integrating Bible values
into everyday life? Is there any area of my life that is untouched
by gospel values? How will I change that? How can I learn to
read the Bible intelligently? What guidance does my faith-
community (Church) offer me in understanding the Bible?
What attracts people to TV evangelists? How can I develop a
better Christian lifestyle? How do I decide if something is in

accord with the gospel? What feelings do I have toward people who differ with me in interpreting the Bible?

Always be ready to make your defense to anyone who demands from you an accounting for the hope that is in you, yet do it with gentleness and reverence (1 Pet 3:15-16).

CHAPTER TEN

Once Upon a Mountain

The Bible speaks through events, prayers, stories, parables, history, and apocalyptic writings. It speaks through miracles, compassion, anger, darkness, light, questions, proverbs, sayings, and teachings. It speaks through confrontations, death, life, frustration, fear, idolatry, and political power. Its words describe human/God and human/human relationships and events.

Journeying Through the Bible

How did the world and life begin? Where is the starting point? In its first pages the Bible says: "In the beginning when God created . . ." (Gen 1:1). The person writing these words was not present at creation. But the writer observed the world he knew, a planet set in a vast universe. He heard stories about creation and how others explained a vision of God-at-work. In prayerful wonder he gave us the story of creation. The writer used his creative talents to express awe at what God had done. The creation story is a marvel of truth clothed in images of the writer's skill. It is not science but theology. It is not technology but wonder. It is not eyewitness reporting but clear-cut portrayal of the truth about our creator God. It shows with startling clarity the power of a creative God at work. It speaks of a Creator whose desire for intimacy moves God to create people in the image of God: "So God created humankind in his image, in the image of God he created them; male and female he created them" (Gen 1:27).

The scriptural writer knew God. His God made everything. He says as much in his writings. God makes light where there was chaos and darkness. God separates the waters and creates the vaults of heaven. God's earth produces fresh growth with seed-bearing plants. God fills the waters with fish. God fills the earth with living creatures who would reproduce themselves. God makes the sun, moon, and stars the sources of light and beauty. God makes human beings to dwell on this earth and be responsible for it. People are made in God's image — male and female God made them. They too would reproduce themselves.

God is the creator of all things, says the author of Genesis. The details of creation are not as important as the message — God is a creating God. Nothing lives without God. That is what we believe. That is how we see things! Whether or not scientists ever prove a "big bang" theory of creation, Genesis remains true. God created the world. An imaginative and caring God shares life with all that is created. "God saw everything that he had made, and indeed, it was very good. . . . So God blessed the seventh day and hallowed it, because on it God rested from all the work that he had done in creation" (Gen 1:31–2:3).

Sabbath, Etc.

■ *God, creator of everything, rested (Gen 2:2-3).*
The writer inserts an important message for his readers: "Take time to rest. Keep the sabbath!" We easily resist rest. Some people think the world will not function without their work. Yet the sun will rise, the clouds roll in, the moon light the night independently of what we accomplish. We indulge in a bit of

idolatry when we consider ourselves indispensable. God, in the beginning, shows that rest from work is important. We need to surrender the headlong desire to control everything. What a challenge for workaholics! God delights in the person who uses leisure well. We need a respite from the pressures of everyday life. Leisure re-creates both body and spirit. It is healthy to take time to rest, relax, and surrender to God. Stressed-out people of today are learning this lesson. "Burnout" is teaching us to slow down and live!

God asks that we allow God to be in control. But we scramble to work in the pressure-cooker of weekends before returning to "work" on Monday. "In the beginning" we learn an important lesson. Rest, relax, and enjoy the sabbath gift of leisure.

A text in Isaiah offers another lesson:

> I am the LORD, and there is no other;
>> besides me there is no god.
>> I arm you, though you do not know me,
> so that they may know, from the rising of the sun
>> and from the west, that there is no one besides me;
>> I am the LORD and there is no other. . . .
> Does the clay say to the one who fashions it, "What are
>> you making?"
>> or "Your work has no handles?" . . .
> I made the earth,
>> and created humankind upon it;
> It was my hands that stretched out the heavens,
>> and I commanded all their host. . . .
> I am the LORD, and there is no other (Isa 45:5-6, 9, 12, 18).

■ *God enjoys being God and seeks no replacement.*
God has no desire to be replaced by anything or anyone else. Repeatedly, the Scriptures shout that there is only *one God* and there is no other. This God enjoys creation and creating new wonders for people. God looks for a response of praise and thanks. God's only Son, Jesus, gives praise and thanks to his Father. "Father, I thank you for having heard me. I knew that you always hear me, but I have said this for the sake of the

crowd standing here, so that they may believe that you sent me'' (John 11:41-42).

Jesus reveals his ''Abba'' as a caring, loving person inviting us to the conversion that brings new life. The Father of Jesus trusts Jesus with everything. God raised Jesus from the dead after his death and burial. What intimate love exists between Father and Son!

Our personal conversion moves us to abandon things that offer a false sense of life. It is difficult to implement the *vision* when we refuse to acknowledge that God alone is God! *I am God. There is no other. I am the creator and I love my creation!* ''So acknowledge today and take to heart that the Lord is God in heaven above and on the earth beneath; there is no other'' (Deut 4:39).

There is another ''in the beginning'' in the Bible. It occurs in the Gospel of John. It reveals another dimension of the *vision*.

> In the beginning the *Word* already was. The Word was in God's presence, and what God was, the Word was. He was with God at the beginning, and through him all things came to be; without him no created thing came into being. In him was life, and that life was the light of mankind. The light shines in the darkness and the darkness has never mastered it. . . . So the Word became flesh; he made his home among us, and we saw his glory, such glory as befits the Father's only son, full of grace and truth (John 1:1-5, 14 — REB — italics mine).

■ *Jesus is the Word-made-flesh, God dwelling with us.*
Jesus is God living among us as a human being. God comes among us for a variety of reasons. Jesus comes as savior. He comes as one who reveals the way of the reign of God. He comes to establish a community to implement his teachings. He comes to heal us, to lift burdens that hinder commitment to the revealed word. Jesus comes as Lord as well as teacher and friend. Jesus comes to call people to be faithful and responsible to their part of the covenant. Jesus comes to teach us the ways of forgiveness and to offer us forgiveness. Jesus comes to give us his Spirit as power to live the gospel. Jesus

comes to share his *vision* with us — the *vision* he received from
his Father:

> No one has ever seen God. It is God the only Son, who is
> close to the Father's heart, who has made him known (John
> 1:18). . . . for this I came into the world, to testify to the truth.
> Everyone who belongs to the truth listens to my voice (John
> 18:37). All things have been handed over to me by my Father;
> and no one knows the Son except the Father, and no one knows
> the Father except the Son and anyone to whom the Son chooses
> to reveal him (Matt 11:27).

> He unrolled the scroll and found the place where it was written:
>   "The Spirit of the Lord is upon me,
>   because he has anointed me to bring good
>   news to the poor.
>   He has sent me to proclaim release to the
>   captives and recovery of sight to the blind,
>   to let the oppressed go free,
>   to proclaim the year of the Lord's favor.
>   . . . Today this scripture has been fulfilled in your
> hearing!' '' (Luke 4:17-19, 21).

The Bible contains many statements by and about Jesus.
Sent by the Father, Jesus comes to touch the lives of his people.
He reveals the truth about himself, about his Father, about a
mission of compassion, about how he wants his people to live.
To believe in Jesus will require us to listen to the word. Our
identity as Christians is spelled out in the Bible. Jesus gives
us his Spirit to enable us to live the *vision*. Jesus shares with
us what the Father shares with him. The Father's dream for
people is an exciting one.

> For I will pour water on the thirsty land,
>   and streams on the dry ground;
> I will pour my spirit upon your descendants,
>   and my blessing on your offspring.
> They shall spring up like a green tamarisk,
>   like willows by flowing streams (Isa 44:3-4).

> The wolf and the lamb shall feed together,
>   the lion shall eat straw like the ox;
>   but the serpent — its food shall be dust!

> They shall not hurt or destroy
> on all my holy mountain,
>   says the Lord (Isa 65:25).

These words give a glimpse of God's vision for us. Jesus invites us to make this *vision* a reality. After two thousand years the work is still unfinished. Our task is to give flesh to the gospel *vision* in today's world.

Once Upon a Mountain
Jesus Spoke the Beatitudes

The Beatitudes (Matt 5:3-12/Luke 6:20-26) express some of the basic ingredients of the gospel vision. They summarize the Christian life. The Beatitudes spell out attitudes of gospel people. These gospel attitudes give us a way to evaluate life. Don't be surprised if you resist some of these ideas. They do not conform to many of the values we learn from society. "Blessed are the poor in spirit, for theirs is the kingdom of heaven" (Matt 5:3). "Blessed are you who are poor, for yours is the kingdom of God. Blessed are you who are hungry now, for you will be filled" (Luke 6:20-21).

"Those who know their need of God" is another way to define *"Poor in spirit."* Jesus is not blessing destitution and impoverishment. Nor does he call for the abolition of all riches. But riches can be a hindrance to gospel living. Too much reliance on wealth makes it hard to follow the gospel. Possessiveness and power lead us to deny our need for God. Blessedness comes to people who know they need God.

Lacking wealth and power, the poor are specially loved by God. They are *open* to accept good things from God. When good things come, the genuinely poor in spirit rejoice and thank God.

People living in poverty may or may not be gracious. But they are poor. They are in need and know it! When gifts are given, the gospel poor respond with rejoicing. Poor people with faith understand that God-is-with-them. The good news

is directed to them. Gospel people make common cause with
the poor. Gospel people lift the burden that poverty and hunger bring. Gospel people seek to liberate everyone from the
indignity of destitution. We get involved because we believe
in the Scriptures. Our task is to make this world reflect the
words of Scripture: "to bring good news to the poor" (Luke
4:18).

Jesus is consistent in his own life. In his society some people
were considered "nobodies." Jesus clearly acknowledges these
folks as "somebodies," deserving of compassion, respect, and
dignity. He associates with sinners and prostitutes, tax collectors and lepers. He has the audacity to confront legalists. He
stands free before the power of Pilate. He knows his Father
and knows the subjects of his Father's compassion — the poor
and powerless. Of all people, they will be given the word of
hope.

The poor will be required to abandon resentment, anger,
and hatred. The gospel does not tolerate such things. If lions
and lambs will eat together, then God's people can dismantle
violence and hatred. It is part of the *vision!* Hunger and poverty are not virtues. But the hungry and poor are loved by God.
They have a special place in God's heart.

> His mercy is for those who fear him from generation to genera-
> tion. . . . he has scattered the proud in the thoughts of their
> hearts. He has brought down the powerful from their thrones,
> and lifted up the lowly; he has filled the hungry with good
> things, and sent the rich away empty (Luke 1:50-53).

God wishes to free the poor from the burden of poverty.
It is senseless to claim that the poor are always with us and
excuse ourselves from doing anything. That is not the message of Jesus. His message focuses on the worth of people.
Neither the rich nor the poor gain anything by ignoring one
another. Neither can grow in faith if they see themselves as
nobodies. The rich cannot use the poor as scapegoats to work
out guilt. The poor cannot become passive victims, full of self-
pity, blaming others for their plight. Jesus asks everyone to

face reality and *choose* to relate to one another. Jesus calls us to see each other as real people with a dignity that is God-given. Otherwise life will become meaningless for everyone. Antagonism, scapegoating, blaming, using one another to work out guilt, or self-pitying passivity is nowhere supported in the gospel.

What is valued is the freedom to love one another without distinction. What is valued is to relate to one another without barriers. What is valued is life itself, whether in the poor or the rich. Without such valuing, the *vision* can get lost in meager hand-outs, long-distance planning, and refusal to let others know their dignity as human beings. "The ultimate injustice is for a person or group to be treated actively or abandoned passively as if they were nonmembers of the human race. To treat people this way is effectively to say that they simply do not count as human beings" (*Economic Justice for All*, Bishops' Pastoral Letter 1986 — NCCB, par 77).

> My brothers and sisters, do you with your acts of favoritism really believe in our glorious Lord Jesus Christ? For if a person with gold rings and in fine clothes comes into your assembly, and if a poor person in dirty clothes also comes in, and if you take notice of the one wearing the fine clothes and say, "Have a seat here, please," while to the one who is poor you say, "Stand there," or "Sit at my feet," have you not made distinctions among yourselves and become judges with evil thoughts? (Jas 2:1-4).

Gospel people cannot be indifferent to the needs of the poor, the homeless, the hungry. Whether political, economic, spiritual, or charitable action is needed, Christians prove their identity by *doing something!* "Dealing with poverty is not a luxury to which our nation can attend when it finds the time and resources. Rather, it is a moral imperative of the highest priority" (*Economic Justice for All*, par 170).

Biblical poverty frees the heart to love. It removes barriers to freedom by removing possessiveness and ideas that are contrary to the gospel. The reason for renouncing "things" is to possess a greater value and *vision*. The gospel offers a *vision* where people can live without fear of one another; where people can approach one another for help, knowing that resources will be shared; where people value relationships over acquisitions; where transformation is more important than preservation. Our task is to share the gospel life in its fullness. Our mission is to be one people, united in Jesus.

This is no easy task. People often desire a religion that is comfortable rather than demanding. People may prefer security to the radically risky journey of conversion. Gospel people, on the other hand, accept the consequences of following Jesus and his gospel *vision*. Jesus surprises and delights them with his gift of joy!

> Blessed are those who mourn, for they will be comforted. . . .
> Blessed are those who hunger and thirst for righteousness, for they will be filled (Matt 5:4, 6). Woe to you who are full now, for you will be hungry. Woe to you who are laughing now, for you will mourn and weep (Luke 6:25).

Mourners have reasons for mourning — the loss of a friend or a family member, a crisis situation, a tragedy. Each can bring mourning in its wake. Those who refuse to mourn bottle things up inside. They "grin and bear it." But sooner or later the wound opens up. If we choose *not* to mourn, we suffer for it. Even psychology tells us of the deadly effects of suppressing hurt and pain.

This Beatitude also invites us to mourn for whatever hinders peace and freedom. We mourn social sin that oppresses people. We mourn personal sin that hinders our growth in the Lord. Mourning pushes us to deal with reality rather than evade it. In doing so, it brings the beginning of comfort. No longer does "it" control us. We begin the process of dealing with our reasons for mourning. We then begin to experience the comfort promised by the Beatitude. We are a people of God. Our mourning brings a beginning of the end to our pain over a loss. Personal mourning may free us to put our inner gifts at the service of others.

The Beatitudes push even farther. To "hunger and thirst for righteousness" shows a passionate concern to make the gospel a reality. A gospel person cannot tolerate delay in the coming of the reign of God. Passionate dedication to gospel living brings mourning when there is delay. Delay in lifting the burden of oppression, whether emotional, psychological, economic, political, or spiritual; delay in offering dignity to people who have a God-given right to human dignity; delay in seeking forgiveness and remaining in the bitterness, hatred, and anger of unforgiveness; delay in showing compassion to those in need; delay in supporting things that bring life to people; delay in fulfilling the gospel vision; delay in caring for our earth's environment; delay in praising God for the wonders of our mother, the earth; delay in honoring the God who is present to all people. Indifference or protectionism that causes such delay is reason for mourning among gospel people.

We critique life in this world in the light of the gospel vision. When anything in our world, secular or sacred, hinders the gospel life, the Christian takes action to correct the situation. The passionate hunger and thirst to put things right never grows dim. This is especially true for the community of believers. It is also true of the individual Christian. Passionate concern can be diminished through failure, disappointment, low morale, and other debilitating factors. When we mourn such situations, the beatitude calls us to deal with these painful issues in realistic ways.

In confronting issues, we discover the comfort promised by God. When we wallow in self-pity, things get worse. Beatitude-mourning deals directly with loss/failure and does it with faith. When we are realistic about our mourning, the burden begins to lift. Comfort enters. We may pass through denial and anger, bargaining and depression (Dr. Elisabeth Kübler-Ross). But the final step is acceptance. With acceptance comes the comfort of peace. Acceptance is a positive choice, not passive resignation. Acceptance chooses life. It will not allow evil or pain to be the power that controls life. Only when we face reality do we find God and God's gift of *shalom*.

But strive first for the kingdom of God and his righteousness,
and all these things will be given to you as well (Matt 6:33).
As you go, proclaim the good news, ''The kingdom of heaven
has come near.'' Cure the sick, raise the dead, cleanse the lepers,
cast out demons. You received without payment; give without
payment (Matt 10:7-8). For I am convinced that neither death,
nor life, nor angels, nor rulers, nor things present, nor things
to come, nor powers, nor height nor depth, nor anything else
in all creation, will be able to separate us from the love of God
in Christ Jesus our Lord (Rom 8:38-39).

Prayer

This brings us to a vital dimension of the *vision*. We get nowhere without incorporation into Jesus. No matter how many
different ways we say it, intimacy with Jesus is the source of
our strength. Intimacy with Jesus is the source of our *vision*.
Intimacy with Jesus is the source of our power. The Holy Spirit,
sent by Jesus, gives us power to live as gospel people. We are
called to communion with Jesus. This is one way of saying we
must be a prayerful people.

To attain communion requires contact and communication.
Contact means taking time with the beloved. No friendship
blossoms or grows without communication. Verbal expressions
mean little if they are not linked with communication of one's
real self. No friendship can survive non-communicative silence.
No relationship can continue when sharing breaks down. No
growth in the Lord can blossom without communication with
Jesus in prayerful communion.

> In the morning, while it was still very dark, he got up and went
> out to a deserted place, and there he prayed (Mark 1:35). ''When
> you are praying, do not heap up empty phrases as the Gen-
> tiles do; for they think that they will be heard because of their
> many words. Do not be like them, for your Father knows what
> you need before you ask him. Pray then in this way: Our Father
> in heaven . . .'' (Matt 6:7-9).

There are many forms of prayer. Each Christian will discover the way to intimacy with Jesus that fits his or her per-

son. What is not negotiable is the need to pray. When we work for justice or seek the ways of peace; when we deal with the foibles of rich and poor, homeless and housed, sick and healthy, we discover a lot of pettiness. Without consistent prayerfulness, we will fall by the wayside. Without communion with Jesus, we are weakened by the energy drain that love and justice require. Without intimacy with Jesus, we grow weak-kneed very quickly. A Christian needs communion with Jesus to be faithful to the gospel *vision*. Intimacy with God comes through the surrender of contemplative communion. Joy and peace are God's gifts to those who are faithful to prayerful communion.

Prayer and ministry are partners who deal both with failure and success. We know whose ministry it is. Prayer makes us real. It keeps our perceptions centered on God's way of seeing things. Prayer forces us to face issues. We discover whether we are faithful because of good feelings we *get* or because we do it for God alone. When God seems distant, will we continue to be faithful? When nothing is working for us, when no glittering feelings make us feel good, will we be faithful for God's sake? Will we choose in favor of God and the gospel *vision* with or without personal rewards? Without mature faith and consistent prayerfulness, it is difficult to be faithful to God and the gospel *vision*.

On with the Beatitudes

"Blessed are the gentle; they shall have the earth for their possession. . . . Blessed are those who show mercy; mercy shall be shown to them. Blessed are those whose hearts are pure; they shall see God" (Matt 5:5, 7, 8 — REB).

Gentleness (meekness) has not always received a good press. The word "meekness" indicates an attitude more like that of a doormat than of a mature person. It seems like weakness rather than strength. The dictionary gives this meaning for meek: ". . . easily imposed upon, spineless, spiritless." Such a description hardly fits Jesus. He was *not* a doormat.

Anything that touched his ministry for the Father was defended and proclaimed with courage and strength. "Gentleness" is the ability to see reality clearly and react realistically.

If we link this beatitude with "those whose hearts are pure" we get a sharp picture. The pure-hearted cut through gobbledegook and doubletalk to get at the heart of things. They are not misled by lies, half truths, negative humor, or violent reactions. They "see through" such smokescreens and get to the core of issues. Instead of hiding behind words, the gentle and pure-hearted use words to communicate reality. They get to root causes rather than symptoms. They are not afraid to stand before the threats of the powerful. They are not put off by the trembling of the weak. Reality is their home, for God is there. The gentle person, perceiving what is real, reacts with righteous anger, gentle compassion, loving confrontation, or strong affirmation. The gentle person deals in reality, whatever it may be. What a change gentleness could bring to many areas of societal life. Imagine what advertising, politics, economics, or church life would look like if gentleness and purity of heart were the norm. Consider what our discussions about sexuality and prejudice would look like if touched by this reality. Such maturity is another brushstroke in the picture of the gospel *vision*.

When we see clearly and react realistically, we will know how to show mercy. Mercy is not one-sided or unilateral. The person who shows mercy receives mercy. Mercy does not overlook wrongdoing or sweep issues aside in a grand gesture of forgiveness. True mercy flows from justice tempered by love. It offers a way for fractured relationships to be healed. It invites someone with self-doubt and guilt to the freedom of wholeness and self-confidence. It touches individual aggressions as well as the aggression of nations.

> Thus, the fundamental structure of justice always enters into the sphere of mercy. Mercy, however, has the power to confer on justice a new content, which is expressed most simply and fully in forgiveness. Forgiveness, in fact, shows that, over and above the process of "compensation" and "truce" which is

specific to justice, love is necessary so that man may affirm himself as man . . . he who forgives and he who is forgiven encounter one another at an essential point, namely, the dignity
or essential value of the person . . .'' (*Rich in Mercy*, John Paul
II, USCC 1981; p. 49, par 14).

An attitude of mercy will grow in a Christian as faith-
maturity grows. We face many issues requiring decisions
reflecting the quality of mercy. Capital punishment needs to
be looked at in all its realism. The welfare system needs a realistic look. Our manner of defending ourselves needs to be examined in the light of gentleness, purity of heart, and mercy.
It is never enough to have good *ideas* about mercy. Our Christian living ''gives skin'' to mercy in everyday life. If we are
evangelized, i.e., ''gospelized,'' we develop a lifestyle that
reflects the quality of mercy. Life and gospel come together
in a person of integrity.

''Blessed are the peacemakers, for they will be called children of God. Blessed are those who are persecuted for righteousness' sake, for theirs is the kingdom of heaven'' (Matt
5:9-10).

Some companies fabricate steel, making it into a usable form
for constructing buildings. Peacemakers are people who ''fabricate'' issues and attitudes in a way that builds peace. This Beatitude relies on the other Beatitudes. It presumes a Christian who
is living the Beatitudes. Their perceptions and interpretation
of events and issues are colored by the gospel truth. Injustice,
oppression, violence, fear, hatred, uncontrolled anger, isolation, dependency, inhumane attitudes and actions, destitution,
greed, the military-industrial complex (President Eisenhower's
phrase), addictions, unforgiveness, and a host of other issues
are hindrances to peace.

Gospel peace requires an atmosphere in which people can
achieve a sense of wholeness and joy (*shalom*). Peacemakers
create an environment that is conducive to healthy growth.
Peacemakers deal with all the issues mentioned above . . . and
then some!

It is vital to create a favorable climate for people to live a human and creative life. The technique used or the method embraced may be clear-cut or questionable. Human beings do not always choose the best or the most effective means to "build peace." Methods that are oppressive or foment violence are not the way to "build peace." Sometimes defensive reactions to peacemakers create oppression and violence even when there is a nonviolent attempt to seek peace. It takes a solid, holistic, believing community to develop methods and techniques that are healthy and prompted by the Holy Spirit.

Gospel peace differs from political peace. When politicians and others-in-society speak about peace, it often means the cessation of fighting or war. If there is no killing going on, we have peace. This is *not* the gospel ideal. Of course, gospel peace does not allow for war or killing and encourages its cessation. But it is more than that. It requires the building of a society where people feel free, where people trust one another, where people make their needs known and are satisfied. It is a society where justice is both fair and prompt. It is a society that knows how to show mercy. Gospel peace requires honesty that does not hide the truth in a deluge of words or bury it in doubletalk and artificial image-building.

Gospel peace deals with differences and arguments in a way that brings about friendly relationships rather than continuing enmity. It is no simple thing to be a peacemaker. But if we never bother to work for peace, we will never experience it. Listen to Paul's way of dealing with the issue of justice leading to peace. Onesimus is a runaway slave befriended by Paul. Philemon is the owner of Onesimus and has a "right" to him. Paul attempts to go beyond justice to mercy and peace, even playing on Onesimus' name (useful one) in his words to Philemon:

> I am appealing to you for my child, Onesimus, whose father I have become during my imprisonment. Formerly he was useful to you, but now he is indeed useful both to you and to me. I am sending him, that is, my own heart, back to you. I wanted to keep him with me in your place during my imprisonment

for the gospel; but I preferred to do nothing without your consent, in order that your good deed might be voluntary and not something forced. Perhaps this is the reason he was separated from you for a while, so that you might have him back forever, no longer as a slave but more than a slave, a beloved brother — especially to me but how much more to you, both in the flesh and in the Lord (Phlm 1:12-16).

Creative Christians find ways to build peace in our world. If things run true-to-form, they will find themselves not only a minority but often a persecuted minority. The world may not value what Christians have to offer. Christians are often considered naive, out-of-touch, and a nuisance. Sometimes we are tolerated. At other times we are ignored. Sometimes we are hauled into court. At other times we are harassed by verbal abuse or ostracized by "friends." Authorities are frequently uncertain how to deal with us and may rely on force as their tool of choice. If we remain passive and quiet, we are readily accepted. If we do "our thing" off in our own world, folks will leave us alone.

We become a problem when we publicly express what we believe. When we offer our gospel alternatives to society's way of acting, we are labeled as "radicals" who are disrupting society. If we refuse to accept such conflict or are fearful of the consequences of gospel reality, it will be difficult for us to embrace wholehearted rootedness in a gospel lifestyle.

Christians are called to *do something* to build a gospel style of society in their world. Different people do different things. What is not tolerable in gospel people is a do-nothing attitude.

Jesus did not accept the status quo of his society. Not only did he claim to be God's son, but he started talking about the way God wanted things to be. That was unacceptable to those in authority. They developed a plan to get rid of Jesus. In their short-sightedness, they did not realize the weakness of such action. The authorities knew Jesus was a threat to structures that were dear to them. Such a threat cannot be tolerated!

Every day he was teaching in the temple. The chief priests, the scribes and the leaders of the people kept looking for a way to kill him; but they did not find anything they could do, for all the people were spellbound by what they heard (Luke 19:47-48). So they watched him and sent spies who pretended to be honest, in order to trap him by what he said, so as to hand him over to the jurisdiction and authority of the governor (Luke 20:20).

Things have not changed a great deal since the time of Jesus. Christians are told by Jesus that they will suffer persecution. Don't be surprised when it happens. At the same time, be sure that what you do is gospel-based and not simply ego-based. Both ego-based and gospel-based actions can be persecuted. You are blessed only if what you do flows from a gospel *vision*.

It is no easy thing to confront people or nations with our vision of peace. When the Gulf War was at its height in early 1991, I grew more and more uneasy with what was happening. I knew people from Iraq. They were people like me. They were being killed to convince their dictator to stop his aggression. At the same time, families with men and women in the Gulf were fearful that their relatives might be killed. What is a peacemaker to do in such a situation?

When the war was over, we honored our returning soldiers. But what had we gained with all the violence? What had we accomplished that had required such bloodshed among so many people? People who are brothers and sisters according to the gospel. I was unhappy with what we had done. The war seemed almost inevitable; it seemed the only way to deal with the issue — according to our politicians. I wasn't certain what I could do, but I mourned our inability to find a peaceful settlement. I mourned my inability to find alternatives. Yet the gospel kept calling me to care for everyone involved. Trying to be a Christian peacemaker was (is) no easy task. It is, in fact, a very uneasy task.

In such a reality case, how does a Christian peacemaker act? Can we support what the gospel abhors? It is obvious that I need to deepen my faith and face the practical implications of peacemaking in such situations. Lots of people would wave the flag and tell me to "love it or leave it!" But it's not that simple. Trying to discover *how* to love my country in these situations is difficult. The gospel may not allow me to support violence. If I choose a way that objects to war, am I less patriotic or more so? Gospel people cannot give up seeking ways of peace. But what a struggle it can be!

To Summarize

1. We have only one God. God alone deserves our worship. God does not tolerate false gods, no matter how attractive they may be.

2. God does not want to be replaced by anything or anyone else.

3. God invites us to allow leisure to be part of life. It is healthy for both body and spirit.

4. Jesus is God's son, come among us as revealer, savior, healer, teacher, and friend. Jesus, in his humanity, is the sacrament of the presence of God. Without Jesus, nothing else makes sense. Jesus, in his humanity, offers us the way to communion with God. There is no other savior, no other way to salvation. Jesus saves us. Jesus is the center and core of our faith.

5. The gospel reveals God's way of life that Christians are called to follow.

6. The Beatitudes offer attitudes and viewpoints that identify the Christian.

　　a) The ability to acknowledge dependence on God;

　　b) A willingness to mourn when either personal or social conditions do not fit God's will. There is a passionate desire in the Christian to replace inequities with justice;

　　c) Christians ''see through'' dishonesty, rationalizations, escapism, passivity, and other ways of hiding from the demands of the gospel. Christians "see into" the ways of the gospel in specific situations, and apply gospel principles and values;

d) Christians recognize mercy as having an intimate connection to justice and love. Mercy outlaws such things as retribution, revenge, and aggression as ways of solving human problems;

e) Peacemaking is tough business. It dreams of a world that allows for human growth and development. It builds an environment that nurtures the human spirit. Absence of conflict is never enough for the peacemaker of the gospel. Peacemakers seek to build a world that allows freedom and joy to blossom;

f) Gospel people will face persecution and pain. Jesus does not have a pie-in-the-sky approach in his *vision.* There will be plenty of resistance to the gospel approach to life.

7. Because resistance to the gospel is not only external, but also internal, Jesus gives us his Spirit as the power that enables us to continue on the path of gospel living.

8. Without communion with Jesus, we are weakened in our ability to live a gospel lifestyle. Prayerfulness, tailored to fit each person's approach to God, is an essential ingredient of the gospel *vision.*

9. In order to follow the gospel, we need the support and strength, the loving confrontation and affirmation of a faith-community. The call of Jesus is a call to unity and communion. We join together to achieve the vision. We are not meant to be loners on the journey. Community is a gift of the Holy Spirit, bonding us to one another. We are one people.

10. It may seem obvious, but a Christian needs to hear the word of God, listen to it in solitude, and reflect on

it personally and with others. We will not be able to follow the gospel if it is unknown to us.

11. Surrender is an essential ingredient of the gospel vision. As intimacy with Jesus grows, we more readily surrender to Jesus. Anything that is an obstacle to intimacy will be discarded. We have many personal ideas, opinions, desires, and attitudes. If they become an obstacle to a gospel life, we surrender them. Our surrender occurs because we freely *choose* gospel ideas, opinions, desires, and attitudes when our own are in conflict with them.

12. The faith-community will speak out with boldness because of Jesus. In his name the powerful word of the gospel will be proclaimed. We will not conform to anything that is counter to the gospel. Hard as this may be, it will be done. We bring a gospel alternative to the conformity that uses brutality or isolation to deny the truth. Our power is the Holy Spirit. All things are possible!

13. The Blessed Mary is honored because she is the mother of Jesus. Her dignified and strong faithfulness to God's word is a model for men and women. Her deliberate choice to trust God in difficult circumstances is a model of courage. She shows the power of a woman freely choosing to surrender to a God she loves. Her prayer shows a strong sense of Scripture wisdom and tradition. "My soul tells out the greatness of the Lord, my spirit has rejoiced in God my Savior . . . the mighty God has done great things for me. His name is holy" (Luke 1:46-47, 49 — REB).

Reflection

How do I react to the Beatitudes' approach to being a Christian? How would I describe a Christian? How does being dependent upon God affect my daily life? What changes do I need to make to be more God-centered? If I mourn about the rejection of God's kingdom, what do I intend to do about it? Is sin a purely personal thing? How do I understand "sin" in my life or the life of the community? How do mercy and justice connect in my life? Do I use mercy to avoid justice? How willing am I to engage in gospel peacemaking? How will I deal with the consequences? What will enable me to be faithful to the gospel when I am persecuted for my faithfulness? Why is the faith-community important to me? What contribution do I make to the faith-community? Do my riches get in the way of trusting God? What can I do about it? How well do I "see through" things and get to reality? Am I easily fooled by specious arguments? How do I react to the influence of advertising? How clear am I about the difference between my needs and my wants? How can I build better ways of peace within my personal relationships? How can I build better ways of peace on a social, national, or international level? How do I feel about this "community" stuff? Can I hope to grow without prayerfulness? How does prayer affect my ability to develop a healthy Christian lifestyle?

———————

We Christians have great power through the Spirit and the Word. The *vision* can stimulate a reappraisal of our way of life. The good news can make a difference in our world. Jesus calls us to be faithful to the *vision* he has shared with us. As the king wrote to Mrs. Anna in the musical *The King and I:* "All that shall matter about man is that he shall have tried his utmost best!"

CHAPTER ELEVEN

Vital Signs

Jesus and his *vision* are at the heart of the Christian life. In ordinary faith-life, special signs reveal the presence of Jesus. These "signs" of Jesus' presence touch us at significant moments of life.

We call these signs "Sacraments." Through words and actions, through the touch of "earthy" things, the faith-community experiences the presence of Jesus. In significant moments of life Jesus touches us with his caring presence and power.

The Sacraments

There are seven special life-signs (sacraments) in the Church. Prior to these seven, Jesus, in his human nature, is the "fundamental sacrament." In his humanity, Jesus reveals in a clear way who God is and what God is about. Jesus builds on the revelation of the Hebrew Testament and enriches its images and ideas of God. Jesus brings to light new aspects of God's own life. No one has or will ever reveal God as clearly as did Jesus. Most especially did Jesus reveal God as an "Abba," a close-at-hand "Father." Jesus is rightly called the "fundamental sacrament." Jesus' words, actions, passion, death, and resurrection reveal the presence, power, and love of God.

The Church is the "Sacrament of Jesus." Without Jesus there would be no sacraments at all. When the Church acts like Jesus, she is "sacrament" of Jesus. The Church is the moon reflecting the light of the son, Jesus Christ. Church has both positive and negative experience in its long lifetime. It has experienced many ways that lead away from the Lord. Hence, Christians are constantly prodded to choose the light rather than the darkness. These sacraments proclaim Jesus, the light, to the faith-community. They present visible images that speak of God at work among us.

There is both revelation and mystery in the sacraments. The signs accomplish more than we can explain. There is power at work that is not subject to human analysis and understanding. God touches human life in a special way through these "signs." The signs can be seen by human eyes and examined by human science. But what happens in the heart and spirit of people is not subject to the rules of science.

Something real and powerful occurs when God's power touches human life. The mystery of God's love goes beyond human "seeing" and examination. More happens than the signs can say. But they point the direction for us. They tell us of something special that God chooses to do. The more pliable our minds and hearts, the more we experience the love of God made present in sacrament.

> But we speak of God's wisdom, secret and hidden, which God decreed before the ages for our glory. . . . "What no eye has seen, nor ear heard, nor the human heart conceived, what God has prepared for those who love him" — these things God has revealed to us through the Spirit (1 Cor 2:7, 9).

To the scientist, things are just things. Words are just words. That is one dimension of truth. But things also contain another message and have another voice. A mountain may be a pile of volcanic rock to a scientist, but it can speak to me of experiences on mountains that have changed my life. Water may be a chemical composition to the scientist, but it speaks to me of cleansing and refreshment that is not contained in a scientific analysis of water. Things can speak to us and offer signs of meaning that go beyond scientific explanations.

They speak to the heart. They communicate a reality that is seen only with the eyes of faith. Sacraments proclaim a rich wisdom that cannot be analyzed by science. "But we have this treasure in clay jars, so that it may be made clear that this extraordinary power belongs to God and does not come from us" (2 Cor 4:7).

Human relationships are vital for human life. People are at their best when they have healthy relationships. They feel least human when they lack relationships and experience terminal loneliness. Jesus seeks to relate to us. Union with Jesus enables us to experience God's love. Jesus is "sacrament," making God's love present to us. "Everyone who believes that Jesus is the Christ has been born of God. . . . Who is it that conquers the world but the one who believes that Jesus is the Son of God?" (1 John 5:1, 5).

The Church is sacrament for all people, not just for Catholics. When its actions reflect those of Christ, it reflects the light of Christ to all. The sacraments proclaim "Jesus is present to his people!"

Baptism

Baptism is a sign that says "You are marked, embraced, and loved as a member of our faith-community." The Church offers the gifts of the community to the baptized. In return, it expects the baptized person to be a responsible Christian. The faith-community teaches and shows the baptized person the way to be a Christian. Simple signs of water and words, anointing and embrace, proclaim that the baptized person belongs to the community. You are not an outsider or merely tolerated. You and we are one. The baptismal action proclaims this in a public way. You are named a child of God. The faith-community passes on to you the gospel teachings and traditions.

These signs speak of being embraced by God in a special way. Externally, there are only words and signs. What is seen is the gateway to a fuller meaning. God speaks to the baptized. God chooses to proclaim union with the baptized through the signs. A heart of faith "sees through" the signs to the reality of God at work. There is mystery here and realistic truth.

After people are baptized it is vital that they grow up in a faith-filled family and community. To isolate them from the faith community is to deprive them of part of the gift of baptism. The new member of the community needs to learn the ways of the community. They need models for following Jesus. Isolation from the community is a disservice to the newly baptized. As the newly baptized grow in their response to the gospel, the community supports their efforts to be faithful.

Confirmation

We live in a world that does not always support Christian development. Alone, we would be no match for unhealthy influences. Another sign of initiation in the faith comes with confirmation. In a community action, we proclaim "You are not alone." The Spirit of Jesus dwells in you. Confirmation tells us we are empowered for the faith-journey. With ritual and word, we affirm that the Holy Spirit is our source of power. In the battle with evil and temptation, we are strengthened by the Holy Spirit. Initiated into community life, we can do what Jesus asks of us in the gospel! Again, something special happens that is spoken in sign and word. Faith stands in awe at the mystery of God's care for the continuing growth of the Christian.

At this point of Christian growth, the *vision* should be part of the one who receives confirmation. The gospel vision is now proclaimed as the vision of this Christian. Now, life is lived in the light of the vision of Jesus. The Spirit within continues to strengthen the Christian in his or her development and ability to proclaim the gospel.

Penance

Honesty is a realistic policy on the faith-journey. We acknowledge we are not always faithful to our baptismal call. We find ourselves seduced by many things. Sometimes we choose little gods in preference to the real God. We choose anger and revenge rather than forgiveness and reconciliation. We allow resentment to linger in our hearts. We find ways of "getting" people we dislike or who hurt us. We get caught in a mesh of false sexual ideas and actions. We lose respect for our bodies and the body and person of others. We find ourselves cutting corners on honesty in order to get ahead. We use deceit and lies to avoid reality. We neglect the needs of others, condemn the poor, and support programs that bring death rather than life. We invest energy in anti-life programs. We look down on the "thems" we consider inferior to ourselves. We seek power to dominate rather than serve. We are not always faithful to spouse or to vows we made as Religious. Despite our community ties, despite the power of the Spirit, we are unfaithful. Unfaithfulness diminishes our ability to live a gospel life.

Jesus invites us to deal with this unfaithfulness. Both privately and communally, Jesus offers his gracious, freely given forgiveness. The offer is freely made by one who chooses to offer forgiving love. We do not earn forgiveness by our actions. We are forgiven by a gracious God who loves us. In the sacrament called Penance (Reconciliation) we receive forgiveness. It frees us to be faithful gospel people. "Conversion" enables us to rely more consistently on the Spirit of Jesus rather than on our own spirit. When we separate ourselves from Jesus and community by sin, God offers forgiveness and reconciliation.

It is good to hear the words "Through the ministry of the Church (faith-community) may God grant you pardon and peace. . . ." No matter how often we come to this sacrament, we are embraced, forgiven, and refreshed in order to continue our gospel growth. A gracious, generous God offers such reconciliation repeatedly. It is a freely given gift that enables us to come to deeper communion with God, neighbor, and self.

The sacrament of penance goes beyond mere words and signs. Something is done that is mystery. It is similar to the sign that Jesus gave to Peter after Peter's denial. Scripture says:

> But Peter said, "Man, I do not know what you are talking about!" At that moment, while he was still speaking, the cock crowed. The Lord turned and looked at Peter. Then Peter remembered the word of the Lord, how he had said to him, "Before the cock crows today, you will deny me three times." And he went out and wept bitterly (Luke 22:60-62).

Practically speaking, we observe only a look between two people. But it is obvious that this "look" touched Peter's heart. It was more than just the eyes of two people looking at each other. It caused Peter to remember and to mourn his weakness. The look was a sacrament of something more real than eyes seeing one another. Something bigger happened in this moment of communication. Power moved Peter to know and repent his sin. Likewise, in the sacrament, the signs point to things that are unseen but real. We are faced with the mystery of God's forgiving love at work through this sacrament.

Matrimony

A special relationship may bring another person into our life in an exclusive communion. Here, too, the faith-community plays a role. The exclusive love of two caring people establishes a bond that requires a lifetime commitment. Even before the community affirms this love, the bond is real. The couple affirm their love in a public way. They publicly proclaim their commitment to one another. They come before the community and acknowledge their love for one another. That love is witnessed and strengthened by the community.

This bond is relational as much as it is contractual. For many years we spoke of marriage as a contract. Breaking the contract was bad news. It was often punished by society and the faith-community. Couples were expected to grit their teeth and remain together no matter how debilitating the relationship became. But we are regaining a renewed gospel understanding of marriage.

The relationship between couples is vitally important and affirmed by the Church. The Church affirms that this relationship is meant to be permanent. At its heart is love, not mere bonding. It is a covenant love that demands more than any contract could spell out. Marriage partners bring to one another a supportive presence that helps the spouse sustain a life commitment. Partners offer each other a safe space that allows for forgiveness and healing. They bring to each other a relationship that creates an atmosphere for growth. As intimacy blossoms, the couple reflect the love of Jesus more clearly.

What the couple do together will touch this community. Their love will reflect the love that Jesus has for all of us. The path of faithful marriage (matrimony) needs support, models, and affirmation from a caring faith-community. In the sacrament of marriage, a mutual proclamation takes place. The couple proclaim their mutual love for one another. The community proclaims this love as a sign of Jesus' love for all his people. Fidelity requires faith. That faith is supported by the faith-community. This dimension of the *vision* of Jesus is difficult to achieve without such support. No one is ever perfectly prepared for all that marriage may bring.

The sacrament of matrimony is a proclamation of faith and love both by the couple and by the community. There is mystery in the sign of a couple's mutual love that reveals the love of Jesus for the Church. "This is a great mystery, and I am applying it to Christ and the church. Each of you, however, should love his wife as himself, and a wife should respect her husband" (Eph 5:32-33).

Holy Orders

God's call to minister within the community as priest brings another service to the community. Called from the community, the priest serves the community. The priest (presbyter) shares in the ministry of the local bishop. The bishop pastors the "local church," and the priests are joined with the bishop in ministering to the faith communities. Priests are servants of the people, available to lead in ways that enable the community to grow. The servant-leader called "priest" gathers the community in prayer. The servant-leader called "priest" proclaims the presence of God among us. The priest is dedicated to a personal gospel life that encourages others. Brokenness is shared and God's power is revealed in the healing of brokenness. The servant-leader called "priest" calls the community to the ways of justice. The servant-leader called "priest" ministers to the community in a dedicated and faithful manner.

Without good leadership, a community easily disintegrates. The servant-leader called priest is one (among others) who invites the community to faithfulness to the gospel. The servant-leader called priest (and others) ministers and proclaims the sacramental encounters that empower the community. The sacrament of holy orders offers a signed way of calling servants to minister within the faith-community. Ordination empowers the person to reflect in life what is done in word and action.

At the ordination rite of a deacon, the bishop hands a book of the Gospels to each deacon. The bishop urges them to "believe what they read, teach what they believe, and practice what they preach." This phrase can easily apply to the priest. Servant among the people, the priest is one with the people of God. Together they believe what they proclaim, teach what they believe, and practice what they preach!

Anointing of the Sick

On our journey, we face weakness and sickness. We face illnesses that bring the threat of death or diminish our capacity to live a full life. Jesus knows his people and sees their need for healing. We are overwhelmed by tragedy and pain. It is enough to diminish or stifle our faith. Jesus comes, in a community setting, to proclaim that he is with us. In the sacrament of the anointing of the sick, he surrounds us with his love and the love of the faith-community. Whatever it takes to help us walk with our pain and hurt, Jesus is present to proclaim that we are not alone. His power is present to heal (if we need that) or to assure us of his loving presence (if we need that).

In a community setting, with loving people gathered round, we proclaim Jesus' love for the sick and suffering. What seems impossible alone is possible as the community makes Jesus' presence real to us. The words and signs proclaim the presence of the compassionate Jesus. This sacrament proclaims the worth of those who suffer. It proclaims the worth of those who can give only their presence and pain. The sacrament tells society that no one is worthless, not even the most helpless among us.

I remember one experience of the power of this sacrament. I was chaplain at a county nursing home. We used to have a communal anointing once each month during Mass. Part of the ritual calls for a silent time when all are quiet. All present laid their hands on the shoulder of the one next to them. Every person was feeling a human touch. In the silence of this community, attentive to God, the presence of the Spirit was palpable.

It was in this quiet time that I experienced a sense of Jesus' presence. The power of Jesus, working in this broken, prayerful community, was clear to me. God's love for those who are poor and powerless was clearly felt. Many volunteers spoke of a similar experience in this sacramental moment. The power of Jesus, poured out on this community, was felt by many, not only the sick. It made us aware that God loves to be with people in their brokenness.

Eucharist

Of all the signs of friendship, none surpasses the Eucharist. In this sacrament, the communion of community is proclaimed. It is nourishment, true. It offers forgiveness of sin, true. It is sacrifice. It is meal among friends. But Jesus is especially delighted to proclaim in word and sign, "I am with you." Like no other sacrament, the Eucharist is all Jesus. It is the sign of communion with his people. It is proclamation of his word that calls to conversion. It is presence in a way that enables us to *be* faithful Christians. It is a call for us to be "one" with all people.

Our covenant with Jesus is a new covenant. Jesus will never break this covenant with us. His word is true and he is faithful. His words, actions, death, and resurrection speak to us of faithful love. Jesus saves us. He is our redeemer. Jesus heals us. Eucharist shouts out the wonder of Jesus — present to us here and now.

In Eucharist, we can contrast the sign of Jesus' faithfulness with the image of our weakness. Over and over, Eucharist after Eucharist, we are confronted and affirmed by faithful love. At the table of love, we gather as friends. Our common gathering-action says we are to be a community that loves. We are to be a community that hears the word of God and acts on it. We are to be a community that offers a gospel vision to the human family. At this table we pray in the name of the whole human family. Their joy and their pain is our joy and our pain.

The scriptural word often confronts our failures. In this place of acceptance, Jesus is with us to deal with failure. This is a community whose faith will get me through my doubts. This is a community whose acceptance will enable me to love myself. This is a community whose members will struggle alongside me. Together we will follow the gospel we hear proclaimed here. This gathered community is a vital ingredient of worship.

We gather as one people, united to each other by the Holy Spirit. What is done here, in this setting, is to be done in the setting of everyday life. But consider who gathers with us. Consider the people Jesus calls to be his friends and to be friends to each other.

There is the woman whose tongue sharpens itself on gossip. Here is a young man with needle marks on his arms. We catch a glimpse of a young person who long ago left the Church. There are people here who have had abortions. Others are unwed mothers. Someone else has been arrested for fraud and just got out of jail. There are beggars here as well as single mothers. There are divorced people here and kids whose noisy behavior annoys those around them. There is a couple here who have cared for a child affected by Down's syndrome, and another whose child ran away from home. Another single person lives with an elderly parent, giving compassionate care. There are parents here who are interested only in academics; others for whom sports is an idol. There are people here who have abused children. Some have known few sober days. There are couples with healthy families and children who make them proud. Many people here are involved with parish activities. Others are only involved in criticizing everything that is done in the parish. Some people here haven't spoken to each other for years. Prayerful and dedicated people are here. There are Native Americans here as well as African Americans. People from Southeast Asia and Haiti gather around this altar. Some people are Spanish-speaking, others speak with an Irish, Polish, or German accent. There are grandparents here who care for grandchildren because mother and father both work. There are the widows and widowers here, barely able to survive on a meager income. There are good and mediocre presiders here as well as exciting and boring preachers.

In short, around this table are gathered people from all walks of life. People who are attractive and people who are rigid and opinionated. People whose company we enjoy as well as those whom we would rather avoid. People who are honest and helpful as well as people who lie and ignore needs. We are gathered together and called to be *one* family. Jesus counts us all as friends. Jesus invites us to do the same. We need Jesus if we are going to embrace such a motley group of people. Jesus comes to us in communion. What we could not do alone becomes possible because of Jesus. To remain separate from others would deny the reality of what we do at this table of the Lord.

I am always learning how to be "sacrament" to these people and to let them be "sacrament" to me. I need the reminder and nourishment of Eucharist over and over. I need to hear the word of God in the Bible. I need to hear the word broken open and shared. I need to offer a sign of my giving of self. I am at the table as Jesus touches my spirit to transform me. I need to experience unity in communion with Jesus and my brothers and sisters. Jesus accepts me the way I am. He calls me to do likewise for the people in my life. To be sent, at each Eucharist, is a regular reminder of who I am. "The Mass is ended, go in peace to serve the Lord" [and one another!].

> Do you not know that you are God's temple, and that God's Spirit dwells in you? If anyone destroys God's temple, God will destroy that person. For God's temple is holy, and you are that temple" (1 Cor 3:16-17).

Issues in a Gospel Community

Jesus addresses issues that hinder growth in gospel people. Jesus is realistic about his human family. He realizes they do not always relate well to one another. He knows how easily the appeal of power and wealth can override the call of the gospel. Jesus is practical in dealing with issues of anger and enmity. He deals with attempts to domesticate God and manipulate people to achieve selfish goals. The gospel teaches about such things. These teachings call people to greater fidelity in living the gospel. Jesus addresses both positive and negative issues touching our lives as Christians.

Arrogance

Arrogance or image-making to achieve a reputation is not tolerated in gospel people. Jesus addresses this issue in a parable
that speaks for itself. Listen to the message about judgment
and arrogance.

> He also told this parable to some who trusted in themselves
> that they were righteous and regarded others with contempt.
> "Two men went up to the temple to pray, one a Pharisee and
> the other a tax collector. The Pharisee, standing by himself, was
> praying thus, 'God, I thank you that I am not like other people;
> thieves, rogues, adulterers, or even like this tax collector. I fast
> twice a week; I give a tenth of all my income.' But the tax col-
> lector, standing far off, would not even look up to heaven, but
> was beating his breast and saying, 'God, be merciful to me, a
> sinner.' I tell you, this man went down to his home justified
> rather than the other; for all who exalt themselves will be
> humbled, but all who humble themselves will be exalted" (Luke
> 18:9-14).

Authority

Jesus addresses the issue of authority. He does not speak of
destroying authority. Jesus addresses the manner in which
authority is to be exercised. Jesus sees people who have
authority as servants in the community. Listen to the words
of Jesus:

> A dispute also arose among them as to which one of them was
> to be regarded as the greatest. But he said to them, "The kings
> of the Gentiles lord it over them; and those in authority over
> them are called benefactors. But not so with you; rather the
> greatest among you must become like the youngest, and the
> leader like one who serves. For who is greater, the one who
> is at the table or the one who serves? Is it not the one at the
> table? But I am among you as one who serves" (Luke 22:24-27).

Relationships

Jesus speaks of the value of relationships. Such a fundamental element of the gospel deserves rich treatment. Jesus knew

the human heart. He knew how difficult it is to develop and maintain sound relationships. At the same time, he realized how important relationships are for personal growth and development. What do we do when we have a "falling out" with another person? How does Jesus expect us to act?

> "If another member of the church sins against you, go and point out the fault when the two of you are alone. If the member listens to you, you have regained that one. But if you are not listened to, take one or two others along with you, so that every word may be confirmed by the evidence of two or three witnesses. If the member refuses to listen to them, tell it to the church; and if the offender refuses to listen even to the church, let such a one be to you as a Gentile and a tax collector" (Matt 18:15-17).

> "So when you are offering your gift at the altar, if you remember that your brother or sister has something against you, leave your gift there before the altar and go; first be reconciled with your brother or sister, and then come and offer your gift" (Matt 5:23-24).

> "Why do you see the speck in your neighbor's eye, but do not notice the log in your own eye? Or how can you say to your neighbor, 'Friend, let me take out the speck in your eye,' when you yourself do not see the log in your own eye? You hypocrite, first take the log out of your own eye, and then you will see clearly to take the speck out of your neighbor's eye" (Luke 6:41-42).

Power

Power seduces us. We begin to think we are the "savior." We cannot tolerate opposition to our ideas. We act as though we are infallible. We use force to impose our will on others. So subtle is the temptation that we rationalize the most oppressive activity through some justification. Whether we are parents or teachers, police or mayors, presidents or pastors, pope or bishop, student leaders or mother's guild president, gang leader or head of a pro-life organization, we are subject to the temptation — use power to control and dominate others.

Thus says the Lord GOD: Ah, you shepherds of Israel who have been feeding yourselves! Should not shepherds feed the sheep? You eat the fat, you clothe yourselves with the wool, you slaughter the fatlings; but you do not feed the sheep. You have not strengthened the weak, you have not healed the sick, you have not bound up the injured, you have not brought back the strayed, you have not sought the lost, but with force and harshness you have ruled them. . . . Therefore, you shepherds, hear the word of the LORD: Thus says the Lord GOD, I am against the shepherds; and I will demand my sheep at their hand, and put a stop to their feeding the sheep; no longer shall the shepherds feed themselves. I will rescue my sheep from their mouths, so that they may not be food for them (Ezek 34:2-4, 9-10).

Wealth/Riches

The accumulation of wealth can be an obstacle to following the gospel. Like power, wealth gives the impression of wisdom. As Tevye says in *Fiddler on the Roof,* ''When you're rich they think you really know!'' Wealth provides money to buy whatever is needed for the ''good life.'' It provides material luxuries that can become necessities. It creates a myth about one's talents and abilities. Wealth makes us feel secure, untouchable, and free to do whatever money can achieve. Wealth is sometimes gained at the price of other peoples' freedom. It can be preserved at the cost of other peoples' work. It can lead to injustice and oppression in order to preserve a rich lifestyle. It need not do this, but it can. Wealth subtly deceives us. The danger must be faced and dealt with. Jesus is clear in addressing this issue:

As he was setting out on a journey, a man ran up and knelt before him, and asked him, ''Good Teacher, what must I do to inherit eternal life?'' . . . ''You know the commandments: 'You shall not murder; You shall not commit adultery; You shall not steal; You shall not bear false witness; You shall not defraud; Honor your father and mother.' '' He said to him, ''Teacher, I have kept all these since my youth.'' Jesus, look-

ing at him, loved him and said, "You lack one thing; go, sell
what you own, and give the money to the poor, and you will
have treasure in heaven; then come, follow me." When he
heard this, he was shocked and went away grieving, for he had
many possessions (Mark 10:17, 19-22).

Then Jesus looked around and said to his disciples, "How hard
it will be for those who have wealth to enter the kingdom of
God!" And the disciples were perplexed at these words. But
Jesus said to them again, "Children, how hard it is to enter the
kingdom of God! It is easier for a camel to go through the eye
of a needle than for someone who is rich to enter the kingdom
of God." They were greatly astounded and said to one another,
"Then who can be saved?" Jesus looked at them and said, "For
mortals it is impossible, but not for God; for God all things are
possible" (Mark 10:23-27).

Part of the reason is that when we have wealth we tend
to rely on it. It pushes God out of the picture. It becomes a
"strange god" that replaces the real God. When we experience
what wealth can do, we give it more worship than it deserves.
It is a concrete, in-the-hand resource. It is easier to accept and
rely on wealth than on a God who seems distant and mysteri-
ous. Caught in this trap, wealth replaces God. We can deal
with this temptation with the help of the Spirit of Jesus. As
Jesus says: "For mortals it is impossible, but not for God; for
God all things are possible" (Mark 10:27). "Take care! Be on
your guard against all kinds of greed; for one's life does not
consist in the abundance of possessions" (Luke 12:15).

The Poor

There is a gospel word about relating to the poor. Jesus loves
the poor. He gathers them in the arms of his concern. They
are people to be treated with dignity and respect. The climb
up the ladder of financial or social success can create attitudes
of elitism. "You grease my palm, I'll grease yours" expresses
part of what we accept as "normal." To such an attitude Jesus
offers this advice:

He said also to the one who had invited him, "When you give a luncheon or dinner, do not invite your friends or your brothers or your relatives or rich neighbors, in case they may invite you in return, and you should be repaid. But when you give a banquet, invite the poor, the crippled, the lame, and the blind. And you will be blessed, because they cannot repay you, for you will be repaid at the resurrection of the righteous" (Luke 14:12-14).

I appreciate that the gospel is hard to follow. Jesus is direct and clear. It is hard to find a way around his words. We need not isolate one text and force it to say more than it can. But each text speaks loudly. It critiques many of our contented attitudes. Our conversion has a long way to go to make us total gospel people. The Lord invites us to rely on his power and his Spirit. Jesus offers these directions when he sends his disciples out to preach. They are armed only with his power.

"As you go, proclaim the good news, 'The kingdom of heaven has come near.' Cure the sick, raise the dead, cleanse the lepers, cast out demons. . . . Take no gold, or silver, or copper in your belts, no bag for your journey, or two tunics, or sandals, or a staff; for laborers deserve their food" (Matt 10:7-9).

When they returned, they told Jesus of their delight in using the power he had given them:

The seventy returned with joy saying, "Lord, in your name even the demons submit to us!" [And Jesus said to them] ". . . do not rejoice at this, that the spirits submit to you, but rejoice that your names are written in heaven." . . . "I thank you, Father, Lord of heaven and earth, because you have hidden these things from the wise and the intelligent and have revealed them to infants; yes, Father, for such was your gracious will" (Luke 10:17, 20-21).

Fear

Fear is a common feeling for us. We fear rejection and do things simply to please others. We fear the consequences of growing old. We fear a nuclear confrontation that could destroy us all.

We fear risking too much in faith lest God do things differently than we anticipate. We fear for our children, growing up in a world full of things that can destroy them. We fear for our marriages and whether we can continue in love for a lifetime of commitment. We fear new knowledge that may require a change in our lifestyle. We fear to let loose of the past lest we wind up empty-handed. We fear letting loose of anger and hatred lest we seem to be pushovers. We fear crime and distrust strangers. We fear death and accidents and avoid taking chances. We fear revealing our fears lest we look weak. We fear revealing addictions lest we be judged or our denial-escape be destroyed. Our fears touch us often. We want to be accepted and loved, cared for and respected. We will do anything to achieve such acceptance. Fear is no stranger to us.

Jesus knows us and our fears. He addresses this issue in the gospel:

> While he was still speaking, some people came from the leader's house to say, "Your daughter is dead. Why trouble the teacher any further?" But overhearing what they said, Jesus said to the leader of the synagogue, "Do not fear, only believe." . . . they came to the house of the leader of the synagogue . . . and went in where the child was. He took her by the hand and said to her, "Talitha cum," which means, "Little girl, get up!" And immediately the girl got up and began to walk about (Mark 5:35-36, 39, 41-42).

Jesus invites us to replace fear with trust. No matter what the source of our fear, Jesus acknowledges it and calls us beyond it. His acceptance of who we are, brokenness and all, builds our self-acceptance. His assurance and presence make it possible for us to go beyond fear to confidence and trust. We need not be ashamed that we are fearful. Jesus will help us deal with fear and achieve freedom and peace. With God all things *are possible!*

> When it was evening on that day, the first day of the week, and the doors of the house where the disciples were had been locked for fear of the Jews, Jesus came and stood among them and said, "Peace be with you" (John 20:19).

The gospel is filled with the wisdom of the Holy Spirit. To live a gospel life, we return again and again to the gospel. We will never exhaust the vision given by Jesus. We continue to go to the gospel, finding there a way of life that leads to wholeness and joy. Let the gospel be a stimulus to your desire to live a full Christian life. Continue to stretch your ability to live a gospel lifestyle.

> "What then is Apollos? What is Paul? Servants through whom you came to believe, as the Lord assigned to each. . . . So neither the one who plants nor the one who waters is anything, but only God who gives the growth. . . . For we are God's servants, working together; you are God's field, God's building" (1 Cor 3:5-7, 9).

Reflection

Who is the fundamental sacrament? How is the Church a sacrament? In what way is the Christian a sacrament? What is the role of the seven signs/sacraments in the life of the faith-community? How often do I use the sacrament of penance? How can I use this sacrament more effectively? Does God always heal physical illness? What does God always do when asked for healing? How does the sacrament of matrimony contribute to building a gospel community? Is God more concerned with sin or faithfulness? Why did I answer the way I did? How would I describe "faithfulness"? What does the gospel say about the exercise of authority? How does the gospel address the issue of animosity/enmity/resentment toward my neighbor? What process does the gospel offer for dealing with problems that arise between people? How do I deal with feelings that accompany hurts? Why can wealth be a problem for the Christian? How can wealth be used constructively by Christians? What is the danger that power brings? How do I use my power? What power does Jesus ask us to rely on? How do I use my authority as parent, leader, boss, pastor, supervisor, teacher, etc.?

How do I experience the power of the Holy Spirit in my life? How does my local faith-community reflect the gospel? How can I contribute to developing a caring faith-community? How do I approach the Eucharist? . . . With a sense of obligation? . . . With a sense of my need? . . . With a recognition of its power to confront me and nourish me for life? How would I describe the role of the Eucharist in my life? How well do I share the message of the gospel in everyday living? How well do I "know" the gospel message? What do I intend to do (or continue to do) to deepen my gospel lifestyle? Why do I think relationships are important? How well do I listen to God and the people in my life? How well do I understand others? Am I always giving advice before actually hearing the problem? Do I use "canned" responses when talking about the gospel? How can I be more genuine in sharing the gospel? Do I realize that all ways of sharing the gospel — words, experience, life itself — are ways of evangelizing? Do I believe in the power of the Holy Spirit dwelling within me? How real is my relationship with Jesus? What is the role of the priest in the faith-community? How often do you affirm others in their call to ministry?

If then there is any encouragement in Christ, any consolation from love, any sharing in the Spirit, any compassion and sympathy, make my joy complete: be of the same mind, having the same love, being in full accord and of one mind. Do nothing from selfish ambition or conceit, but in humility regard others as better than yourselves. Let each of you look not to your own interests, but to the interests of others. Let the same mind be in you that was in Christ Jesus, who, though he was in the form of God, did not regard equality with God as something to be exploited, but emptied himself, taking the form of a slave, being born in human likeness. And being found in human form, he humbled himself and became obedient to the point of death — even death on a cross. Therefore God also highly exalted him and gave him the name that is above every name, so that at the name of Jesus every knee should bend, in heaven and on earth and under the earth, and every tongue confess that Jesus Christ is Lord, to the glory of God the Father (Phil 2:1-11).

CHAPTER TWELVE

The Impossible Dream

I've written of many issues in the course of this book. This chapter gathers together some problems we face in today's world. Christians today have the opportunity to bring hope to our world. Even in the face of a multitude of problems, a pessimistic Christian would be a contradiction in terms. Faith in Jesus offers hope and is the foundation for our hope. No matter how dark the situation, we bring the light of Jesus to it. If we fail to bring the lived gospel to our world, we are useless Christians.

On the One Hand

Our world has many problems. It is filled with violence, loneliness, anger, addiction, poverty, hopelessness, isolation, war, a faltering economic system, political corruption, threats, ecological disasters, and a host of personal problems. It would seem that the power of evil is dominating our world and its people. The thousands of people who face the consequences of abuse and rejection, divorce, and dysfunctional family life form an ever enlarging community. The gap between rich and poor grows wider. Greater portions of wealth in America are held by fewer people, while the majority struggle for a piece of the economic pie. Unemployment and lack of job security does psychological and economic damage to thousands of people. There is a powerful ripple effect on families and children.

The sexual exploits of people in positions of trust has eroded confidence in priests, ministers, teachers, coaches, day-care people, doctors, and other professionals. Pedophilia has entered our vocabulary, as has the disease AIDS. Divorce and separation touch many families. Many of the next generation are growing up without benefit of healthy parenting models. A groping generation finds escape in noise and violence, drugs and emptiness.

This scratches the surface of the destructive elements unleashed in our world today. It nudges us into paralysis, a feeling that we are helpless. The stories of hurting people touch us, especially when they are family and friends. It is not different from many other times in history. But it is happening to us. It bombards us. TV brings gruesome pictures into our homes. Newspapers regularly comment on the problems. Graphic pictures of starving children with bloated bellies are commonplace.

There is a sense of indifference in the Church. We fight with one another over what direction to take in Church life. Many people simply drop out, finding religion boring and irrelevant. Documents are issued that competently address modern problems. But few people read them. Fewer, still, implement them. They are voices crying in a wilderness of indifference and unbelief. Hope is not a prominent virtue in our time.

Many people live in the cauldron of things that destroy hope and life. People living in urban slums and farmers on bankrupt homesteads feel powerless. Life is becoming cheap. Abortions, euthanasia, doctors assisting people to commit suicide, suicide among the young, drive-by killings, homelessness for more people — these facts support the conclusion that life is cheap. No instant, magical solutions come to mind. Yet we act as though some magic method will appear to make everything right. People cling to the feeling that some brilliant formula will be discovered that will make the darkness go away.

What we suffer because of Church and society's dysfunctional behavior, we experience on a personal level as well. We are beginning to understand the powerful impact of the experiences of childhood. When our need was to be hugged and accepted, many children experienced rejection. The little child inside an adult body may still be looking for acceptance. So the adult person conforms or agrees with everyone, suppresses anger, and becomes aggressively controlling or manipulative in a desperate search for self-worth and acceptance. These tricks of the trade are ultimately unsuccessful in the search for intimacy. Manipulation drives people away. Controlling behavior scares people off. Our inner child, yearning for acceptance, again experiences rejection.

Children grow up in families in chaos because of adult addictions. A child may feel responsible for a parent who is out of control. If the child had been more obedient or smarter, Mom or Dad wouldn't have to drink! Guilt and shame show their ugly heads in the child's life. The beginning of a lifetime effort to "make up" for the guilt of another's addiction is born. Divorce may be a necessary step for the safety and health of the people involved. But for both child and parents, there is a sense that something awful has happened. Marriage is such a personal investment that its death devastates the people involved. Children often feel responsible or cannot understand. So much is lost. The adult wants to change such patterns. Yet habits of early life mangle such hopes. We continue to do the things we said we would never do. It is not easy to change perspectives that grow out of a broken or dysfunctional home life. Some people accept this as "normal" because it is the only model they know.

Sometimes people work at being "fixers," trying to save people. In modern jargon, it is called co-dependence. Our actions, attitudes, and responses enable others to evade responsibility for their addictions, habits, actions, compulsions, and behaviors. We are controlled by events and people outside ourselves. We cannot allow people to bear the consequences of their choices. We hold them up when they need to fall. We cover up for them when they need to be exposed. We support them when we ought to let them stand alone to face their "problem." We become dependent on our need to be the "fixers and saviors." We are afraid to stop such behavior because we don't know what life would be like without it. A false idea of gospel love supports such behavior. In the process, everyone experiences less life and more frustration and emptiness.

Some people get caught in the cycle of sexual dysfunctions and unhealthy sexual action alone or with others. Pornography feeds a distorted picture of reality. Respect for men and women breaks down. People are objects to be used for personal satisfaction. They cease to be human beings whose dignity demands respect. At its extreme it leads to the gruesome murder of others in an out-of-control ritual of sexual excess. Torture, pain, masochism become everyday needs in order to get excitement. Adult book stores furnish the tools for encouraging such misguided search for sexual excitement. The perpetrators may even be outstanding members of the community. Sooner or later their lack of integrity takes its toll.

Sexual dysfunctions touch people of all classes, from clergy to truck drivers, from pre-school teachers to housewives, from politicians to reporters. Men and women find themselves enmeshed in a web of destructive sexual behavior. They often use children to satisfy sexual aberrations. The cycle of destruction touches the lives of thousands of people.

People who have been the subject of sexual, emotional, or psychological abuse as children are often scarred for life. In the early years of adulthood such experiences are often pushed to the background. But the time comes when the experiences resurface. We can explore what others have done to us. We begin the process of forgiving people (often relatives) who have abused us. We deal with our own inner feelings and find ways of health. We address issues from childhood that may still influence our lives. It is no easy process. It *is* a freeing and affirming process. Denial will get us nowhere. Dealing with the issues and their consequences brings a new level of freedom. Self-worth flourishes as we realize we are not evil people.

The awful power of sexual and emotional abuse makes people feel that they are bad persons. Not just that they did bad things, but that they are bad persons. It is called "shame." It can touch the core of our inner self. It touches the way we live and relate to others. It colors the picture we have of ourselves. To deal with shame is a tough but life-giving experience. The help of a competent, compassionate guide is a practical necessity. With thousands of people being touched by such experiences, we face a problem of monumental proportions. Some researchers say that at least 25 percent of people (1 in 4) suffer some form of sexual or physical abuse. In some groups it may even reach 80 percent!

Many people refuse to accept the reality of AIDS in family members or friends. Feelings of rejection and isolation grow in the infected person. People become outcasts even to their family of origin. Some families even refuse to accept the body of an AIDS patient for burial. Denial is common. Judgment is frequent — deciding on the "badness" of the person with AIDS. The heart breaks in the face of compassion denied. Denial and cover-up take their toll on everyone involved. There is no joy here.

None of us is free from some baggage that burdens us. All of us yearn for acceptance. All of us yearn for relationships that offer life. All of us yearn for the solitude that brings us in touch with God. We may realize intellectually that behaviors which control us bring impossible stress. Yet we continue to do them. We lie to avoid reality. We pick fights to avoid honesty. We use aggressiveness to hide insecurity. We put on a good front to hide sinfulness — even from ourselves. We refuse association with the family skeleton, now out of the closet. Our need for a savior is abundantly clear.

Society also needs the perspectives and directions of a savior. We have yet to find the perfect society. Some may be better than others, but all systems have clay feet. Our savior's perspective allows us the space and freedom to question anything that fails to give dignity to people. The distribution of wealth and goods that denies anyone their dignity creates jealousy and anger. Government policy that promotes violence (or supports its pursuit) leaves corpses in its wake. Economic policies that make welfare recipients out of entire nations create a reservoir of hatred. Politicians who destroy each other with character assassination leave a residue of mistrust. Government decisions based on protecting assets of the rich while ignoring the needs of the poor give birth to deathly skepticism. Human systems repeatedly prove their inadequacy.

Around the world, violence and war lead to bloodshed and death. Nationalities slaughter one another. Centuries of hatred break open into a melee of aggressive behavior. Religious fanaticism boils over into a slaughter of the unbeliever. Quest for power uses violence and deceit to attain its goals. Ordinary people keep getting caught in the crossfire of inner and outer warfare. No one is exempt from the consequences of violence. Young and old, people of every color and economic status bear the burdens of this systemic violence. Cemeteries are populated by people of all races and creeds, of every age and ideology. Greed and power-seeking continue to support this death-dealing activity. Religious fanaticism adds fuel to these fires in the name of God. Gang rape and violence toward women leave thousands of women in a limbo of self-hatred and abandonment.

We face a plethora of problems. We Christians may not ignore them. We must deal with systemic structures that leave people out in the cold; with policies that leave people subject to manipulation by political power; with decisions that create war and violence; with the choices that leave people deprived of their freedom. Anything that requires change or new direction is a legitimate Christian concern.

Jesus had no hesitancy in forcefully declaring that people are what life is all about. Relationship is what life is about. Healthy concern for one another is what life is all about. "Just as you did it to one of the least of these who are members of my family, you did it to me" (Matt 25:40). Any system that denies human dignity to anyone needs to change. Christians with a gospel spirituality do not piously mouth prayers without also getting involved in issues that touch human life. We may not settle everything, but we will not hide behind pious clichés and personal "holy" experiences. As Paul said to Timothy: "Teach and urge these duties. Whoever teaches otherwise and does not agree with the sound words of our Lord Jesus Christ . . . is conceited, understanding nothing, and has a morbid craving for controversy and for disputes about words" (1 Tim 6:3).

A brief look at the level of violence in our world confirms a lack of respectful relationships. Children grow up in an atmosphere that shouts out "Might (guns/machoism/war machines/violence) is right." Adults feel the same way. Power is used to dominate others. When words and dialogue fail, violence is used to solve things. Centuries of hatred continue to influence the present generation. People on every side fear to give in lest they appear to be "pansies" or "sissies" in the face of power. The awful destruction of people as a way to achieve peace seems an awesome price to pay. The violence spills over into peacetime as physical and psychological problems proliferate among soldiers and civilians alike.

Gang warfare in our cities traps people in their homes. Drive-by shootings make anyone a target. Fear escalates. It may finally explode in a reactive violence. The last state is worse than the first. Violence in families is common. Domestic violence grows as unemployment and hopelessness blossom. To ignore the impact of this violence is to be an ostrich with our heads in the sand. The portrayal of violence in films and on TV only cements an attitude that violence is a tool for solving problems. Little wonder that respect for life is growing dim.

> Woe is me because of my hurt!
>   My wound is severe. . . .
> My tent is destroyed,
>   and all my cords are broken;
> my children have gone from me,
>   and they are no more;

> there is no one to spread my tent again
>   and to set up my curtains.
> For the shepherds are stupid,
>   and do not inquire of the LORD;
> therefore they have not prospered,
>   and all their flock is scattered. . . .
> Correct me, O LORD, but in just measure;
>   not in your anger, or you will bring me to nothing (Jer
>   10:19-21, 24).

Then there are the pictures of starving people. Flies crawling across the emaciated faces of children. People living on garbage heaps, getting food from dump trucks that haul the garbage from the cities to their shantytowns, shacks that barely protect people from sun and rain. Water rises and spills raw sewage into shanty houses. No electricity, no running water, no baths, nothing safe to drink. People facing these issues day after day after day. No nutritious food to eat, no place to play, no schools to attend, no stores, no money to buy with — these are people with dignity (?). How many countries have squandered their resources for a quick profit? How many people suffer because of tribal antagonisms and violence. Nations refusing to allow "such people" to enter their shores. A protectionism that blocks the pathway of compassion to maintain a lifestyle to which people have become accustomed. The problems are awesome in their magnitude — both in the "outer" world of society and in the "inner" world of the heart.

The USSR breaks up. Economic chaos follows in its wake. Awesome difficulties arise in dealing with the problems of newfound freedom. Hunger stalks the streets. Continued power struggles divert the focus from human need. Generations of silence break open into revenge on the oppressors. There is a mangling of the human spirit in the struggle for rights and human dignity. It seems safe to say that we have problems on planet earth!

On the Other Hand

Our exploration into the destructive side of life gives only a portion of the story. Life-giving things are also happening in our world.

We live in a time when both medicine and psychology have blossomed. Illnesses that only recently were death-dealing are now healed by medicine. In the course of a few decades we have come to a point where organs can be transplanted; where research is diminishing the rate of terminal cancer; where effort and money are being spent to find a cure for AIDS. Many ailments are being handled in new and better ways through the science of medicine. Psychology is developing better understanding of the human person. Many psychologists are beginning to realize the need to treat the whole person, not just psychological symptoms. There is a growing understanding of the limitations of psychology. Many holistic clinics and practitioners are springing up around the country. These incorporate practices that deal with the physical and spiritual as well as the psychological. Common sense is coming to the fore in many places.

There is growing awareness of the need to deal with grief. After a long period where extraordinary things were done to prolong life, we are beginning to deal with death more realistically. The desire of many people not to be kept alive by extreme artificial means is growing. This gives some fresh direction to the medical community. We approach death with less fear and more realism and dignity. The hospice movement is spreading in our country. People with terminal illnesses can spend their last days in a caring community. Family and friends are free to visit the sick person in a homelike setting. Rules and regulations are geared to giving people all the independence they can handle. Caring people are present to listen and help.

We have seen the breakup of a dictatorial empire in the USSR. What seemed unbelievable not many years ago has happened. Though we also see the difficulty that freedom brings, we stand in awe that an "enemy" has begun to respond to the human yearning for freedom. But their struggle reminds us that freedom takes dedication to maintain. Many of us have roots in the "old country." We wait to see how freedom will develop in former dictatorships. Countries that have been at civil war for years finally begin to make small gestures toward peace. We recognize the fragility of peace when power and control are at stake. Yet, peaceful possibilities are present.

Support groups are blossoming. In a country whose culture preaches independence, people are learning that we need one another. Consider the vast variety of people who help one another through crisis situations. Alcoholics, sex addicts, drug addicts, the divorced and separated, abused people, overeaters, work addicts, compulsive shoppers and gamblers, people dealing with grief, all finding groups to support them in seeking freedom. Alcoholics Anonymous, Overeaters Anonymous, Sexual Addicts Anonymous, Gamblers Anonymous, etc., dedicated to offering supportive help. People with AIDS find support groups as do cancer patients. People dealing with handicapped children or developmentally disabled family members find helping hands. Families dealing with Alzheimer's disease in a loved one help one another. Such compassion reflects the vision of the gospel.

More and more young people are taking time to volunteer their help in various ways. Some work with established religious groups to help the poor. Some tutor poorer students. Some work in nursing homes. Some paint and fix homes for senior citizens. The energy of many young people is pointed in the direction of helping others. Students Against Driving Drunk (SADD) provides a necessary service and goal for young people. Peer pressure can and is used to accomplish good things. Teachers and parents are working together to create an educational climate to help young people deal with tough life issues. More and more we are accepting the fact that we need to work and walk together in dealing with problems.

Habitat for Humanity and similar groups gather people together to build housing for the poor. Service to shut-ins and homebound people is common. Eucharistic ministers in many parishes provide a link to people unable to leave their homes. Parishes often have volunteers who visit lonely and forgotten people. Many people use vacation time to help in poor areas of our own and other countries. Doctors as well as nonprofessionals give time to serve people who cannot pay for services. It is done in a way that does not diminish the dignity of those who are served. Enhancing human dignity is a part of such service.

There are people who give help and support when tragedy strikes, people who continue caring long after the burial of a loved one. There are thousands of people who show their love by caring action. There are parents who band together to confront drug dealers and crack houses in their neighborhoods, strong and brave people who stand up to urban gangs and work to make their neighborhoods safe places. It takes courage to stand up to violence and crime. Many good people are doing it.

On the economic front there are companies who have begun a profit-sharing contract with employees. Union and management in some industries have begun to work together to create a better climate of dialogue that benefits everyone. Economists are beginning to talk of new ways of dealing with the problems of work and unemployment. Shorter workweeks may allow more people to have an opportunity to work. A lessened demand for wage increases may keep a business operating rather than going into bankruptcy. Better working conditions can provide incentive for better work. The issues of women in the workforce are being addressed. Facing the problem of sexual harassment will bring deserved dignity to both men and women.

Our government has been generous with food and other help when tragedy strikes foreign nations. People support generous use of surplus foods to help starving people. Flights of mercy are commonplace. People pitch in to help when earthquake and tornado devastate homes and lives. Government stands firm in confronting naked aggression. It has put aside political wrangling to achieve needed legislation. There is light in the darkness.

All problems are by no means solved. We are not out of the woods. But people are beginning to see the need for basic changes in the system. Christians realize that this kind of change touches our lifestyle. It also helps us return to basic Christian values. Within the Church we are dealing with systems that do not measure up to the gospel. Significant steps are happening that will alter the face of the Church. Their historical impact will be felt in future generations. We do not have solutions to all our problems. But we are beginning to address issues that touch the lives of many people. Being in a transitional stage may leave us uneasy. But there are signs that people are taking responsibility for their faith-life. In what is sometimes called our dysfunctional Church, there are people willing to address issues that hinder the gospel. We have a wealth of human resources to bring new life to the Church. We recognize the resource called the Holy Spirit at work among us.

Many places around the country help people in need. Soup-kitchens sprout up to offer food for people in need. Many of these places offer shelter and counseling as well. Shelters are provided for the homeless. Families open their homes to other families who have lost house and shelter. There are places where runaways can find housing. Many areas have established safe houses for people who suffer from physical and emotional abuse. Many urban areas have established legal help for those unable to afford large lawyer fees. In rural areas people are addressing the issue of the bankruptcy of farm families. People are becoming aware of the importance of talking with others about the crises that face them. There is a growing hope that we can help one another. Compassion has made us more aware of the extent of the problem. God is leading us to the light. We "see" with new eyes. We bring the strength of companionship to deal with apparently unsolvable problems.

In religion there is a dynamic searching that brings people to acknowledge their need of God. Retreat centers have programs that deal with everything from prayer to co-dependency, from alcoholism to contemplation. People-needs are being met more directly. Pious clichés are in less abundance and solid fare is becoming part of religious sharing. Groups dedicated to teaching the ways of contemplation are growing.

Ordained preachers are joining with lay people in offering programs to parishes and congregations. Men and women are working together, realizing the balance that is needed in proclaiming the message of the gospel. Lay men and women are training to become spiritual directors, competent companions on the gospel journey. We are blessed with an abundance of people who gather together to pray. Numerous twelve-step programs blossom throughout the churches to help people with addictions and as a means of growth. Many people are taking the gospel more seriously. Groups dedicated to gospel living are growing.

In the face of a world that sometimes seems out of control, many people are realizing the need for a savior like Jesus. Events are convincing many of the need for a power beyond ourselves to help us. Though the images of God vary, there is a growing hunger for God's unconditional love.

While many in positions of authority still try to maintain a controlling approach to things, many others in authority realize the need for collaboration. No one person, no matter how high their position, has all the answers. A desire for control can become addictive for people in authority, whether in Church or family, government or the local bridge club. Power-seeking for one's own advantage is a human problem. The gospel image of power for service is growing in many places. Collaboration and collegiality are no longer "bad words." Often done with hesitation, beginnings are being made. Paradise has not arrived. But there is movement that is beginning to bear fruit.

The gospel says that it is God's grace that transforms people. Laws and regulations do not have that power. At best they can create a structure and a climate for transformation. Laws whose sole purpose is control cannot transform people.

Even when people seek to assert and dominate others through control, people see through the façade. Healthy authority needs to be respected. Oppressive authority must be transformed. Otherwise, everything is lost in a "We and Them" battle. We don't want to say "We have met the enemy and they is us!" Authority used with wisdom and compassion is a gift to all. Organizations need a power source and someone to speak for the group. A good leader will not be a dictator but a servant. The good of the whole and respect for the dignity of the individual is important. Domination and manipulative control is not the gospel model for the practice of authority. With a healthy understanding of the gospel, we limited humans are giving flesh to the gospel ideal of authority. It is another sign of the Holy Spirit at work among us.

> If they make you master of the feast, do not exalt yourself; be among them as one of their number. Take care of them first and then sit down; when you have fulfilled all your duties, take your place, so that you may be merry along with them and receive a wreath for your excellent leadership (Sir 32:1-2).

In preaching around the country I meet hundreds of people whose lives are living examples of faith. I have listened to divorced people talk about the way pastors/parishes treated them. In some instances it was shabby at its best and un-Christian at its worst. Yet here they were, refusing to leave the Church that was their heritage. Having experienced rejection by the community, they refused to abandon their faith heritage. Many found gentle pastors whose concern helped make the difference. I have walked with people who lost spouses and felt absolutely stunned. Some couldn't even go shopping without being paralyzed into immobility. Yet they struggled through this awful period of grief and became compassionate companions for others who experienced loss. I have listened to stories of ordinary folks whose lives touched an entire community — like the story of Gro.

Gro was considered retarded. Gro picked up the mail for housebound people and shopped for them. He had a card that read: "If you have a need, please call. . . ." Anyone who called received whatever help Gro could give. He earned some money by cleaning a hardware store. One day an aggressive shopper made fun of Gro, telling him how dumb he was, how all he could do was to sweep floors. Gro said nothing. The storekeeper was ready to kick the man out! The next day the same thing happened. Then it happened a third time. The angry owner was ready to tell the man to leave. But Gro looked up from his sweeping and spoke directly to the man: "You have no idea how much I love you. I pray for you every night!" Needless to say, the man was dumbfounded. When asked about the incident later, Gro said quite simply: "The gospel tells us to love one another and forgive our enemies and those who persecute us. That's all I did!"

> But I say to you that listen, Love your enemies, do good to those who hate you, bless those who curse you, pray for those who abuse you (Luke 6:27-28).

When Gro died, the church was packed with people who had received his simple message of love. Gro did the simple things demanded by the gospel. There are lots of Gros in our world who will outlast the ego-centered and power-hungry. No one can block the power of such love and integrity.

The stories could continue. My point is simple. Good is truly as plentiful as evil. Hope is growing in the lives of many faithful people. We have no need to stand in a corner twiddling our thumbs while the world burns. The power of God's love is and always has been more powerful than the power of evil. That is as true today as it has ever been. Empires come and go, but the message and presence of Jesus continue to touch lives. The powerful die and are forgotten, while many little people live in the memories of those they have loved and served. "The light shines in the darkness; and the darkness did not overcome it" (John 1:5).

Dedication is a commodity that is still alive and well in our world. Good people network with one another and become a force that evil can neither tolerate nor defeat. Confronting evil may bring repression and persecution. But faith-filled dedication cannot be stilled or killed. It is enlivened by the Spirit, and no human force can bury it. It is God at work among and within a people in love with God.

> Woe to the faint hearts and nerveless hands and to the sinner who leads a double life! Woe to the feeble-hearted! They have no faith, and therefore will go unprotected. Woe to you who have given up the struggle! What will you do at the Lord's coming? (Sir 2:12-14 — REB).

Family life is being nourished by people willing to face modern issues head-on and develop an atmosphere for dealing with them. Retreats for family groups go on from Massachusetts to Wisconsin to California. Many places offer programs to deal with family life. Youth ministers invest energy and concern in dealing with adolescents. In many ministries with young people there is more acceptance and less bossiness. We are not doing enough, but much is being done. Instead of bitching about it, many people are creating positive programs to help families and young people.

Men and women are learning ways of communication. Both the women's movement and men who seek better understanding of their role have developed an atmosphere where dialogue is possible. Spirituality programs for men and women are giving us a richer sense of self-identity. These movements will improve communication between men and women. Nondefensive communication, listening without prejudice, suggesting without demanding — these are tools that make a difference in relationships. We are aware that churches do not always have their house in order. People are showing responsibility for what happens within their church/parish/congregation.

> Be quick to hear, but deliberate in answering. If you know what to say, answer your neighbor; but if not, put your hand over your mouth. Honor and dishonor come from speaking, and the tongue of mortals may be their downfall (Sir 5:11-13).

As we face the future, necessity and theology are forcing us to rethink many of our ideas and structures. My personal opinion is that necessity will change us as much as theology. Both can push us to new, creative ways of facing the future. The Holy Spirit at work is astounding to see. What seemed impossible becomes possible.

> For all who are led by the Spirit of God are children of God. For you did not receive a spirit of slavery to fall back into fear, but you have received a spirit of adoption. . . . We are children of God, and if children, then heirs, heirs of God and joint heirs with Christ — if, in fact, we suffer with him so that we may also be glorified with him (Rom 8:14-17).

A widening interest in contemplative prayer and the realization of God's presence and love among us is growing. Even the attraction of many so-called "visions" indicates how powerfully people are attracted to signs of God's presence. Such enthusiasm can be channeled in ways that can help build healthy communities.

The widespread interest in small faith communities indicates a hunger to be with folks willing to discuss Scripture, faith, and life. The people who are dedicated to the cause of justice offer another sign of God at work among us. They refuse to be silent as long as people are being hurt, killed, oppressed, and denied human dignity.

An honest critique of our times shows it to be a mixture of good and bad, light and darkness. Our Christian task is to keep bringing light and life to people. Our name for light and life is Jesus. The power of faith to transform our world is real. God is no less powerful than when David faced Goliath, or the slaves of Egypt outlasted Pharaoh under the protection of God. God is no less loving than when God proclaimed a new vision through Jesus. The Holy Spirit is no less powerful than when the words of a fisherman changed the hearts of five thousand people in one day.

Our task is to be hope-givers to our world. We will contribute positively to a world often filled with negatives. Where darkness lives, we will bring light and insight. Where destructive values dominate, we will bring the values of life. Where people deny their goodness, we will bring our acceptance. Where criticism and gossip destroy, we will bring the critique and affirmation that builds. Where fear pushes people to cower, we will bring the power of trust to overcome fear. Where violence and hatred shatter lives, we will bring the power of peace to rebuild lives. Where power has become nakedly self-serving, we will bring an authority that serves. Where economic inequalities have fractured families and people, we will bring a spirit of sharing. We have a great gift for a world in need. We share what we have received. We are caretakers of the message of the gospel. Through word and life, that message will be proclaimed to a world in need.

> For to this end we toil and struggle, because we have our hope set on the living God, who is Savior of all people, especially of those who believe (1 Tim 4:10).

> . . . so that you are not lacking any spiritual gift as you wait for the revealing of our Lord Jesus Christ. He will also strengthen you to the end, so that you may be blameless on the day of our Lord Jesus Christ. God is faithful; by him you were called into the fellowship of his Son, Jesus Christ our Lord (1 Cor 1:7-9).

Reflection

I invite you to reflect on the following Scriptures. They are a potpourri of texts from the Bible. Since each of us is unique, different texts will touch us in different ways. Allow the power of the word to give insight to your reflection. Your spirit-journey will be nourished by God's word.

> But the Lord God called to the man and said to him, "Where are you?" He said, "I heard the sound of you in the garden, and I was afraid, because I was naked; and I hid myself." He said, "Who told you that you were naked? Have you eaten from the tree of which I commanded you not to eat?" (Gen 3:9-11).

And the LORD continued, "See, there is a place by me where
you shall stand on the rock; and while my glory passes by I
will put you in a cleft of the rock, and I will cover you with my
hand until I have passed by; then I will take away my hand,
and you shall see my back; but my face shall not be seen" (Exod
33:21-23).

Now the LORD came and stood there, calling as before, "Samuel,
Samuel!" And Samuel said, "Speak, for your servant is listening" (1 Sam 3:10).

. . . and I will abolish the bow, the sword, and war from the
land; and I will make you lie down in safety. . . .
 And I will have pity on Lo-ruhamah [Not pitied],
  and I will say to Lo-ammi [Not my people],
   "You are my people";
  and he shall say "You are my God" (Hos 2:18, 23).

"You are light for all the world. A town that stands on a hill
cannot be hidden. When a lamp is lit, it is not put under a meal-
tub, but on the lampstand, where it gives light to everyone in
the house. Like the lamp, you must shed light among your
fellows, so that, when they see the good you do, they may give
praise to your Father in heaven" (Matt 5:14-16 — REB).

"You are my friends, if you do what I command you. No longer
do I call you servants, for a servant does not know what his
master is about. I have called you friends, because I have disclosed to you everything that I heard from my Father" (John
15:14-15 — REB).

"See, the home of God is among mortals.
He will dwell with them as their God;
  they will be his people,
  and God himself will be with them;
he will wipe every tear from their eyes.
Death will be no more;
mourning and crying and pain will be no more,
for the first things have passed away. . . ."

"It is done! I am the Alpha and Omega, the beginning and the
end. To the thirsty I will give water as a gift from the spring
of the water of life" (Rev 21:3-4, 6).

Now concerning love of the brothers and sisters, you do not
need to have anyone write to you, for you yourselves have been

taught by God to love one another. . . . But we urge you, beloved, to do more and more (1 Thess 4:9-10).

If a widow has children or grandchildren, they should first learn their religious duty to their own family and make some repayment to their parents, for this is pleasing in God's sight. . . . And whoever does not provide for relatives, and especially for family members, has denied the faith and is worse than an unbeliever (1 Tim 5:4, 8).

"And now, my children, listen to me: happy are those who keep my ways. Hear instruction and be wise, and do not neglect it. Happy is the one who listens to me, watching daily at my gates, waiting beside my doors. For whoever finds me finds life and obtains favor from the LORD; but those who miss me injure themselves; all who hate me love death" (Prov 8:32-36).

———————

CHAPTER THIRTEEN

Ways and Means

Many "helping" programs grace our landscape. You may be familiar with particular ones that have been helpful to you. Choose the program that best fits your needs.

The twelve-step program of Alcoholics Anonymous (AA) contains a solid and realistic process. The program can help in many situations other than alcohol addiction. One gift of the twelve-step program is a caring honesty, the ability to be direct without being destructive. It is an honesty with self, with others, and with God.

Some of the reflections on the twelve steps of AA in this chapter were stimulated by the book *Hunger for Healing: the Twelve Steps as a Classical Model for Christian Spiritual Growth* by J. Keith Miller (San Francisco, Harper, 1991). I offer you my ideas, but Miller's book often served as stimulus and guide.

The principles of Alcoholics Anonymous are designed around some simple steps to a healthy life. We *acknowledge* the harmful effects of an addiction/compulsion and its power over our life and decisions. We *recognize our inability* to deal with the problem alone. We *seek a spirituality* that fits our needs and enables us to deal with the addiction/compulsion. We develop sound relationships. We choose not to be controlled and dominated by addiction. We *reach beyond ourselves* to help others. Jesus spells it out for us:

> "If any want to become my followers, let them deny themselves and take up their cross and follow me. For those who want to

save their life will lose it, and those who lose their life for my sake will find it. For what will it profit them if they gain the whole world but forfeit their life? Or what will they give in return for their life?" (Matt 16:24-26).

Addictions

When we speak of addictions, we speak of an attachment to specific kinds of behaviors, things, or people. They begin to rule our lives with their insidious ways of control. Addictions are serious roadblocks on the way to intimacy with God.

I am not being flippant when I say that all of us suffer from addiction. . . . I mean in all truth that the psychological, neurological, and spiritual dynamics of full-fledged addiction are actively at work within every human being. The same processes that are responsible for addiction to alcohol and narcotics are also responsible for addiction to ideas, work, relationships, power, moods, fantasies, and an endless variety of other things. We are all addicts in every sense of the word. Moreover, our addictions are our own worst enemies. They enslave us with chains that are of our own making and yet that, paradoxically, are virtually beyond our control. Addiction also makes idolaters of us all, because it forces us to worship these objects of attachment, thereby preventing us from truly, freely loving God and one another. Addiction breeds willfulness within us, yet, again paradoxically, it erodes our free will and eats away at our dignity. Addiction, then, is at once an inherent part of our nature and an antagonist of our nature. It is the absolute enemy of human freedom, the antipathy of love. Yet, in still another paradox, our addictions can lead us to a deep appreciation of grace. They can bring us to our knees. . . .

Addiction exists wherever persons are internally compelled to give energy to things that are not their true desires. To define it directly, addiction is a STATE of compulsion, obsession, or preoccupation that enslaves a person's will and desire. Addiction sidetracks and eclipses the energy of our deepest, truest desire for love and goodness. We succumb because the energy of our desire becomes attached, nailed, to specific behaviors, objects or people. (Gerald May, M.D. *Addiction and Grace*, Harper & Row, 1988, pp. 4 and 14).

Addictions are serious problems. Dr. May's opinion offers ample material for serious reflection. Addictions cause much pain for many people.

Addiction and Twelve-step Spirituality

The twelve-step approach of Alcoholics Anonymous is primarily directed to the addiction of alcohol. But it can readily be applied to other situations of addiction, compulsion, sinfulness, or unhealthy patterns of behavior.

In a society where control and independence are rampant, dealing with personal addiction(s) is not an easy path to follow. Society supports many of our controlling and addictive behaviors. People deny that their behavior is a problem. Some people believe that working harder at control will eliminate personal problems. Even more satisfying (falsely) is a belief that our problems are somebody else's fault. Addictive people are skillful in laying guilt on others. Denial keeps people in the quagmire of personal problems. Since we do not acknowledge personal responsibility, we do nothing about the problem. We create a "reality" to fit our perceptions. The addiction is given new life by our denial.

Anyone trapped in addictive behavior uses many patterns to avoid facing the issue of personal helplessness. The first step of the twelve-step program is essential. There comes a point when we are miserable enough (or wise enough) to start being honest. At this point we begin to walk the path of taking responsibility for our personal problem(s). We acknowledge our powerlessness to handle our problem(s). We face reality. Our lives have become unmanageable!

We come to believe that we are powerless over our addiction, whatever it may be. Life has lost its zest and become unmanageable.

Family chaos, broken relationships, unfulfilled promises, job-related problems, depression, loneliness, exhaustion, unemployment, feelings of isolation and hopelessness are the levers that finally break through our wall of denial. Reality sets in. We acknowledge our responsibility for what is happening in our lives. Without this acknowledgement of powerlessness progress is stymied. Accepting the consequences of such an admission, we begin to live again.

This first step is crucial. Until we acknowledge that we cannot handle our problem alone, we walk in the quicksand of false bravado. When we accept the truth of our helplessness, we begin to take personal responsibility for our lives. We seek help. Hope has a new birth in us. When we drop the ''I can do it myself'' lie, we experience light and hope. It is a painful time and frightening to face, but it breaks open the gateway to health.

If acknowledgement of reality is the first step, the second flows quite naturally. I am personally unable to solve my ''problem.'' I need help. I conclude that a power greater than myself is needed to restore me to sanity. The second step makes good sense to me.

We come to understand and believe that God (a greater power than ourselves) can help us deal with our addiction in a healthy manner.

Humility sometimes gives the appearance of being the doormat virtue in the Christian basket. Too often, our definition of humility makes it sound as if we must become nobodies in order to please God. There is a healthy sense in which this is true. God *is* the source of all life and holiness. Life and holiness come to us through Jesus Christ and by the sending of the Holy Spirit. We are not our own savior. In this sense, humility *does* mean that we are powerless without God.

In another sense, humility is the ability to see and acknowledge reality. It is the earthy virtue that lives in the light of God. It acknowledges God as God and that's the truth! It acknowledges that God can help me face life and my problem(s). Whether I call God a Higher Power or some other name, the truth remains — I believe that God can restore my sanity. Out of the shambles of life God can build a new temple. Our God is willing and able to lead us from the darkness of unrealistic perspectives to light and life. Chaos and darkness are transformed by the power of God. "Little children, you are from God, and have conquered them [spirits of the Antichrist]; for the one who is in you is greater than the one who is in the world" (1 John 4:4).

Our readiness to call on God is a step in the right direction. But it is not easy to acknowledge our need. Step One makes Step Two viable. American individualism and a "me-alone" attitude can hinder acceptance of God's help. When we let loose of isolation and realize our need for help, progress is being made.

We decide to surrender our lives to God (as we understand God).

Decision time. Time to "put our money where our mouth is." This decision has far-reaching effects. It allows us to deepen our touch with reality. If we cannot handle things alone, it is obvious that we need help. In seeking help, we go right to the source — God. The directness of this step is healthy for growth. We begin to relate to others rather than remain in isolation. We seek companionship and obedience rather than go-it-aloneness and independence. No little accomplishment! It opens the door for us to seek the human help God offers. Sincere acknowledgement of need puts us in the category of the "poor in spirit" who know their need for God.

Surrender does not make us slaves. Rather it is an acknowledgement of reality. This Greater Power is a friend ready to walk with us, not a dictator trying to manipulate us. God knows we have needs. God gives gifts to make us whole. God provides people and opportunities for growth. Surrendering to God is a smart investment. It offers the way to life.

Now there are varieties of gifts, but the same Spirit; and there are varieties of services, but the same Lord; and there are varieties of activities, but it is the same God who activates all of them in everyone. To each is given the manifestation of the Spirit for the common good (1 Cor 12:4-7).

Decisions require follow-through. If we are going to be freed of our addictive behavior, or at least limit its control over us, we must continue the process.

We make a searching, fearless, and honest inventory of ourselves.

If we hope to surrender our lives to God, we need to know what is being "turned over." An inventory allows us to look at both the good and the bad elements of our lives. Without it we are unrealistic about what is being surrendered to God. This step is ongoing and never quite finished. Honesty is a key word. No more lame excuses that evade responsibility. No more blaming others. No more nonsense about our willpower. No more neglecting the abilities we have. No more feeling sorry for ourselves. No more refusals to recognize the strengths that are ours. Just plain honesty, period.

Many of us retain behaviors that were appropriate when we were younger but now need to be discarded. Being a flirt at sixteen may be cute. When you're married and have two children, flirting is definitely immature. It may be normal to shout and yell to get your way at three. Doing it at thirty-three is out of place. Uncontrolled anger and abusive behavior is somewhat less dangerous in a five-year-old than in a fifty-five-year-old. We find ourselves continuing childish behaviors as adults. Our personal inventory will help us discover what is happening. Immature behavior needs to be left behind when we grow up.

Our sensitivity to others, our compassion for the needy, our ability to listen, our skill at organizing, our gift of speaking, our ability to "feel" with others, our insights in prayer, our competencies are part of our inventory. The inventory must be balanced. We surrender both good and bad to God. In the surrender, we discover that God returns gifts with one simple request — "Use them to live the gospel of my Son." The bad things will be diminished and the good things nourished. We live the gospel and serve God more effectively.

> Work out your own salvation with fear and trembling; for it is God who is at work in you, enabling you both to will and to work for his good pleasure. Do all things without murmuring and arguing, so that you may be blameless and innocent, children of God without blemish in the midst of a crooked and perverse generation, in which you shine like stars in the world (Phil 12:12-15).

This moral inventory gives us better self-knowledge. It enables us to see and deal with our behaviors, values, and attitudes, good and bad. It puts us in touch with the truth that sets us free. Without self-knowledge, we remain stuck in behaviors that are self-defeating and destructive. We fail to nurture behaviors that bring light and life to ourselves and others. This reflective step is a regular part of life. We are so wonderfully created that a lifetime is hardly enough to discover our whole self. Add to it as new insights come to you. It is worth your investment of time and energy.

Take a look at people you like or dislike. Discover why you feel as you do. You may have resentments that color your judgment. Where did they come from? Why do you feel resentful? What fears do you have? What kind of sexual behaviors are inappropriate? Appropriate? How powerful is your need for financial security? How does it influence you and your relationships and use of time? How much power do your emotions have on your decisions? . . . on your reactions to others? How would you evaluate your emotional life? What behaviors or actions are you most proud of? Which ones are you ashamed of? What attitudes would you like to keep? . . . would you like to change? Do you have unhealthy perfectionist tendencies that dictate reactions and choices? Do you carry unresolved guilt ("I did bad things!") or live in shame ("I'm no good!")? Do you accept responsibility for your life? What degree of compassion do you have? How sensitive to others are you?

Do you find yourself ready to forgive rather than resent or hate others?

We admit, to ourselves, to God, and to another person, the results of our inventory. Together we find ways of freedom and growth.

Confession is healthy. It allows us both to hear ourselves revealing what we have discovered and get feedback from the listening person. We may catch ourselves trying to justify our behavior. Don't! Acknowledge what happened, how you acted, what you said or did. The goal is insight, not guilt. Avoid judging yourself or others. Bring the facts into the light. Deal with them. Take your written inventory when sharing with another person. Choose someone with whom you are at ease, someone you can trust. If a person seems reluctant to listen or tells you that "God forgave you, so this is not necessary," find someone else!

What benefits/values come from this step?

1. You are required to be clear about what goes on in your life.
2. You allow another person to reflect with you about your life and behavior. A second opinion of this kind is helpful.
3. You realize how easy it is to rationalize unhealthy behavior. You are forced to acknowledge your role in the situation(s).
4. A wise companion can offer insights you may have missed.
5. A trusted companion will offer acceptance that diminishes the power of your addictions/compulsions/sin and brings a sense of freedom and self-worth.
6. You will experience the relief of being heard and accepted.
7. You experience a new sense of conversion and of God's love for you.

8. Your perception of reality becomes sharper.
9. You feel good about "you" and find it less necessary to keep proving yourself to people.
10. You discover that "having fun" is okay. Workaholism has less power over you.

Some people experience shame at this point. They even wonder if they should have done this step. If such is your reaction, it may be that you have not *really* finished the first steps. There may be things you are afraid to face — and you need to talk about your feelings with a trusted, competent friend.

> "Is there anyone among you who, if your child asks for a fish, will give a snake instead of a fish? Or if the child asks for an egg, will give a scorpion? If you then, who are evil, know how to give good gifts to your children, how much more will the heavenly Father give the Holy Spirit to those who ask him" (Luke 11:11-13).

We ask God's help in dealing with our destructive actions/behavior and allow the power of the Holy Spirit to remove them.

This is a natural consequence of our recognition of reality. If we cannot solve problems of addiction and sin by ourselves, it is reasonable to ask for God's help. This is not a magic step. It does not mean that we are passive and that God does everything. It does acknowledge our need for God. We grow more open to the working of God in our lives. Our focus is not on what "I want" but on what God wants. The power of the Holy Spirit does more than we could ask or imagine.

> I pray that the God of our Lord Jesus Christ . . . may give you a spirit of wisdom and revelation as you come to know him, so that, with the eyes of your heart enlightened, you may know what is the hope to which he has called you, what are the riches of his glorious inheritance among the saints, and what is the immeasurable greatness of his power for us who believe (Eph 1:17-19).

If this step is going to happen, we need to be ready for it. We may not, for example, be ready to forgive an enemy. Other people don't magically change and make forgiveness easy. Perhaps we must *wait* until we are ready to forgive ''enemies.'' Sensitive awareness of your present feelings will help you choose good ''timing'' for this step. But stick with the process that leads to forgiveness.

Our growth in virtue will require patient practice. This is not accomplished by a simple mental decision. God often offers *more* opportunities for practicing the virtue we need. If we ask God for patience, we may be given countless opportunities to practice it! We come to realize that this process takes time. When we are ready to let God work, God works. As we deal with a problem(s), God is working in us. Eventually we recognize God's wise timetable as well as God's healing presence throughout the process.

An experience of freedom comes as ''gift'' with this step. We need not be our own savior. We allow God to do what God does so well — saving us through Jesus Christ. The burden of doing it alone is lifted. We walk with confident hope, knowing that the power of the Holy Spirit will accomplish what needs to be done.

If, however, we surrender all these things to God and don't replace them with positive behavior, we are worse off than before. If we stop trying to control people but become indifferent, there is little gain.

> ''When an unclean spirit has gone out of a person, it wanders through waterless regions looking for a resting place, but it finds none. Then it says, 'I will return to my house from which I came.' When it comes, it finds it empty, swept, and put in order. Then it goes and brings along seven other spirits more evil than itself, and they enter and live there; and the last state of that person is worse than the first'' (Matt 12:43-45).

If we tidy up our house but leave it empty, the same problems can recur. If we leave a vacuum, it will be filled with something. Unless we determine what fills it, we may find ourselves trapped all over again. We need to fill that empty space with positive qualities and actions. Otherwise, the process of growth may come to a screeching halt. We may revert to behaviors as destructive as the ones we surrendered.

For example: we have managed to let go of our violent anger. We have made good progress. However, we still get angry. Surrendering the destructive dimensions of anger is not enough. We need to discover ways to use the power of anger in a positive way. If we don't, our next bout with anger may again become violent. Then the old cycle begins anew. "I can't win. I never get ahead. This is a hopeless situation." We play the same old broken record of the past. Instead of hopeful progress we wind up with fresh feelings of hopelessness.

When we disagree with someone's poor decision, we need not clam up and say nothing. Neither is it helpful to control them. If we disagree, we need not scream and shout about their stupidity! It is better to express your concern about the issue without laying guilt on the other person. Some friends, for example, decide to go into farming because they like chickens. They have no farming experience at all. You need not call them stupid! You might share some issues involved in chicken-farming. You might invite them to do some research on what is needed financially to run a successful chicken farm. The key is to make certain that their decision is based on facts and not simply on desires. Share what you feel and let them free. If you dictate their decision, defensiveness is what you will get. If you share your ideas without manipulation, it may move them to reconsider.

People feel more understood when they are listened to than when they are given advice that "manages" their lives.

After listing people we have harmed, we are willing to make amends to them. Forgiveness is offered to self and others where needed. We do this with sensitivity to others so that we avoid doing more harm than good.

People are not always ready to receive our "amend." We need to be sensitive to others when implementing this principle. It is important to acknowledge that forgiveness is necessary before reconciliation can happen. We let loose of the power that the hurt has given us. Our anger, frustration, resentment, or irritation has a power of its own. When we forgive, we surrender this power. We may still feel some feelings of hurt. We gradually deny them any more power as we forgive others. We may never forget the hurt. But we gradually diminish its power to control us. Freedom enters our lives when we forgive. We have the possibility of reconciling. We no longer allow the ''enemy'' to control us.

There are situations where disclosure to another may do more harm than good. For example, a spouse has a one-night affair that calls for making amends. Direct disclosure to the spouse might ruin the marriage. Make amends as best you can. But don't do it so that someone else is badly hurt by it. Understand the limitations of making amends when it can only be done at another's expense. There may be times when direct honesty is called for. But go about making ''amends'' with a sensitive heart.

Making amends may include returning money. It means replacing stolen items or their equivalent. It may require apologizing to a friend. Do the best you can in these situations. The key? Do what you can to make amends. Your actions will free you from past burdens. It will allow you to live in the here and now. This is an important step.

> ''Be on your guard! If another disciple sins, you must rebuke the offender, and if there is repentance, you must forgive. And if the same person sins against you seven times a day, and turns back to you seven times and says 'I repent,' you must forgive'' (Luke 17:3-4).

These steps require a new life-style that deals with life-issues as soon as possible. We keep in touch with the light and darkness in life and admit them in a way that leads to healthy growth.

There is something wonderful about being me. Each year of life has brought some new insight into who Lester is. I am quite a complicated person. But I'm excited about learning more about me. It allows me to move in new directions that were unthinkable a few years back. I remember that I thought I trusted God. Then I tried to "live in the present moment" that one of my Capuchin brothers spoke about. I quickly discovered that I managed a "whole minute" before I was looking ahead to next week's work. I could control the work. I couldn't stay with the present moment and let God have control. That opening led to a further inventory of my actions. In reality, my trust was weak and my need to control was strong. I really depended on my appointment book to regulate my time. I let God in but not in a primary spot. The insight is helping to make a few changes in me. It is a struggle, but downright worth it. I sense that my integrity as a Capuchin is growing. I'm downright upright in new ways!

New insights continue to come when I am faithful to reflection on my gospel journey. Honesty with self and others makes life richer. It makes relationships more real. It brings joyful peace. Some people find it helpful to do a short reflection a couple of times each day. At noon ask yourself: "What did God do in my life this morning? What people/events spoke to me of caring? Did I fail to catch God's presence? Why?" Use a few minutes to stay in touch. Doing it again in the evening helps to situate my day in the presence of a loving God. Don't make it an analysis, but rather a gentle reflection that keeps life properly tuned.

> A king is not saved by his great army;
> > a warrior is not delivered by his great strength.
> The war horse is a vain hope for victory,
> > and by its great might it cannot save.
> Truly the eye of the Lord is on those who fear him,
> > on those who hope in his steadfast love. . . .
> Let your steadfast love, O Lord, be upon us,
> > even as we hope in you (Ps 33:16-18, 22).

God is so important that I take time to communicate with God. I ask God to teach me the gospel way and give me strength to live it.

How long it has taken me to realize how important God is to a real life! For many years I filled my life with work and obedience and doing what I thought was right. I don't regret those years. But now I know they could have been richer and filled with more joy. There was (and is) too much ''Lester-concern'' in what I have done. I like my independence even when I obey. No one can see how I feel about obeying. I kept that corner of motivation hidden. I still do — but not as much as before. God is teaching me that being Lester-for-God is my best gift to the Lord. I know better how to allow God to teach me and how it happens in everyday life.

Moreover, keeping in touch is easier than it used to be. I have fewer illusions about how it ''should'' be. Prayerfulness comes wandering into my life more naturally. It is not a grudging time given to a demanding God. Now it is a natural listening to Jesus, my Jewish friend. Prayerfulness is becoming more a part of who I am. Even when I fail, I sense a presence that confronts and forgives at the same time. I am never coddled, nor are my sins overlooked. Yet I am never ''put down'' or made to feel worthless. Prayer is still sometimes (too often) ''putting in time.'' But it is also good time with the Beloved whose love is life. There is less concern for my needs and a stronger awareness of the need to listen to God. Being quiet before God allows God's word to penetrate my life.

> Rejoice always, pray without ceasing, give thanks in all circumstances; for this is the will of God in Christ Jesus for you. . . . May the God of peace himself sanctify you entirely; and may your spirit and soul and body be kept sound and blameless at the coming of our Lord Jesus Christ (1 Thess 5:16-18, 23).

What we have received freely, we share freely. We take the gospel message to others.

Step by step we are surrendering to God. Though we are not yet finished, we learn to share what we have received. What has been gift to us we now offer as gift to others. Frequently, we discover people walking the path we have walked. We offer hope by sharing our story about how God has worked in us. When we get too "self-centered" again, it helps to share with others who are in need. Too much self-analysis tends to frustrate progress. Too little reflection does the same. But sharing has a way of balancing things. It helps us to realize how human we all are. Without judgment or elitism, we confidently carry the gospel message to others. It is a natural consequence of all we have learned.

A few cautions are in order. Don't force yourself on others and become a nuisance. Don't presume to have answers for people and speak from your high place of wisdom. Don't tell people what they have to do. Don't use your sharing to get them to join a group or practice your favorite way of prayer. Don't overwhelm them with your holiness and insight or tell them how God wants them to act. People will discover this for themselves. Don't try to be their savior.

Develop healthy qualities as you grow. Learn how to listen without interrupting. Learn to be sensitive to the pain of other people. Learn to share in a gentle way the portion of your story that may help others. Allow yourself to be vulnerable, realizing your limitations without anxiety. In the very best sense, try to "get under the skin" of the other person. Try to feel as they do, perceive as they do, and, perhaps, sense fear as they do. Do your sharing as a free gift not a tit-for-tat demand. Sharing gospel lessons life has taught us offers a realistic gift to people. It also keeps us from over-dramatizing our own hurts and needs. It moves us beyond ourselves to concern for others. Share without making judgments. Our goal is to get at the issues that need to be addressed. We are not interested in imposing guilt or assessing blame or "looking good."

> Then he opened their minds to understand the scriptures, and he said to them, "Thus it is written, that the Messiah is to suffer and to rise from the dead on the third day, and that repentance and forgiveness of sins is to be proclaimed in his name to all nations, beginning from Jerusalem. You are witnesses of these things" (Luke 24:45-48).

Other Ways and Means

We wrote of taking time during the day to see where God is in our lives. For these few minutes, focus on the presence of Jesus. Use some of these questions to help your reflection.

1. Did I feel drawn by the Lord today through a companion? . . . an event? . . . a good book? . . . a difficult time? . . . an enemy?, etc.

2. How did I meet the Lord in my fears? . . . misunderstandings? . . . work? . . . joy? . . . suffering? . . . insights? . . . successes? . . . failures?

3. What have I learned about Jesus in the ordinary happenings of life today?

4. How did the word of God come alive for me today? . . . in prayer? . . . in liturgy? . . . in other readings? . . . in life situations?

5. In what ways have I been a sign of God's presence and love to those I live with? . . . to those I work with? . . . to friends? . . . to family? . . . to others?

6. Am I more aware of the Holy Spirit's lead in my feelings? . . . in movements of conversion? . . . impulses of grace? . . . dealing with others?

Taking time to stay in touch strengthens our awareness of the presence of God. Use whatever is helpful for your life. The tools of growth are most effective when they fit your person.

As an aside about the value of time, this statistical data offers an idea of how time is used by the *average* person (whoever that is!).

■ The average person spends seven years of life in the bathroom.

■ The average person spends six years eating.

■ The average person spends five years waiting in lines.

- The average person spends four years cleaning the house.
- The average person spends two years trying to return telephone calls to people who aren't there to receive them.
- The average person spends three years preparing meals.
- The average person spends one year searching for misplaced things.
- The average person spends six months sitting at red lights.   ˙
- The average person spends eight months opening junk mail.
- Unknown: The time addicts spend on their addictions!

Over twenty-nine years of life are taken up by such things! Add the time spent chauffeuring kids around, time spent sleeping, and other possible uses of time. It is a wise person who uses time well.

Each day, set aside time for enlightenment and insight. Let the sacred space within your heart be filled with the light of Jesus.

As the truth becomes clearer, test it in the gentle presence of people who love you. Unveil it and allow others to reflect upon it with you. Let their words, given in caring love, prove the truth you continue to discover in your inner temple. Each of us is a fragment of a mirror, reflecting light into places of darkness.

Use Scripture as a way of growth. Let your imagination give life to the stories in Scripture. Be present to the stories. Absorb the people and situation of the story. Be one of the people in the story. Allow your imagination to feel the feelings, think the thoughts, experience the pain, celebrate the joy. See how real Jesus is to you. What begins as role-playing often becomes an encounter with the risen Jesus. YOU are present. The person in the story is you — and Jesus is present to you NOW! The word of God is powerful. Enter into the power and light that it brings.

Jesus often challenges things we take for granted. He often did this in the Gospel stories (Carolyn Glynn S.P.).

1. People generally assumed that the prodigal son in the Gospel story would *not* be received back. Jesus explodes that opinion by having the father in the story throw a party for the prodigal. It was totally uncalled for and unexpected (Luke 15:11-32).

2. Ordinarily, people would have expected a priest or a Levite to help the man who was beaten by robbers. In Jesus' story, the ritually unclean and despised Samaritan is the hero (Luke 10:30-37).

3. A Pharisee would be expected to be a master pray-er. Certainly better than a tax collector. But in Jesus' story, it is the tax collector who is pointed out as the good pray-er (Luke 18:9-14).

4. Anyone with any sense realized that adulterous people needed to be stoned as the law required. But in Jesus' story, the woman caught in adultery is forgiven rather than being stoned (John 8:4-11).

Don't be surprised if Jesus explodes some of our pet ideas. Jesus has a tendency to dynamite assumptions that do not fit gospel people. It can happen to us. Don't be shocked when it occurs.

It seems fair to say that some things in life don't change. Try as we might, no remedy seems to work. In such cases we need to remember the story of the man who had dandelions in his beautiful lawn. He tried everything to remove them. But he had little success. Finally, he wrote to the county extension agent for help. The reply came back: "Learn to love them." Some of our dandelions — compulsions, shadow-side qualities, etc. — may not go away. We may die with some of them still unresolved. Learn to love them even while continuing to deal with them in healthy ways. No use being anxious. Anxiety is no help at all.

The Shakertown Pledge contains some solid, down-to-earth principles. They deserve serious reflection.

Recognizing that the earth and the fullness thereof is a gift from our gracious God, and that we are called to cherish, nurture, and provide loving stewardship for the earth's resources, and recognizing that life is itself a gift and a call to responsibility, joy, and celebration, I make the following declarations:

1. I declare myself to be a world citizen.

2. I commit myself to lead an ecologically sound life.

3. I commit myself to lead a life of creative simplicity and to share my personal wealth with the world's poor.

4. I commit myself to join with others in the reshaping of institutions in order to bring about a more just global society in which all people have a full access to the needed resources for their physical, emotional, intellectual, and spiritual growth.

5. I commit myself to occupational accountability, and in so doing, I will seek to avoid the creation of products that cause harm to others.

6. I affirm the gift of my body and commit myself to its proper nourishment and physical well-being.

7. I commit myself to examine continually my relations with others, and attempt to relate honestly, morally, and lovingly to those around me.

8. I commit myself to personal renewal through prayer, meditation, and study.

9. I commit myself to responsible participation in a community of faith.

Wherever we discover the flavor of the gospel, we embrace it. We may need to test it and dialogue about it. But the gospel flavoring of life is given to all people. It is a reflection of the yearnings of the human heart and spirit. We did not create ourselves. We show wisdom when we go to the creator to learn about life. We discover that work which rewards the spirit may be more important than work which makes money. It may be that competition and self-defense are enemies to be shunned, while committed love is an ally to be embraced. Worship of a God who remains a mystery may be most important of all. If this is so, it requires changing attitudes that have grown acceptable without being challenged by reflection. (Cf. Bellah, Robert. *Habits of the Heart*, p. 96.)

Psychology and human programs are good human tools. But the Christian does not stop at the level of psychology and programs. We are children of God, not simply bodies living on a planet in space. That makes quite a difference! We have a God whose unconditional love can do more than human means can accomplish. Christians forget this at their peril. We are friends of Jesus. With Jesus we have an intimacy that gives us dignity and wholeness.

Psychology, process, and programs help clear away debris and open doors to health. But Jesus adds a dimension beyond psychology and programs. Christians receive from Jesus a freely given power for living a gospel life. We blossom best when Jesus is given free reign in our hearts and lives. We are servants of God, sent to do God's will and build the kind of community God designs. Listening and surrender come to mind as ordinary roles of a servant. In short, we delight in the human gifts and discoveries of science, psychology, medicine, and programs of growth. We are delighted that we are not limited to them. As friends of Jesus we have access to a power that goes beyond what human resources can deliver.

Reflection

Once again allow the words of the Bible to stimulate your reflection. Listen to the texts. Let God speak to your heart.

We have not ceased praying for you and asking that you may be filled with the knowledge of God's will in all spiritual wisdom and understanding, so that you may lead lives worthy of the Lord, fully pleasing to him, as you bear fruit in every good work and as you grow in the knowledge of God (Col 1:9-10).

Brothers and sisters, do not be weary in doing what is right. Take note of those who do not obey what we say in this letter; have nothing to do with them, so that they may be ashamed. Do not regard them as enemies, but warn them as believers. Now may the Lord of peace himself give you peace at all times in all ways. The Lord be with all of you (2 Thess 3:13-16).

Now to God who is able to strengthen you according to my gospel and the proclamation of Jesus Christ, according to the revelation of the mystery that was kept secret for long ages but is now disclosed, and through the prophetic writings is made known to all the Gentiles, according to the command of the eternal God, to bring about the obedience of faith — to the only wise God, through Jesus Christ, to whom be the glory forever! Amen (Rom 16:25-27).

But to all who received him, who believed in his name, he gave power to become children of God. . . . From his fullness we have all received, grace upon grace. The Law indeed was given through Moses; grace and truth came through Jesus Christ (John 1:12, 16-17).

Whoever loves discipline loves knowledge,
    but those who hate to be rebuked are stupid.
The good obtain favor from the Lord,
    but those who devise evil he condemns.
No one finds security by wickedness,
    but the root of the righteous will never be moved. . . .
From the fruit of the mouth one is filled with good things,
    and manual labor has its reward.
Fools think their own way is right,
    but the wise listen to advice (Prov 12:1-3, 14-15).

CHAPTER FOURTEEN

Pass It On!

Sharing the faith is an important part of following the gospel. Jesus gave us responsibility for passing on the gospel message. This is not a luxury for a Christian. It is our duty. Those who hold God's word in their hearts pass it on to others. We are channels of the message. Our lives and words are the means by which we pass on what we have received and are receiving. We call this process "evangelization."

Evangelization is not possible without the help of the Holy Spirit. The techniques of evangelization are helpful tools. But they cannot replace the action of the Holy Spirit in the work of evangelization.

We share the word in many ways. As we develop a gospel lifestyle, we influence other people. Our compassion, our willingness to give people a second, third, and fourth chance, has its effect on people around us. Our willingness to share with the needy or stand up for the homeless has its impact. Our ability to cut through double-talk and deal with basic issues does not go unnoticed. Neither does our concern about social problems that touch peoples' dignity. We do not influence everyone equally, but we do influence people. The more genuine our gospel lifestyle, the more influential is our example.

And you became imitators of us and of the Lord, for in spite of persecution you received the word with joy inspired by the Holy Spirit, so that you became an example to all the believers in Macedonia and Achaia. For the word of the Lord has sounded forth from you not only in Macedonia and Achaia, but in every place your faith in God has become known (1 Thess 1:6-8).

Witness is not sufficient by itself. We must be ready to offer the reasons for our way of life. If the influence of Jesus and the gospel are not proclaimed, there is no true evangelization. We need to offer the reasons and motivating force for our actions. Witness is helpful but requires a clear explanation of *why* we live this way.

Do not be intimidated, but in your hearts sanctify Christ as Lord. Always be ready to make your defense to anyone who demands from you an accounting for the hope that is in you; yet do it with gentleness and reverence (1 Peter 3:14-16).

Some ministries offer the opportunity to speak directly to others about faith and the gospel. A verbal proclamation of the gospel is a vital way to share the faith. Sometimes this is done in formal teaching situations. At other times it is accomplished through ordinary conversations. Use opportunities to speak up when it seems appropriate. Evangelization is inadequate unless it is listened to and accepted. This takes time. We need to be patient.

In the presence of God and of Christ Jesus . . . I solemnly urge you: proclaim the message; be persistent whether the time is favorable or unfavorable; convince, rebuke, and encourage, with the utmost patience in teaching (2 Tim 4:1-2).

There are many direct ways of sharing the word with others. Teaching young people about the faith offers the opportunity to pass on our values and convictions. It also can refine our convictions through the questions young people may pose. We are not answer-people so much as joyful people who desire to share the message. We choose to dialogue about the gospel message. Sometimes faith-sharing finds expression in Bible-study groups, prayer groups, and other spiritual growth groups. Interchange with others opens the door to fresh ideas. Each of us brings a unique reflection of the gospel to such sharing situations.

Men and women preach the word at liturgical gatherings. This is an opportunity to share our understanding of the message of Jesus. Breaking open the word at Eucharist can enliven faith. A wedding, a funeral, a jubilee Mass offer opportunities for sharing the word. These occasions are times when people are open to a fresh hearing of the word. We do this with sensitivity to people's needs. It is a gentle sharing that fits the occasion and the people.

Current events in our world offer occasions for proclaiming the Christian message. Riots, war, tragedies, natural disasters, and celebrations are part of life. They offer opportunity to reflect on such events from a gospel perspective. How do we see the hand of God at work? Is there a message of conversion being offered by such events? Are we being called to compassion and understanding for the people involved?

We bring Jesus' perspective to assess national and international policies. We try to make gospel values heard where policy touches the lives of people. We may not always succeed in what we seek, but we cannot be silent! We will do what we can to create a world where human dignity is respected. We believe in the presence and power of the risen Jesus. We believe such power can make a difference. We are sensitive to the demands of reality. We don't bring religious "magic." We do bring honest gospel reflection to crisis situations.

We Are Learners

Whenever we are in a position to share our faith, we are also called to deepen our personal understanding of faith. Sharing faith almost inevitably demands that we become learners. We are quickly made aware of how much we have to learn. Putting our convictions into words for others requires clarity in our own thinking. Good teachers soon learn how much they do not know. Gospel people understand that the pursuit of wisdom is a lifetime search. Personal struggles with faith help us to be patient with the struggles of others. Force and domination should be unknown in our sharing.

> Conduct yourselves wisely toward outsiders, making the most of the time. Let your speech always be gracious, seasoned with salt, so that you may know how you ought to answer everyone (Col 4:5-6).

Sharing the "gospel truth" is meant to bring people to Jesus. It is not an exercise in self-aggrandizement. We are often the instrument of the Holy Spirit in bringing Jesus' message to others. Sponsors in the Rite of Christian Initiation of Adults (RCIA) are companions for people seeking Jesus. Our Catholic faith-tradition offers rich insights into the Bible message. Friendship often results as we share faith with others. Friendship is best when it brings friends to know and follow Jesus. The faith-community brings people to communion with each other. The Holy Spirit is at work drawing us to be one people in Jesus. We share both friendship and freedom in sharing the message of Jesus.

> For the grace of God has appeared bringing salvation to all, training us to renounce impiety and worldly passions, and in the present age to live lives that are self-controlled, upright, and godly, while we wait for the blessed hope and the manifestation of the glory of our great God and Savior, Jesus Christ. He it is who gave himself for us that he might redeem us from all iniquity and purify for himself a people of his own who are zealous for good deeds (Titus 2:11-14).

Telling a Faith Story

One way of sharing faith is by sharing a personal faith story. In a conducive setting, it is one way to open the way to evangelization. It is natural to speak about one's own faith-experience. It is often more easily received than a dialogue on doctrine.

Not everyone is comfortable talking about religion. Many people feel ill at ease talking about their religious experiences. Yet most people have such experiences. What most people don't do is to share those experiences. There is a fear of being labeled a religious fanatic. Our task is to create an atmosphere in which people feel comfortable sharing their religious ideas and experiences. We understand their fear. We have our own fears about sharing personal faith-experiences with others.

It is important to create a trusting, non-judgmental atmosphere. We listen to the religious experiences of others without judging them. When we create this atmosphere, people feel free to share with us. When they know we will listen with gentle hearts, they are more comfortable sharing their stories.

Experiences, visions, apparitions, and inner feelings need a reality check by the faith-community. Personal religious experiences are not automatically healthy reflections of God's message. We need the reflection of people gifted with wisdom to test our experience. Wisdom helps us assess our experience and test its authenticity.

We do *not* respond like gangbuster-saviors, overwhelming people with our faith-experiences. Ordinary stories are often more effective than dramatic conversions. Most of us are ordinary people. We are impressed with human stories of God working in ordinary lives. Instead of pressuring others to share their stories, we share our own story. Surprisingly, our sharing often opens the door for sharing by others. Sharing a personal faith story gives others freedom to do the same. A mutuality grows in this accepting atmosphere. There are moments when a simple "praying with" someone can be helpful. Especially when someone is hurting, a gentle prayer reveals a caring spirit. This, too, can open hearts to the message of Jesus.

> Beloved, you do faithfully whatever you do for the friends, even though they are strangers to you; they have testified to your love before the church. You will do well to send them on in a manner worthy of God. . . . Therefore, we ought to support such people, so that we may become co-workers with the truth (3 John 1:5-6, 8).

Some Guidelines for Telling Stories

Follow some practical, sensible rules when sharing. Your story should be true and it should be yours. If you exaggerate or make up a story, it has little power. Your story should be short. Don't spend thirty minutes telling your faith story. If it takes that long you will probably put people to sleep. Say what you need to say and stop. The longer the story gets, the less effective its impact on the listener. A faith story can focus on three points:

1. What kind of Christian were you before your faith-experience, i.e., in a particular area of your life?

2. Briefly describe the faith-experience — what happened? How were you touched by God?

3. What difference did it make in your life? A faith-experience generally brings some change in its wake.

Another way to share is to use a Scripture story as the vehicle of sharing.

1. Select a story from your life — one that was meaningful to you.

2. Find a Scripture story that is similar to your own story.

3. Share the way in which you see how the two are linked to each other. Keep it simple but real!

4. You can reverse the process and begin with a Scripture story and then insert your own story. Discuss how they are similar or different from each other.

Use whatever process is helpful to you. Show how God has touched your life and made a difference in some area of your life. Choose a story that fits the person(s) with whom you are talking.

You may have other ways of sharing that you have found helpful. Use whatever is most effective for you and your lis-

234 Pass It On!

tener(s). Your story is a gift given to the other. It does not carry any demands. If it results in a response by the listener, give careful attention to the story that is shared. There is no need to comment on another person's story or offer interpretations. Simply accept it with attentive care.

God is at work in our faith stories. Give God the credit. Many groups or individuals may have helped us. Retreats, cursillos, marriage encounters, Secular Franciscan experiences, and other movements may have helped us. But God is the one who does the work. Acknowledge that fact when you tell the story.

Use language that is understandable. Do not lace your stories with churchy language that is gobbledegook to your listeners. I remember talking about the ''homily'' of the Mass with people down South who were not Catholic. Afterwards they asked someone if ''homily'' was something to eat with grits!

If your story triggers a listener's story, listen with attention. Accept the story without critiquing it. When people initially open their heart to you, they need gentle acceptance. As your relationship grows there will be time to share insights that sharpen or refine the sharing. Respect and reverence are the best first responses.

Some Essential Truths of Faith

It may happen that your rapport with someone permits them to ask questions about the faith. Even Catholics often have questions about the faith. If sharing opens the door to dialogue, be prepared to explain the faith that is yours. If there is something you don't know, say so. Don't guess or waffle. Tell them you will try to find the answers and get back to them. At times, family or marital difficulties need more skill than you have. Acknowledge that fact and suggest someone who might help. Offer to help them get in touch with that person. Courteous honesty is an important virtue in these situations. Encourage them to deal with whatever problem is present. Don't become their savior! Be a good companion and help them to help themselves.

Sometimes we are overwhelmed with the vast amount of data we know about our faith. If someone asks us what are the essential elements of our belief, we feel lost. There is so much we have read and learned and heard about faith. We have a sense of not seeing the forest for the trees. Faith can seem quite complicated when we're asked to give the essential elements of our belief. Here are some thoughts on the essentials of our faith.

God looms large among the fundamental elements of our faith. We believe in God. We believe God is creator of all things. We believe that God's creative love is still at work. We believe that God's nature is such that God loves us unconditionally — because that is the only way God knows how to love. God is present to all people. God wants all people to experience the joy of the vision of God's glory. It is a well-known fact that belief in God is essential to our faith-life.

When I look up at your heavens, the work of your fingers,
    the moon and the stars you have established;
what are human beings that you are mindful of them,
    mortals that you care for them? . . .
Yet you have made them a little lower than God,
    and crowned them with glory and honor.
You have given them dominion over the works of your hands;
    you have put all things under their feet. . . .
O LORD, our Sovereign,
    how majestic is your name in all the earth (Ps 8:3-6, 9).

There is a gap between our way of living and the way God calls us to live. The gospel is not always our mode of operation. Even when our minds understand, we have no guarantee our behavior will follow. We make many choices that are not life-giving. We may choose things that are mean-spirited, self-centered, and unconcerned for others. We do many things that are more like death than life. We name these things "sin." They not only separate us from God but also from one another.

They can also break us apart inside. A brief look around our world offers substantial data to prove the presence of sin. We are a fallen people. We have a problem!

We are all sinners. We commit sin in varying degrees or categories, but we are sinners. Adam and Eve may get the blame. Their fall from glory may help explain the facts. But the truth is — we are sinners and need help to be saved. Our faith teaches us about this reality.

> Those conflicts and disputes among you, where do they come from? Do they not come from your cravings that are at war within you? You want something and do not have it; so you commit murder. And you covet something and cannot obtain it; so you engage in disputes and conflicts. You do not have because you do not ask. You ask and do not receive, because you ask wrongly, in order to spend what you get on your pleasures. Adulterers! Do you not know that friendship with the world is enmity with God? (Jas 4:1-4).

> You stupid Galatians! You must have been bewitched — you before whose eyes Jesus Christ was openly displayed on the cross! Answer me one question: Did you receive the Spirit by keeping the law or by believing the gospel message? Can you really be so stupid? You started with the spiritual; do you now look to the material to make you perfect? Is all you have experienced to come to nothing — surely not! When God gives you the Spirit and works miracles among you, is it because you keep the law, or is it because you have faith in the gospel message? (Gal 3:1-5 — REB).

We have a problem. How are we saved from the power of sin and evil? How do we deal with sin in ourselves and others? Are we competent to banish it single-handedly? Are we intellectually astute enough to rationalize it away? Can we meet it head-on and defeat it? What data do we have about our efforts to overcome sin and its consequences with our own power?

History does not support a theory that we are successful in eradicating sin and its consequences. Quite the contrary. Even a casual look at history convinces us of the staying power of sin. Even hermits might conclude that sin is a problem as they struggle in their solitude. If that is so, how can we be saved?

God's answer to that question is Jesus.

> For while we were still weak, at the right time, Christ died for the ungodly. . . . God proves his love for us in that while we still were sinners Christ died for us. . . . For if while we were enemies, we were reconciled to God through the death of his Son, much more surely, having been reconciled, will we be saved by his life (Rom 5:6, 8, 10).

God chooses to be visible on earth through Jesus. The life, passion, death, and resurrection of Jesus is God's chosen way to save us. The power of evil and sin succumbs to the power of God. Jesus is savior. Jesus shares with us what he receives from the Father. Jesus glorifies the Father by his faithfulness. After the resurrection Jesus ascended to the Father. Jesus sends the Holy Spirit to us. The Holy Spirit is the power that enables us to deal with sin and evil. We become a Spirit-filled gospel people.

> When the Advocate comes, whom I will send to you from the Father, the Spirit of truth who comes from the Father, he will testify on my behalf. You also are to testify because you have been with me from the beginning. . . . When the Spirit of truth comes, he will guide you into all the truth (John 15:26-27; 16:13).

Finally, there is the truth that we are called to respond to the gospel. Jesus reveals the heart and mind of his "Abba." He sees this as the way to joyful living. Jesus offers humankind a vision that gives dignity to all. Jesus reveals a vision that sees forgiveness as a natural quality in godly people. Jesus proclaims a vision that creates an atmosphere of acceptance in order to diminish the need to hide our real selves. Jesus speaks of a community where genuine care for one another is the hallmark of his people. Jesus creates an atmosphere where tough issues are dealt with compassionately and realistically. Jesus speaks of a society where power is used to serve people. Jesus calls for a community where destitution is eradicated because greed and possessiveness are discarded. Jesus wants a gentle place where fear is diminished because violence is transformed into peacefulness. Jesus proclaims an inclusive community where undesirables find a home and acceptance. Jesus calls a people who care for Planet Earth and all its inhabitants. Jesus proclaims a law of love where justice blossoms and mercy finds a home. Jesus cries out for a community where love is the cornerstone and where light and life are possible for all people.

The unbelievable fact? Jesus has given us the vision and power to build this kind of community. He desires our response and invites us to be faithful to the vision. When we believe in Jesus this is our life-task. Wherever we live, our task is to create a community that reflects the vision proclaimed by Jesus. Much of what we shared in this book relates to our response to Jesus. To say that we are a special people is too mild a term. We are a people of God. All people of all nations and tribes and color are called to be part of this people. No one is excluded. On Planet Earth we are the body of Christ.

To Summarize

Our basic beliefs include:

1. A belief in God, creator, lover of all of creation, a God who loves us unconditionally.

2. A belief that we are a fallen people and we sin. Sin is a real problem. It keeps us from experiencing God's love or being free enough to love self, God, and neighbor in life-giving ways. We experience the consequences of the fall.

3. A belief that Jesus came among us to teach us, heal us, and save us. It is Jesus who is the answer to our needs. Jesus is the one whose presence, vision, and Spirit enable us to give flesh to the gospel vision in our lives and our world.

4. A belief that our task is to respond to the vision of Jesus with faithfulness, and joyfully share it with others.

There are many more dogmas and doctrines within our framework of belief. But these few are the essentials of what we believe. They are the basic beliefs we share with others. They offer a believable synthesis of our faith.

Our faith is a communal faith. God not only calls us individually but as a people. We work together in the task of building the faith community. Whatever we can do to help one another to be faithful, we WILL DO! We are not meant to be isolated believers, struggling for wholeness in our personal cocoon. We are the body of Christ, called by God, to be united in communion with God and one another. Evangelization anticipates bringing people to a vibrant community. The community is the common gathering place for God's people. Here is where people gather who have heard the word proclaimed.

The gospel spirit-journey lasts a lifetime. Evangelization is also a lifetime project. No single experience can exhaust our discovery of God's love. As long as life is in us, growth is a sign of that life. Growth means change. God's creative love far exceeds our expectations. We may need quiet space to absorb what God gives, but we can never become Rip Van Winkles, sleeping away our faith-lives.

> He (Jesus Christ) it is whom we proclaim. We teach everyone and instruct everyone in all the ways of wisdom, so as to present each one of you as a mature member of Christ's body. To this end I am toiling strenuously with all the energy and power of Christ at work in me (Col 1:28-29 — REB).

(Resource book for some of the ideas in this chapter: Robert Deshaies, Chet Stokloza, and Susan Blum, *Mission Evangelization: A Course to Train Evangelists* [Catholic Evangelism Press, 1984 — Box 1282, Boca Raton, FL 33432].)

Reflection

With gentle reflection, allow the word of God to touch you. These words of Scripture offer an outline of the Christian life.

Be quiet. Listen as the words speak to your heart and call you to new life.

> But we appeal to you, brothers and sisters, to respect those who labor among you. . . . Esteem them very highly in love because of their work. Be at peace among yourselves. And we urge you, beloved, to admonish the idlers, encourage the faint hearted, help the weak, be patient with all of them. See that none of you repays evil for evil, but always seek to do good to one another and to all. Rejoice always, pray without ceasing, give thanks in all circumstances; for this is the will of God in Christ Jesus for you. Do not quench the Spirit. Do not despise the words of prophets, but test everything; hold fast to what is good, abstain from every form of evil.
>
> May the God of peace himself sanctify you entirely; and may your spirit and soul and body be kept sound and blameless at the coming of our Lord Jesus Christ. The one who calls you is faithful, and he will do this (1 Thess 5:12-24).

> "These are the words of the holy one, the true one,
>   who has the key of David,
>   who opens and no one will shut,
>   who shuts and no one opens. . . .
> "I know your works. Look, I have set before you an open door, which no one is able to shut" (Rev 3:7-8).
